AHMANSON · MURPHY
FINE ARTS IMPRINT

THE AHMANSON FOUNDATION
has endowed this imprint
to honor the memory of
FRANKLIN D. MURPHY
who for half a century
served arts and letters,
beauty and learning, in
equal measure by shaping
with a brilliant devotion
those institutions upon
which they rely.

DEMOCRATIC VISIONS

DEMOCRATIC VISIONS

Art and Theory of the Stieglitz Circle, 1924–1934

CELESTE CONNOR

UNIVERSITY OF CALIFORNIA PRESS

Berkeley
Los Angeles
London

The publisher gratefully acknowledges the generous contribution to this book provided by the Art Book Endowment of the Associates of the University of California Press, which is supported by a major gift from the Ahmanson Foundation.

University of California Press
Berkeley and Los Angeles, California

University of California Press, Ltd.
London, England

Library of Congress Cataloging-in-Publication Data

Connor, Celeste, 1961–
Democratic visions : art and theory of the Stieglitz Circle, 1924–1934 / Celeste Connor.
p. cm.
Includes bibliographical references.
ISBN 0-520-21354-8 (cloth : alk. paper).
1. Stieglitz Circle (Group of artists) 2. Stieglitz, Alfred, 1864–1946—Art patronage. 3. Art, Modern—20th century—United States. I. Title.
N6512.5.S75 C66 2000
709'.73'09042—dc21 99-087355

Manufactured in the United States of America

09 08 07 06 05 04 03 02 01 00

10 9 8 7 6 5 4 3 2 1

The paper used in this publication meets the minimum requirements of ANSI/NISO Z39.48-1992 (R 1997) (*Permanence of Paper*).

to Da

If we are to break out of the non-historical fixity of *post*-modernism, then we must search out and counterpose an alternative tradition taken from the neglected works left in the wide margin of the century, a tradition which may address itself not to this by now exploitable because quite inhuman rewriting of the past, but for all our sakes, to a modern future in which community may be imagined again.

RAYMOND WILLIAMS, *"When Was Modernism?"* (1989)

CONTENTS

ILLUSTRATIONS

PLATES *(following page 110)*

FIGURES

ACKNOWLEDGMENTS

I WOULD LIKE TO EXPRESS MY GRATITUDE to the Samuel H. Kress Foundation for its ample support of my research and to the California College of Arts and Crafts for its assistance with the expenses of my illustration program.

I am also indebted to the many helpful curators and staff members of the U.S. museums I have visited who smoothed my path at every step: the Metropolitan Museum of Art, National Gallery of Art, the Whitney Museum of American Art, the Art Institute of Chicago, the Norton Museum of Art (West Palm Beach, Fla.), the Smithsonian Institution's National Museum of American Art and Hirshhorn Museum and Sculpture Garden, the Museum of Modern Art (New York City), the Beinecke Rare Book and Manuscript Library (Yale University), the Columbus Museum of Art, the Phillips Collection (Washington, D.C.), and the Philadelphia Museum of Art. In particular, I am grateful to curators Courtney Donnell, Sarah Greenough, Barbara Haskell, Lisa Messinger, and Mark Rosenthal, all of whom generously shared their time and thoughts on the Stieglitz circle. Special thanks are due David Schoonover, curator of the Collection of American Literature at the Beinecke Rare Book and Manuscript Library at Yale, for his patient and liberal assistance and interest in my project during the months I spent there examining the Stieglitz papers.

I wish also to acknowledge my debt to Stephanie Fay, longtime friend from my days at the University of California at Berkeley, who had the insight to recommend (to a former acquiring editor) my talk on the Stieglitz circle at College Art back in 1988. I am grateful as well to Deborah Kirshman, fine arts editor and my acquiring editor, whose persistence is matched only by her wit and charm, and to Deborah's assistant, Kim Darwin, a source of support throughout. I thank Alice Falk for her admirable editing of the manuscript and Fronia Simpson for her meticulous proofreading.

Without the unflagging interest, enthusiasm, and useful comments of Peter Selz, from the earliest phases of the project to the present, this book might never have come to an effective conclusion. And special recognition must go to Anne Wagner, whose tough criticism of my thesis catalyzed the thoroughgoing revision that has produced the present text.

In the last phase of that reworking, Martha Hollander, Jane McKinne, and the poet Bill Mayer helped me take a fresh look at my introductory remarks. Stephen Berger generously provided technical support throughout the process.

INTRODUCTION

ART HISTORIANS COMMONLY CREDIT the photographer Alfred Stieglitz with introducing into the United States, at his New York gallery, 291, examples of the most innovative European art of the time. They have emphasized Stieglitz's role as the American importer and promoter of significant modern European artists. During the 291 years (1905–17) and later, however, Stieglitz played another role, equally important and more prominent, as he promoted the American artists Charles Demuth, Arthur Dove, Marsden Hartley, John Marin, Georgia O'Keeffe, and Paul Strand, who became known as the Stieglitz circle. After 291 closed in 1917, Stieglitz chose to exhibit only the work of American artists at his Intimate Gallery (1925–29) and An American Place (1929–46); that later period is the focus of this book.

In addition to revising the misleading identification of Alfred Stieglitz exclusively with the ideals and accomplishments of 291, I also seek to correct the familiar assumption that a native art and a related body of theory, global in its ambitions, were created in America only in the 1940s. For in the decades following World War I, the painters and photographers of the Stieglitz group invented unique idioms of pictorial representation. Their artworks of the interwar period eloquently and effectively expressed to a receptive international public a specifically American aesthetic and social philosophy. During the decades following the war, visual artists of the Stieglitz circle found ways to represent the landscape that were as innovative and ambitious as those of any contemporary American or European movement. Depictions defining and celebrating their native land became their forte, indeed their obsession.

Their art was legitimized and disseminated by a series of gallery exhibitions orchestrated by Stieglitz and supported by a coterie of art and cultural critics and writers that included Sherwood Anderson, Van Wyck Brooks, Waldo Frank, Lewis Mumford, and Paul Rosenfeld. These sympathetic literati produced engaged art-critical and theoretical literature that is self-consciously derived from the radical democratic vision of Walt Whitman—a vision of participatory democracy that stressed inclusion and community.[1] These important yet largely forgotten writings not only constituted the dominant American discourse on art of the twenties and thirties but also deeply inform present-day dialogues on American art.

When I first learned of the two later galleries, the discovery raised more questions for me than it answered. Why was there only one brief mention of them in the art-historical literature?[2] What were the concerns of the visual artists, critics, and theorists who reconstituted the circle after World War I? What were their collective goals? How did they propose to reach them? Scholars in my field and in others have long supposed that American artists achieved notable group consciousness only with the government programs of the Depression era, and a style perceived as desirable in the international art market only after World War II.[3] The Stieglitz group's post–World War I collaboration suggests otherwise. Historians of modern art also hold that the abstract expressionism of the 1940s represents the first American avant-garde organized around a group of visual artists and critics with a common ideology and determined to acquire an international reputation. Indeed, even Serge Guilbaut's probing and critical book of 1983, *How New York Stole the Idea of Modern Art*—while conceding that "During the twenties Stieglitz and his modern artists did of course defend modern art"—insists, "but they never dreamed of replacing Paris."[4] But American artists of the Stieglitz circle in the twenties and thirties had succeeded in placing American cultural products before a receptive international public. They deliberately sought to end the Parisian dominance of the international art market. Indeed, a desire for international acclaim led the group to create a native visual idiom, and thus an American cultural identity, before World War II.

The conservative Regionalists (notably the painter Thomas Hart Benton and the critic Thomas Craven) as well as the American dadaists in the 1930s and 1940s denied the circle its international accomplishments. In the early fifties, one of the chief arbiters of modernist taste, Alfred H. Barr, Jr., celebrated the abstract expressionists as America's first truly indigenous painters and presented the Stieglitz circle simply as their distant precursors.[5] Yet the works of those in the Stieglitz circle drew significant audiences of other artists (including the abstract expressionists) at Edith Halpert's Downtown Gallery, where they were exhibited continuously from Stieglitz's death in 1946 until Halpert's in 1970.[6]

By depicting the Stieglitz circle as proto–abstract expressionists, formalist writers implied that most of the group's visual artists never achieved their own compelling modes of representation. To maintain their tendentious view of cultural history, these artists and critics identified the Stieglitz group exclusively with the 291 years, a highly selective account of art-historical events that makes the members of the circle at best "transitional" figures. Formalists like Clement Greenberg, who singled out John Marin's oil paintings for praise because he believed they demonstrated a clear trajectory from impressionism to the abstract expressionism that he passionately promoted, devalued most of the postwar work of visual artists and critics of the Stieglitz circle.[7] The attempts by various rival contingents of the New York art world to write the definitive version of American intellectual and cultural history purposefully and quite effectively minimized the actual range and force of the Stieglitz group's cultural contributions.

The one authoritative scholarly text on the circle to date—*Alfred Stieglitz and the American Avant-Garde,* published by the art historian William Homer in 1977—perpetuates the viewpoint both of the group's contemporary detractors and of Barr in the 1950s by considering in depth only the circle's first little cooperative gallery, 291. Homer's abbreviated coverage, along with his emphasis on form, style, and especially biography rather than historical context, has limited his analysis. In focusing their lenses so narrowly, art historians have distorted the picture of early-twentieth-century American cultural production. Moreover, by considering visual artists apart from the body of critical and theoretical literature that they and their advocates generated, historians and critics have constructed an ideologically disinterested picture of the New York art scene during the first three decades of this century. I offer, instead, a nonchronological social and cultural history, examining the Stieglitz circle from various angles and dispelling the notion of its insularity by revealing its social and economic commitments and the interactivity of its discourses. Knowing the circle's visual and written productions in their full context is essential to understanding the relation between them.

In chapter 1, "Toward a Democratic Art," I suggest that the circle articulated its post–World War I aims in radically democratic art-critical and theoretical writings. Among the advantages of this approach (related to present-day interventionist, or socially engaged, criticism) is its acknowledgment of the spectator's role in making meaning. Members of the circle developed their sensitivity to the varied audience for art in response to the arrival of immigrants who came to the United States from many cultural centers abroad. Especially important to my analysis is the *Seven Arts,* a groundbreaking journal that supported the values of transnationalism, cultural pluralism, and collaboration in the contemporary arts community—values still being explored today in the theory and criticism of art.

The artistic practices of the West during the past two hundred years have inevitably been linked to contemporaneous critical and theoretical discourse within and outside art. In the Stieglitz circle, critical theory interacted with practice (both within and outside the circle itself), a process of appropriation and parody that is worth examining in detail. The conventional forms of art-historical inquiry, the monograph and the biography, tend to obscure both this interaction and the group's collaboration, particularly as it affected the workings of all three galleries.[8] These traditional art-historical genres mask the cooperative element of the marketing structure developed by all the circle's members, though Stieglitz took the lead. As the critic Paul Rosenfeld observed: "Complex works of art speak not through individuals but ensembles."[9]

Chapter 2, "Recycling Whitman," attempts to answer the complex question of purposes. What fueled the immense effort of these visual artists and art writers? What goals did they pursue? what ideas of America's future? It is clear that the circle was moved by Whitman's democratic visions, as interpreted by *Seven Arts* authors. By the 1920s and 1930s Whitman's message of a new kind of democracy had spread across class boundaries, across national borders, and across oceans, thereby expanding the capacity of audiences to appreciate American imagery. Whitman created a template in the social imagination for themes of the desirability of pluralism and the tolerance of difference.

To the Stieglitz circle, Whitman's work successfully integrated aesthetic form with social content, presented a radical democratic ideology, and fused Western and non-Western ideas much as contemporary European visual art practices did. Perhaps most important, his poems provided sketches of a new American iconography, a conceptual map of a transformed, pluralist American future. To members of the circle and their supporters, the poet sang powerfully of American hopes for freedom and equality. Whitman's great critical essay "Democratic Vistas" (from which I have borrowed my own title), proclaims in its first sentence that "the greatest lessons of Nature through the universe are perhaps the lessons of variety and freedom."[10]

Chapter 3, "A Direct Point of Contact," examines the cooperative structure of the circle's galleries as an alternative to the dealership system. This alternative form persists in the artist-run galleries of America's West and East Coasts today. The exploration of new ways to present art to the viewing public went hand in hand in the early twentieth century with a reenvisioning of that same public. At the close of the nineteenth century, close relations (amalgams of friendship and commerce) between artists and patrons gave way to a new arrangement in the art transaction, European in origin, in which the dealer played the role of intermediary between artist and audience. At 291 as well as at the Intimate Gallery and An American Place, however, Alfred Stieglitz enacted yet another role. Although he directed operations of the three galleries, he received no remuneration for this work. Not a dealer in the usual sense (he openly disdained the role), Stieglitz played the part of active patron (a traditional market role), astute collector, and impassioned supporter of the arts—with a decidedly democratic twist. Stieglitz's role as it emerges in this study of the circle's cooperative gallery practices counters the long-dominant notion that this American photographer was an elitist, isolated champion of the arts, as his critics in the thirties maintained.

The circle's cooperative galleries focused not on sales but on exhibits. The most important goal was getting the broadest public for their works of art. Their notion of placing art in the public sphere is a thoughtful updating of William Morris's well-intentioned but unsuccessful effort to place superlative artworks into as many hands as possible. The central role the circle assigned to a redefined, more inclusive public was reaffirmed when Georgia O'Keeffe, in the years immediately following Stieglitz's death, dispersed his own collection, which included works that the photographer had chosen from his colleagues' oeuvres. O'Keeffe gave these works to various public museums, demonstrating the circle's belief that art is not property and cannot be privately owned. Instead, the circle conceived the act of beholding a work of art as equivalent to attending a poet's reading. The ambition was to disseminate ideas; and the received intellectual "property" was, ideally, free and accessible to all. All three galleries were planned, in part, as educational centers to provide such access. The transnational ambitions of all members of the group (except O'Keeffe) led them to participate in international exhibitions in Paris, Germany, Italy, Canada, Mexico, and South America, as well as in their own galleries' exhibitions, from the mid-1920s until World War II.

The New Realism—the notion, embedded in their visual works and critical writings, that art contributes to democracy by helping its viewers see culture and society freshly, as it "really" is—responded to the members' awareness of how American demographics were changing because of immigration and internal migration (especially the "Great Migration" of southern blacks to northern cities). Chapter 4, "Reconfiguring Realism," explores the circle's redefinition of realism after a decade of experiments with abstraction. It was a self-conscious turn to legible representation that would be accessible to a broader community. The circle felt the pressing need for an innovative set of icons to represent the new American sense of self and to bind all parts of the population in a common knowledge and self-understanding.[11]

The popular discovery of the idea of culture in Depression-era America grew out of a search for a cultural identity that gained strength immediately after the war. During World War I, the effort was given life by cultural radicals,[12] and thereafter it took on the dimensions of a crusade that affected every aspect of American inquiry. According to one historian, "The search was to continue throughout the decade in the most overwhelming effort ever attempted to document in art, reportage, social science, and history the life and values of the American people."[13]

The Stieglitz circle's ambitions and social functions come to light in a critical rereading of Regionalist, leftist, modernist, and formalist histories of American culture. Such an analysis reveals the circle's important role in the earliest phases of that culture's development. Members of the circle can finally be recognized as agents in the spread of a visual literacy that helped unify the American community in self-awareness.

All theoretical aims aside, the art produced by the Stieglitz group during the twenties and thirties is indelibly marked not with the latest European accents (as had been the case before 1920) but by a thoughtful synthesis of past and present European and American artistic accomplishments. The postwar art of the circle testifies to its makers' knowledge and absorption of English Arts and Crafts ideals (in their later German and American translations), of the experiments of the dadaists (whom the Stieglitz group occasionally described as carrying on the legacy of 291), of the French purists, and especially of the surrealists, whom they saw as their chief contemporary competitors for international renown.[14] Providing an unparalleled touchstone for artists of later generations, the art that these Americans produced in the interwar period was neither stubbornly and unreflectively provincial nor imitatively and emptily cosmopolitan like the work of less talented disciples of William Merritt Chase.

Another major weakness of previous literature on the Stieglitz circle is scholars' resistance to closely examining and interpreting the works of visual art themselves. My principal method was to look long, sketch, and carefully "read" selected paintings and photographs. Having grown up in the household of an artist, I know that visual works can be read as closely and as profitably as critical, theoretical, or literary texts. Cultural activities like viewing art are in fact designed to demonstrate that ideas are visible. Although my field traditionally assumes that the process works in reverse, my first close encounters in 1981 with artworks by the Stieglitz circle (while helping prepare an exhibition and catalogue for the San Francisco Museum of Modern Art)[15] disclosed to me the ideas that I explore in this book.

Prolonged beholding of works of art is for me the essential method that relates art history to art criticism. The assessments it makes possible cannot be completely objective, since interpretations are not disinterested knowledge; rather they are ideological desiderata, colored by the idea that art can transform social conditions and by the ambition to do so. This partisan way of looking and assessing forms the bridge from the analyses of historical contexts in the first part of *Democratic Visions* to the art-critical readings of the second part. If one looks only for significant form, there is plenty to see in this art; if one looks also for significant thought, the search will be multiply productive.[16]

My discussion of partisan reading calls for an acknowledgment of my debt to Raymond Williams's groundbreaking 1973 literary study, *The Country and the City,* not only because of its profound understanding of the significance of the country-city dialogue but also because of Williams's engaged approach. Both were great stimuli to me in the initial stages of this work. This book, too, is the result of personal pressures and commitments—different from those of Williams but equally felt. I grew up surrounded by painted images of undeveloped rural landscape created in America in the 1930s and 1940s by my father, who celebrated the place as one who belonged there, an insider. I have questions about that approach to representing America that certain works by the Stieglitz circle also evoke. Perhaps above all, I have a deep commitment to understanding and exposing the largely untold history of the economic and social circumstances of American artists in the interwar period and after. How did the well-respected and appropriately remunerated image maker of late-nineteenth-century America fall on hard times? Finally, by reading the images created by the circle as closely as their writings and then interrelating the two, I demonstrate that an effective relationship can indeed be forged between critical theory and artistic practice, a debate that surfaced in the 1980s and thus far shows little sign of abating.

In chapter 5, "The Country," the view of rural America in the twenties and thirties is shown to be a major point of contention among American image makers. The Stieglitz group perpetuated a Whitmanian notion of nature as health-giving and unifying that corresponded to the idea of nature promoted by members of Germany's Bridge and Blue Rider groups. Marsden Hartley, who exhibited with the Blue Rider, discovered and wrote about a salutary nature similar to Whitman's as it was eloquently expressed in the cosmologies of Native American peoples. The circle's images of rural regions often became vehicles of a proto-environmental consciousness. For the American circle, this rural landscape also became the perfect metaphor for the precarious reception of the early modernist artwork. The rapid overdevelopment of land and the greedy exploitation of local resources by interloper businessmen suggest comparison to the growing fad among nouveaux riches business tycoons for buying early modern (especially European) art.

In chapter 6, "The City," I focus on the spectacle of New York in images and on the circle's conflicting feelings toward America's early-twentieth-century cultural mecca. Raymond Williams's 1973 study shows Western culture's views of the metropolis to be historically ambivalent. Williams confides, in discussing H. G. Wells's disapproval of the urban scene, "I find I do not say 'There is your city, your great bourgeois monument, your towering structure of this still precarious civilization' or I do not only say that; I say also 'This is what men have built, so often magnificently, and is not everything then possible?'"[17] The homage interspersed with diatribe that characterizes the left-leaning Stieglitz circle's postwar output attests to similar unresolved and even conflicting passions.

The final chapter of *Democratic Visions,* "The Most American Place," looks at how the circle seized on the newly formed state of New Mexico as the perfect emblem of America's future. New Mexico exemplified successful cultural mixing and provided opportunities to witness ancient, non-Anglo civilizations and to mingle with their descendants. The region also granted one member of the circle, Georgia O'Keeffe, an opportunity to put theory to the test. Perhaps above all, New Mexico necessitated the redefinition of the term "native" in ways that both reaffirmed and expanded the circle's democratic ideology.

Once the interwar change in representation and the meanings of that change for the culture are examined, the main function of the Intimate Gallery and An American Place become apparent. Rather than portray the abstract expressionists of the forties as the first genuine flowering of indigenous American expression, it is more accurate (and indeed more useful) to discuss their participation in the same ambitions and social purposes as the Stieglitz group: the creation of an American iconography to support the collective (but constantly debated) American ideology. The circle undertook mythmaking and symbol coining in part to humanize the modern environment, the new American landscape. Malcolm Cowley affirmed in 1934, with the benefit of two decades of hindsight, his belief in the social value of such intentions:

> Before a man can feel at home in any surroundings, whether those of seaside or forest, metropolis or factory, he must first transform the objects about him by connecting them with human emotions, by finding their purpose and direction, by making them understandable. He repeats the same process in the world at large, by perceiving in it architectural and musical forms, unity and rhythm, by giving it a history, and chiefly by transforming it with myth.[18]

The Stieglitz circle's creation, in collaboration with like-minded radicals, of a cultural mythos for American society sets them squarely among the significant art makers of Western tradition. What distinguishes their accomplishment within that tradition is the modern, democratic accent of the iconology they coined. In their quest for an American identity they fashioned a story of acculturation that was written not to serve a powerful elite but to democratize representational systems and make art more accessible.

The belief that cultural endeavor could transform American society empowered visual artists and critical theorists of the early decades of the twentieth century to produce countless valuable American works of textual and visual art. The critic Lewis Mumford wrote to Stieglitz on his seventy-fifth birthday: "We value you for the faith without which your works would be non-existent. . . . [T]he waves you have set in motion will continue to spread in widening circles and will in the long future touch far distant shores."[19] Indeed, as Mumford predicted, the circles of influence inevitably affected subsequent generations of art makers and art writers, and the search for cultural identity had both far-reaching and enduring effects. The visual culture of subsequent generations echoes its impulses, and its ideology, expressed in countless books and essays, resurfaced with éclat in the 1960s. In that decade radical thinkers, frustrated in part by the inability of contemporary Marxists to accept anything outside the confines of orthodox Marxist thought and acutely aware of the post–World War I intellectual heritage, reexamined cultural expression as an instrument of social change.[20] Although ultimately they did not place their faith in the visual arts per se, radical thinkers of the sixties accepted—and extended—a dominant theme of the Stieglitz group: the primacy of imagination and of vision, the notion that imagination is revolution.[21]

And yet another wave of Stieglitz circle thought washed up on international shores in the 1980s. Artists and critics of the circle spoke throughout their careers in opposition to the narrow formalist and socially disengaged theories that characterized much modernist criticism. In their own interdisciplinary approach, which depended on economic, psychoanalytic, literary, and sociological theories to connect art and society, Stieglitz circle authors are the American predecessors of the politically engaged criticism endorsed by American postmodernists in the eighties.[22] The Stieglitz circle, as progenitors of indigenous cultural expression that has international influence, contributed to American culture artifacts, visual and textual, that embody and attest to the careful crafting of resilient ideals and criticisms. In their own search for a usable past they collaboratively created one for future generations.

1

TOWARD A DEMOCRATIC ART

IN THE CRITICAL AND THEORETICAL writing of the Stieglitz circle we find the antecedents of today's cultural debates on issues of identity and inclusion. Current analysts of American culture and society need not look to structuralism or deconstruction to ground their arguments. Moreover, these writings of literary and visual artists counter the common view that early American modernists generated no critical theory.

While American avant-garde artists of the early 1910s might initially have followed European fashions, soon some were considering what forms of representation and what ideological underpinnings best fit their distinct cultural tradition. Among them were the photographer Alfred Stieglitz and the visual artists associated with him. After World War I, a group of art critics and theorists, along with some American social and cultural commentators, became allied with the artists of the Stieglitz circle. They were united in their deep concern that the practices of industrial capitalism had alienated artists from their audiences and that this relationship had been worsened by massive immigration to the United States. While many contemporary modernists saw this artistic exclusiveness as a virtue, members of the Stieglitz circle and their allies did not.

Emphasizing engagement with the public, the circle took their aesthetic philosophy from the socialism of William Morris—an earlier response by art makers to alien-

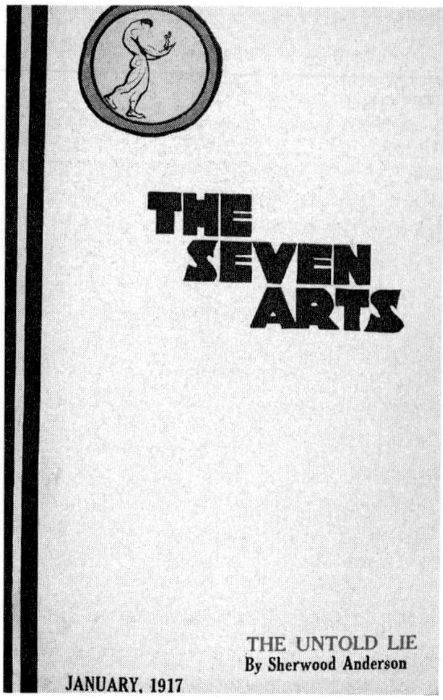

1a. Front cover, *Seven Arts,* January 1917.

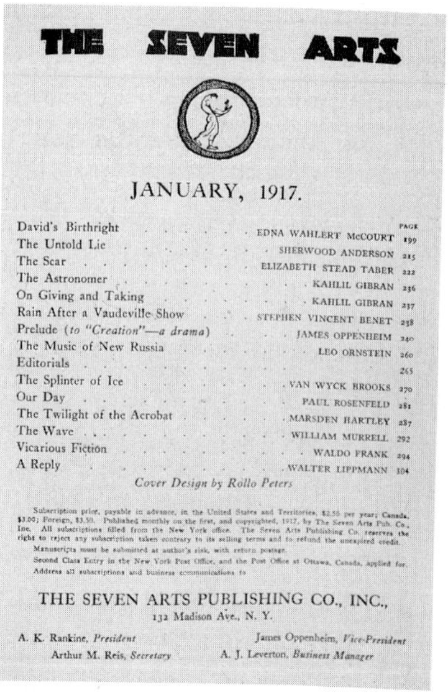

THE SEVEN ARTS

JANUARY, 1917.

Cover Design by Rollo Peters

Subscription price, payable in advance, in the United States and Territories, $2.50 per year; Canada, $3.00; Foreign, $3.50. Published monthly on the first, and copyrighted, 1917, by The Seven Arts Pub. Co., Inc. All subscriptions filled from the New York office. The Seven Arts Publishing Co. reserves the right to reject any subscription taken contrary to its selling terms and to refund the unexpired credit.

Manuscripts must be submitted at author's risk, with return postage.

Second Class Entry in the New York Post Office, and the Post Office at Ottawa, Canada, applied for.

Address all subscriptions and business communications to

THE SEVEN ARTS PUBLISHING CO., INC.,
132 Madison Ave., N. Y.

A. K. Rankine, *President* — James Oppenheim, *Vice-President*
Arthur M. Reis, *Secretary* — A. J. Leverton, *Business Manager*

1b. Table of contents, *Seven Arts,* January 1917.

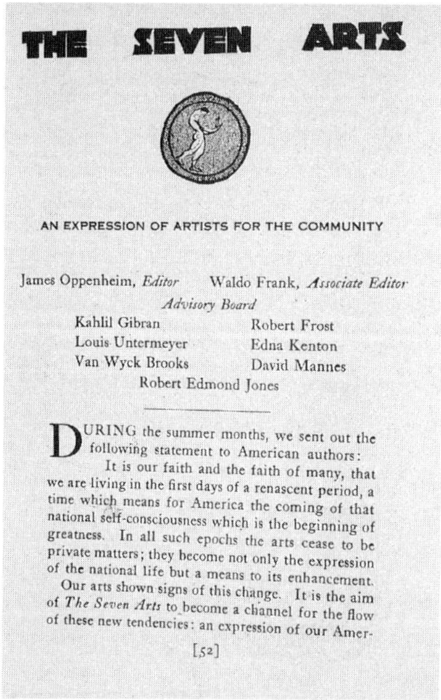

THE SEVEN ARTS

AN EXPRESSION OF ARTISTS FOR THE COMMUNITY

James Oppenheim, *Editor* — Waldo Frank, *Associate Editor*

Advisory Board

Kahlil Gibran — Robert Frost
Louis Untermeyer — Edna Kenton
Van Wyck Brooks — David Mannes
Robert Edmond Jones

DURING the summer months, we sent out the following statement to American authors:

It is our faith and the faith of many, that we are living in the first days of a renascent period, a time which means for America the coming of that national self-consciousness which is the beginning of greatness. In all such epochs the arts cease to be private matters; they become not only the expression of the national life but a means to its enhancement.

Our arts shown signs of this change. It is the aim of *The Seven Arts* to become a channel for the flow of these new tendencies: an expression of our Amer-

[52]

2a. Introduction to editorials section, *Seven Arts,* November 1916, p. 52.

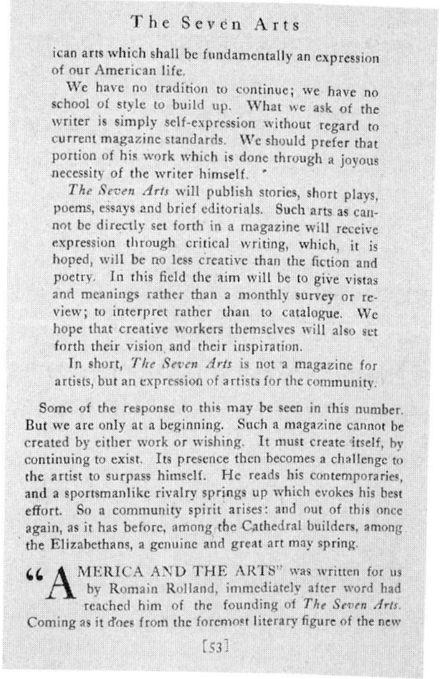

The Seven Arts

ican arts which shall be fundamentally an expression of our American life.

We have no tradition to continue; we have no school of style to build up. What we ask of the writer is simply self-expression without regard to current magazine standards. We should prefer that portion of his work which is done through a joyous necessity of the writer himself.

The Seven Arts will publish stories, short plays, poems, essays and brief editorials. Such arts as cannot be directly set forth in a magazine will receive expression through critical writing, which, it is hoped, will be no less creative than the fiction and poetry. In this field the aim will be to give vistas and meanings rather than a monthly survey or review; to interpret rather than to catalogue. We hope that creative workers themselves will also set forth their vision and their inspiration.

In short, *The Seven Arts* is not a magazine for artists, but an expression of artists for the community.

Some of the response to this may be seen in this number. But we are only at a beginning. Such a magazine cannot be created by either work or wishing. It must create itself, by continuing to exist. Its presence then becomes a challenge to the artist to surpass himself. He reads his contemporaries, and a sportsmanlike rivalry springs up which evokes his best effort. So a community spirit arises: and out of this once again, as it has before, among the Cathedral builders, among the Elizabethans, a genuine and great art may spring.

"AMERICA AND THE ARTS" was written for us by Romain Rolland, immediately after word had reached him of the founding of *The Seven Arts*. Coming as it does from the foremost literary figure of the new

[53]

2b. Introduction to editorials section, second page, *Seven Arts,* November 1916, p. 53.

ation from self and community within a capitalist system of production. Just as American modernists had adapted the new European methods of representation, so the Stieglitz circle imported and transformed the Arts and Crafts aesthetic. At the same time, members of the circle sought an indigenous American social and aesthetic theory—which they found largely in the works of Walt Whitman, whose earlier call for a reformed democratic ethos contained a political element that seemed especially compelling after World War I.[1] Whitman's radical, poetic rethinking of the desirable relationships of self to others (often along transcendentalist lines) depicts a network of disinterested acts, connected by common ties to nature and flowing across class boundaries. The allied critics and visual artists hoped to create a new, more complex American identity, one that accounted for the past yet welcomed cultural diversity and change. Inspired by the historical revisionism of the critic Van Wyck Brooks, they looked at the second great wave of immigrants to America and saw that the Pilgrim story—white, elitist, and exclusive—would no longer suffice. Social theories that applauded cultural mixing and difference were needed to support the kind of cultural pluralism that the Stieglitz circle envisioned.

The critic-theorists who created the periodical the *Seven Arts*—Van Wyck Brooks, Waldo Frank, Lewis Mumford, and Paul Rosenfeld—saw the artists' cooperative galleries as models of collaborative practice (see figures 1a and 1b). In images and essays, members of the circle gave concrete form to the theories elaborated in *Seven Arts*. Artists and theorists alike saw Whitman's art as offering an alternative to alienation from the community and as legitimizing their support of nascent personal liberation movements. His writings gave the younger generation permission to experiment in form and content, suggesting total libidinal freedom—without the neurosis feared by a generation steeped in Freud. *Seven Arts* authors uncovered in Whitman what would become the seeds of the women's and sexual liberation movements. The magazine, which circulated from November 1916 to October 1917, is the first publication that sought to speak for a pluralist American culture; it was itself a collaboration of Christians and Jews. Those artists and writers who had an eye to Morrisian and Whitmanian values began after the war to advocate and create works that did not reflect the assumption of European modernists that the artist intends primarily to express the private, feeling self. They moved slowly and deliberately toward defining the artist's self as more responsive and responsible to the public.[2] Tellingly, the subtitle of the *Seven Arts* was "An Expression of Artists for the Community" (see figures 2a and 2b).

Although all the visual artists of the Stieglitz circle except Georgia O'Keeffe studied abroad, none needed to travel to Europe to fall under the sway of the Arts and Crafts movement's aesthetic and social theory. A highly influential American periodical, the *Craftsman* (published from 1901 until 1916), made William Morris's prescription for modern art practices readily accessible. Its title encapsulates Morris's theory: good craft is a democratizing social force. Its editor, Gustav Stickley, spelled out in the magazine's first issue his intent "to extend the principles established by Morris."[3] Alfred Stieglitz had been fortunate enough to be in the right place (Germany) at the right time (1880) to be exposed to core notions of Arts and Crafts aesthetics and to participate in creating a craft-based means of native expression that might have wide appeal: the supporters of the *Craftsman* made such participation possible for all Americans, if only vicariously. Describing the aesthetic reform movement, by then international in scope, Stickley wrote: "It desires to strengthen honest craftsmanship in every branch of human activity, and strives for a form of art which shall express the spirit of the American people."[4] In their collaborative activities at 291 gallery (1905–17), members of the Stieglitz circle sought to create just such a native form of expression. Their activities shared ideological roots with the labors of Stickley and his colleagues, who were engaged in another cooperative venture called the United Craftsmen of Eastwood. And the *Craftsman* gave voice not just to Stickley and his designers but also to several American supporters of Morrisian socialism; perhaps the most prominent among them was John Spago, author of the influential *William Morris: His Socialism* (1908).[5]

The international Arts and Crafts movement particularly resonates in the work of Arthur Dove and Georgia O'Keeffe, who drew on motifs from Arts and Crafts pottery and fabric design.[6] These members of the Stieglitz circle translated into painting the principles of an essentially decorative arts movement, absorbing "low" forms in their creation of "high" forms just as they had done in translating the aesthetics of the applied art of photography.

In 1911, a decade after the appearance of the *Craftsman,* another periodical critical to the education of American artists was founded. The *Masses* was produced by thinkers influenced by socialism in general and by Marxism in particular; neither the magazine nor its successor of 1926, *New Masses,* developed a consistent aesthetic.[7] Both the *Masses* and its less-known contemporary, the *Seven Arts,* were forced to cease publication because of the wartime economy (in particular, the sharp reduction of Stieglitz's first wife's income caused by the shutdown of her family's brewery). The staff of *Seven Arts* were Morrisian liberals and socialists. Their ideals were echoed in the theory and criticism written by Lewis Mumford, a critic of architecture and urban planning. When the short-lived periodical folded it merged with the *Dial,* whose editorship Mumford assumed in 1919.[8]

Relations between Stieglitz and Mumford were cordial, and the two corresponded extensively from the postwar years until the photographer's death in 1946. In September 1925, Stieglitz raised a particularly important issue: "Of course I am delighted that you feel about our 'work' as you do and that we are to be mentioned in your article in 'Form' [*sic*]—I am glad that you let our friends on the other side understand that America aesthetically is not entirely non-productive."[9] Other letters make it clear that "the other side" is Europe, the competition. The photographer appreciates not simply Mumford's promotion of circle members but his capacity—since Mumford himself commanded an international audience—to defend the quality of American productivity in that marketplace, which was expanding rapidly. Stieglitz in fact wrote that he would provide Mumford with materials to aid his arguments: photographic reproductions of works by visual artists of the circle to accompany future essays. As Stieglitz notoriously distrusted the photographic techniques used for mass reproduction of visual art, finding them inadequate to ensure accurate copies, his offer to Mumford demonstrates his determination to reach an international public.

The dominant figure of the *Seven Arts* group was the socialist literary critic Van Wyck Brooks, whose prose explicitly and implicitly revealed William Morris and John Ruskin to be his guiding lights; his influence on Paul Rosenfeld and Waldo Frank should not be underestimated. Rosenfeld recognized his debt; while preparing an homage to Brooks for publication, he wrote to Stieglitz: "We have so many thoughts in common, or at least his thought has so often stimulated my own, that I have had great difficulty in distinguishing what is properly himself from what is properly me. . . . [M]any of the ideas that I thought his have been added on to what he constructed by Bourne, Waldo and myself; to Brooks of course goes the credit of having done the initial thinking."[10]

The younger generation of socially conscious critics aligned with the *Seven Arts* were inspired by an idea that Brooks shared with visual artists in the Stieglitz circle: "The American renaissance will not get very far unless it develops that guild spirit which is . . . the development of a craft-sense."[11] American artists must engage in cooperative efforts, such as the *Seven Arts* experiment or 291; they must also redefine the function and meaning of their work as craft. The writers who collaborated on *Seven Arts* concurred that the road to America's cultural renaissance had already been embarked on, in the visual arts, by the Stieglitz co-op of painters and photographers.

The continuing experiments of those artists were supported by the *Seven Arts* coterie of theorists and critics long after the periodical itself had ceased publication. Waldo Frank, Paul Rosenfeld, and Lewis Mumford became members of the inner circle when the original band of critics associated with *Camera Work,* the periodical that complemented 291 exhibitions, dispersed. With the aid of these fresh recruits, visual artists and art writers renewed their efforts to inculcate a spirit of community and collaboration to do battle against careless craft.

That new attitude, in accord with their Morrisian beliefs, was not to be limited to the American cultural community. The members of the Stieglitz circle instead took the radical step of including the American public. Waldo Frank represented the intelligent and intuitive visual artist as a "worker" and, conversely, the knowledgeable worker in any field as an artist: "The skilled craftsman becomes an artisan, an artist: the tool holds close to his nature and works his will in ways so immediate that the instinctive love attaching limb to mind goes over, consciously, into the brush, the knife, the hammer."[12] Anticipating the later speculations of conceptual artist theorists such as Joseph Beuys and Alan Kaprow, Frank posits the innate dignity of manual labor and the inextricable bond between the manual and the intellectual, a revolutionary notion countering the dominant idea that separated and ranked them. Like Morris, the circle desired a new synthesis of the creative faculties of humankind through which their ultimate goal—social cohesion—would be achieved. American artists of the early twentieth century were concerned only secondarily about the industrial capitalism that Morris saw as spawning alienation; they primarily blamed the unprecedented mixing of immigrant groups in the domestic industrial labor force. Thus the zeal with which they sought a new American identity, reassessing history and ideology, was a direct response to sociocultural and political issues.

The magazine that competed most directly with the *Seven Arts* for the attention of socially concerned artists was the *Masses*. As already noted, its emphasis was Marxist, though some of its staff subscribed to the ideals of Morris and Ruskin. But a Marxist emphasis on the primacy of economics in social life contradicts a Morrisian emphasis on ethics. And by denying that nature is a determining factor in human social development, Marxist socialists sharply opposed not only the theories of Morris but also the practices of many contemporary visual artists, especially those of the Stieglitz circle. The circle, following the poet Walt Whitman and his interpreters like Brooks, conceived of nature, and indeed human nature, as both determinative and essentially good. This fundamental conflict between the two strains of social thought was played out in print for American audiences again when the *Masses* was resurrected in 1926 as *New Masses,* and its new staff (sometimes including Waldo Frank) refined the ideas of Morris and Marx and also introduced those of Stalin. Like Frank, most of the contributors to *New Masses* in the first decade of its publication were not Communist Party members; many were not sympathetic to the party at all.

Members of the Stieglitz circle read *New Masses* as religiously as they had its forebear, according to their correspondence as well as the reports of their biographers.[13] Although Frank attempted to straddle the two ideological camps, tensions came to a head when Georgia O'Keeffe's works were attacked by critics of the *New Masses* for their purported "social irrelevance" and "exaggerated individuality."[14] In March 1930 O'Keeffe volunteered to debate *New Masses* editor Michael Gold on the subject of her own artistic production as well as that of her colleagues. Though they met in the private dining room of the Hotel Brevoort in New York, we are fortunate that a detailed account appeared in the local press.[15] O'Keeffe both supported Morrisian principles and took advantage of the occasion to promote another cause to which she was equally committed: feminism.

Gold began their argument, stating that the only appropriate subject for contemporary works of art was the most important struggle of the day, that of the oppressed working class. When O'Keeffe asked, "When you name 'the oppressed' do you include women?" Gold retorted that he was not interested in equal rights for the "pampered bourgeoisie." The artist countered by pointing to her own experience: the long oppression of women had left her only male artists as models. All classes of women were affected, and through her work she was trying to redress that wrong. Furthermore, O'Keeffe argued that it was not necessary to paint realistic scenes of the women's struggle, calling such work "glorified cartoons"; instead, she insisted that the form and color of a well-conceived and well-executed object could themselves transform the viewer. Gold attacked O'Keeffe's concern with aesthetics, a linchpin of Morrisian theory, dismissing craft and design principles as "little tinkerings." Precisely because the Marxist socialism of her contemporaries paid no attention to the theory or practice of aesthetics, it had little appeal for O'Keeffe; moreover, as Gold's comments make clear, it had no interest in feminism.[16]

By the mid-1930s, American thinkers with Marxist or Stalinist leanings began to move toward an aesthetic stance quite similar to what those inside the Stieglitz circle had consistently held. The Artists' Union, originally formed in 1933 as a bargaining agent for artists, collaborated with the Artists' Committee of Action to publish a new magazine, *Art Front,* that—unlike other leftist publications, such as *New Masses* or *Partisan Review*—was written exclusively by and for visual artists.[17] The first issue appeared in November 1934. As the artists spoke for themselves, they rejected the position of earlier theorists of social realism. In "Five on Revolutionary Art" (September–October 1936), a respected leader of the public art movement, the Mexican muralist José Orozco, asserted: "It is a vulgar notion that an illustration with a slogan constitutes revolutionary painting. Actually it has nothing to do with art. We have reached a new stage in revolutionary art where we recognize that the painter has the right to be an artist first. We social revolutionary painters need above all now to define our problems within the field of art itself."[18] This "new stage" heralded by *Art Front* in 1936 is very much the old platform of the Stieglitz circle. Orozco affirmed that to be effective as an artist, to have the desired impact on one's audience and the broader society, one must attend first to craft and mastery of expressive techniques. Revolutionary transformation depended not on subject matter but on an ethics of production.

The Stieglitz circle made fundamental contributions to an approach to representation that began with the Arts and Crafts movement in England. The exhibitions, catalogues, and the literature of the Intimate Gallery and An American Place, as well as essays and interviews by members of the artists' cooperative, fostered both New Realist painting and the "straight" school of photography of the 1920s and 1930s. Their Morrisian views pervaded architecture and the fine and applied arts; American social realism, with its underpinnings of Marxist or Stalinist theory, never was as widely accepted by the viewing public or by practicing artists and never produced such durable and creative works. Those in the Stieglitz circle believed that complex ideas about nature (especially human nature) were best expressed in direct representations or abstractions of natural forms. Because nature made individuals interdependent and formed their experiential and psychic worlds, it connected them with a common cord. Its representation could thus be intelligible to the widest possible community of viewers. Members of the circle viewed the murals commissioned for government projects and the standard fare of leftist periodicals not as interpretations but as caricatures of nature—stereotypical statements that condescended to the public.

A sense of their audience affects many choices artists must make, including how they represent their subjects. O'Keeffe, for example, did not see her magnified flowers simply as easily legible and broadly appealing. Rather, she expected that any viewer who had ever produced anything at all would immediately notice her great care in remaking nature in pigment. That is, by virtue of being a "maker," anyone could be an intelligent critic of art. Other members of the Stieglitz circle shared this nineteenth-century sense of the American audience for art; in the early twentieth century, however, advertising was transforming members of that audience from producers to consumers.

The circle's visual artists and theorists found support for their vision of a popular audience for the arts and for their ideas about nature not only in Morris but also in Whitman. They (and the broad reading public) were expertly guided through Whitman's prose by Van Wyck Brooks, the period's most respected exponent of Whitman's art and his idea of how it should function in society. Moreover, he judged the contemporary literary scene by Whitman's standards: "indigenous expression" was as key a phrase in Brooks as in Whitman. Throughout the twenties, while Brooks was still defending contemporary American authors, he remained a model for writers in the Stieglitz circle. When his criticism focused exclusively on the literature of the American past, they viewed him as a defector.

In both Waldo Frank's *Our America* (1919) and Paul Rosenfeld's *Port of New York* (1924), Van Wyck Brooks's figure looms large. He provided these younger critics with a model of a criticism passionately concerned with the sociocultural context in which works of art were produced. Rosenfeld, in *Port of New York,* named Brooks America's first "effective" cultural critic—a term he used in the Whitmanian, ethical sense. Rosenfeld found particularly valuable Brooks's insistence that "every original work of art is to a great degree the evolutionary product of social conditions, deriving many of its characteristics from climate, national character, national manners, politics, and religion."[19] Frank's essays on art and culture and Rosenfeld's essays on music and painting displayed this contextual approach, and their concern with social and historical conditions distinguished their writings from the formalist criticism dominant in the late thirties and forties. The tradition of socially engaged criticism they helped to establish flourished in America in the late sixties and early seventies.[20] The painter-poet Marsden Hartley was also influenced by Brooks's ideas, and like Frank and Rosenfeld he produced manifestos specifically targeted at New York's visual artists. Their tracts played a pivotal role in the cultural conversation between the literary community and contemporary artists, and both groups were represented within the Stieglitz circle. In attempting to democratize the old hierarchical structure of the Beaux Arts tradition, writers and artists often collaborated, meeting as equals.

American debates about the politicization of artists and their products were not new, though they received little attention until the late twenties and thirties. To Brooks, whose adaptation of Whitman's views proved highly influential, an artist's political beliefs could be firm and widely known (the early Brooks, for example, openly adhered to socialism); but politics must not become the exclusive subject of his or her work.[21] Few members of the Stieglitz circle would challenge this credo until well into the thirties, and Stieglitz himself staunchly defended it throughout his career. The true role of the artist was that of ethical leader. Furthermore, Brooks provided a theory that the critical writers of the Stieglitz circle could convincingly apply to the visual artists of Stieglitz's postwar galleries—Charles Demuth, Arthur Dove, Marsden Hartley, John Marin, Georgia O'Keeffe, Paul Strand, and Stieglitz himself.

Brooks's *Wine of the Puritans* (1908) is essentially a diatribe against an American mind-set that originated in the theocracy of the Puritans, who bore the full blame for rendering Americans unimaginative, unaware or afraid of sensuality, and hopelessly engrossed in the work ethic. *The Wine of the Puritans* calls for a reform of the contemporary literary community that would completely sweep away the rationalist, pragmatic thought and ideals associated with the business classes that dominated early-twentieth-century American society. Brooks questioned the motivations of the corporate world and condemned American business practices—with their total lack of spiritual or ethical purpose—for depriving American society of an authentic identity, a common point of view. Without such an identity, no feeling of community or American mythos could take shape. These cultural absences seemed critical to Brooks; as he wrote his reform manifesto in England, he was keenly aware of early modern America struggling to establish itself within an international community.

Brooks believed that identity could be attained through "rootedness," and that the fame of American artists depended on their achieving that rootedness in American society. "In other countries," he observed, "a man seems to win fame precisely because his talent is the blossom of the very deepest roots of national life."[22] Members of the Stieglitz circle took up the notion enthusiastically as they constructed public self-images: the painter John Marin that of a Yankee backwoodsman and Sherwood Anderson (despite his long sojourns in cities—Chicago, New York, New Orleans) that of a "farm boy" from Ohio. This was not localism for its own sake: both authentic and fictive roots in rural America were seen as essential to the effective artist. The organic metaphor of rootedness also provided subject matter for the paintings of O'Keeffe and Demuth, whose depictions of flowers—often literally homegrown blooms—are in part meditations on the value and meaning of fame and talent within American society.

Though he focused primarily on literature, Brooks saw the visual arts as equally in need of reform. In *The Wine of the Puritans,* arguing for native expression grounded on an ethics of production, he found in the cultural wilderness of the Protestant-dominated past one figure of change: Walt Whitman. Brooks revives the poet's image of a stage in the development of American society, rising from its political and material foundations, in which native expression and spirit would become ascendant in the arts (Whitman's "Third stage" is discussed below). Moreover, in appropriating Whitman's term "indigenous," he stresses the sensate over the ideal even more than the poet had. Brooks's notion that artistic ability is literally an extract of one's home turf is itself extracted from "Democratic Vistas":

> Subtly interwoven with the materiality and personality of a land, a race—Teuton, Turk, Californian, or what not—there is always something—I can hardly tell what it is—history but describes the results of it—it is the same as the untellable look of some human faces. Nature, too, in her stolid forms, is full of it—but to most it is there a secret. This something is rooted in the invisible roots, the profoundest meanings of that place, race, or nationality; and to absorb and again effuse it, uttering words and products as from its midst, and carrying it into highest regions, is the work, or a main part of the work, of any country's true author, poet, historian, lecturer, and perhaps even priest and philosoph. Here, and here only, are the foundations for our really valuable and permanent verse, drama, &c.[23]

From Whitman, Brooks (and with him the circle) seized a formula for a type of expression specifically geared to provide American society with a cultural identity. After all, Whitman had used this formula—and it had worked. Whitman's own artistic success was seen as proof that the artist who took America as subject matter could achieve international renown.

Seven years after *The Wine of the Puritans,* Brooks produced one of his best-known works, *America's Coming-of-Age,* further developing the ideas of the earlier book—more urgently now with the onset of war in Europe. Brooks again struck an antirationalist stance against what he saw as a trade-oriented society's overconcern with the "practical" aspects of life. He also railed against philosophies, such as American transcendentalism, that de-emphasize immediate and concrete cultural and historical circumstances. To Brooks, Ralph Waldo Emerson represented the mouthpiece of the "genteel tradition," a set of elite beliefs and conventions that smacked of "an unworldly refinement."[24] Once more recalling Whitman, Brooks demanded a radical democratic ideology, communal and participatory, that would displace the pragmatism of American business (a sphere of pure avidity Brooks famously dubbed "Lowbrow") and the transcendentalism of academia (a sphere of ideas abstracted from their sociocultural contexts that he termed "Highbrow"). The role of the artist, he argued, is to "harness thought and action and turn life into a disinterested adventure" (p. 29). Economic gain could no more motivate one's existence than could the hope of rewards in some afterlife. Instead, each person aims toward a public self-fulfillment that Brooks defines as "the working out of one's own personality, one's own inventiveness through forms that are directly social" (p. 32). Brooks has synthesized

William James's and John Dewey's calls for culturally engaged citizens to work disinterestedly for the public good.[25]

In Brooks we find notions of social imagination and a communal sense of self that—following a long stretch of dominance by formalism—have again emerged in some American artistic communities. But while the socially engaged critical theory of the early 1990s tended to stress conceptualism, to Brooks good craft itself could bring about social ends. He explicitly locates some of the "directly social" motivations of the artist "on the economic plane that implies socialism" (p. 33). Moreover, Brooks engaged directly with the Progressivism of Theodore Roosevelt as he reworked and Americanized European socialism; the discourses of postmodernist critics, in contrast, seem to add little to the national political discourse of the United States. Postmodernism, originally fashioned in direct response to diverse European social, political, and historical conditions, has not been sufficiently recontextualized (and its misconceptions not sufficiently challenged) to contribute to such public discussions.[26] Contemporary theorists could profitably study the hybrid solutions of their predecessors: the Americanized socialism that greatly appealed to most critical writers and visual artists of the Stieglitz circle. Stieglitz himself, even in the years of the first gallery, lent economic and verbal support to its advocates—notably the critic and political activist Benjamin de Casseres—providing them space to air their views in *Camera Work.* Susan Davidson Lowe, in her biography of her uncle Stieglitz, writes that he "regarded himself as an outstanding example of voluntary socialism," making it plain that in the years just prior to the closing of 291 until the opening of the Intimate Gallery in 1925, his daily companions were socialist artists and authors.[27] The Stieglitz circle borrowed not the latest European formal and stylistic devices alone, as later accounts of formalist critics would have us believe, but contemporary social theories and practices as well.

For Van Wyck Brooks, Whitman's function—and the role of any native artist—was to "precipitate" the American character. In this transformative process, "All those things which had been separate, self-sufficient, inco-ördinate—action, theory, idealism, business—he cast into a crucible; and they emerged, harmonious and molten, in a fresh democratic ideal, which is based upon the whole personality" (p. 118). Whitman acted in an exemplary fashion when he bequeathed to America the radical democratic credo that Brooks and his followers Rosenfeld and Frank later welded to the tenets of modern socialism. "All this indicates," Brooks wrote, "a function quite different from that of a poet in any but the most radical and primitive sense of the word. . . . a man, that is to say, who first gives to a nation a certain focal centre in the consciousness of its own character." That "focal centre," he made clear, was not "the sense of national or imperial destiny which has consolidated the great temporal powers of history"; the American identity was instead "that national 'point of rest' . . . upon which the harmony of a work of art is founded" (pp. 119 [his ellipsis], 120).

If this is nationalism, it is certainly the most benign variety. In Brooks's compelling and influential vision, America will come of age culturally, and American artists will mature professionally, when a truly democratic ethos is achieved. Brooks takes Whitman's program a step further, arguing that current conditions make it not simply permissible but necessary for the artist to adopt an active political stance (though still without taking politics as a subject). "Is it possible to get 'civilization' out of the Yankee stock?" he asked rhetorically, then mused, "If something vibrates in the air it is without doubt the expectation of a social ideal that shall act upon us as the sun acts upon a photographic plate" (p. 163). This pointed metaphor undoubtedly caught the imagination of the photographers Alfred Stieglitz and his protégé Paul Strand, and the conclusion of *America's Coming-of-Age* must have seemed to the gallery operator and his circle a personal call to arms:

> To leave behind the old Yankee self-assertion and self-sufficiency, to work together, think together, feel together, to believe so fervently in the quality of standards that we delight in prostrating our work and our thoughts before them—all that is certainly in the right direction[.] . . . [I]ntimate feeling, intimate intellectual contact, even humor . . . [—] these are the enemies of that base privateness which holds the string of what we call publicity; these promote that right, free, disinterested publicity which the real gentleman, the real craftsman, the real civil servant has always had in his blood. (p. 180)

Brooks speaks forcefully to a specific audience: the artistic community, whose "workers" traditionally used both heads and hands in the service of their profession. The Stieglitz circle took the critic's image as their self-likeness, a representation of the ideals they were collaborating to establish. It is quite possible that the Intimate Gallery derived its name as well as its guiding sentiments from this fervent passage.

Brooks's calls for reform affected American producers of culture outside the Stieglitz circle as well. A number of intellectual and artistic circles vied for, and won, attention from the American press immediately after World War I.[28] After their prominent part in the war, Americans found themselves playing a new role on the international stage, and new voices—many from the artists' groups clustered in Manhattan—spoke of culture in both little magazines and popular journals. The result was not an instantaneous upheaval but what one historian has called "a notable quickening of the pace of change, a period when things began to move so fast that the past, from then on, looked static."[29] The heightened pace was reflected in the growing urgency in Brooks's tone; the transformation to modern modes of thinking and behaving was matched and aided by changes in modes of artistic representation.

In the years just after the closing of 291, Stieglitz continued his voluminous correspondence, keeping family, friends, and professional associates abreast of his latest works and ideas from a ground-level office in the same building that had housed the gallery. The little room was dubbed "The Tomb" by intimates of the circle, and Stieglitz was indeed all but dead to public life until he orchestrated exhibitions of his own work and O'Keeffe's in 1921, 1923, and 1924, and then in 1924 opened the circle's second exhibition space, the Intimate Gallery. Thus we must look to the private correspondence to learn the issues that concerned the photographer and his colleagues during this transitional period. Brooks and Mumford wrote regularly, but it was mainly with Paul Rosenfeld, Waldo Frank, and Sherwood Anderson that Stieglitz established the theoretical foundations of the Intimate Gallery and An American Place.

These letters of the late 1910s and early 1920s underscore the cooperative nature of their undertaking. In a letter he wrote to Stieglitz on December 29, 1921, Waldo Frank, who was in Paris at the time, marks the end of his European sojourn by prophesying a new journey. As was often the case within the circle, the writer cast himself in the role of representative citizen, and in fact Frank voiced impressions and intentions that would be repeated by scores of American artists through the twenties and well into the thirties (most popularly in Malcolm Cowley's *Exile's Return*). Frank depicts postwar Europe as a culture in decline, a world "[i]nevitably past its climax, whose fire has begun to recede, whose light goes out in colors marvelously intricate and fair of gloaming. All of them . . . from the exquisite Gides and Dadaists to Rolland . . . are brothers in deep extinction." These impressions, based on his own investigation of the contemporary Parisian art scene, convinced him to "come home to America, and begin what I see more clearly than ever to be my work." Frank's belief that the war had ended European culture may have been wishful thinking, but it had a productive result, inspiring him to actively compete with the Europeans in producing culture and to stimulate other Americans to do the same. The prewar image of Europe, with its rich, historically layered culture, had daunted Americans: the postwar image, however inaccurate, was definitely psychologically empowering.

Both in and outside academic communities, the cultural and intellectual position of America vis-à-vis Western Europe was the topic of lively debates, in which artists took great interest. American visual artists, in particular, feared that controversial European works might prove so popular that their own income and prestige would diminish; and American authors found the vogue for modern French prose no less intimidating. Stieglitz and his group frequently offered insights into this perceived crisis—though sometimes in an envious tone, as when Stieglitz encouraged Paul Rosenfeld to make haste with the manuscript of *Port of New York:* "It *must be*—and *can be completed*—as contracted for. Yes, you have struck it—why it's so important: America without that damned French flavor!"[30] By the letter's conclusion, the tone was more tempered, more modulated:

> But when the world is to be France I strenuously hate the idea quite as much as if the world were to be made "American," or Prussian . . . that's why I continued my fight single-handed at 291—that's why I'm really fighting for Georgia. She is American. So is Marin. So am I. Of course by American I mean something much more comprehensive than is usually understood. . . . Of course the world must be considered a whole in

the final analysis. . . . But there is America—or isn't there an America. Are we only a ranked down bargain day remnant of Europe? Haven't we any of our own courage in matters "aesthetic"?

In *Port of New York* (1924), Rosenfeld followed Stieglitz's lead as he took Frank's image of a fading Europe a step further and claimed a high cultural profile for the United States.

Stieglitz makes clear that members of the circle did not envision a world "made 'American'"; cultural hegemony, while in fact achieved by the United States by the late 1940s, was not part of their agenda. Such an idea was incompatible with other democratic ideals. Instead, the group intended to win a fair slice of the international pie, a portion of the artistic power and status that Western Europeans had been the first to win and traditionally had solely possessed—a state of affairs that seemed to early-twentieth-century American visual artists to have gone on far too long. In 1925 Stieglitz confided to Sherwood Anderson that the trend toward modernism in the arts, especially its European variants, had become "a worse academy than the old." What Stieglitz saw in the new galleries now flourishing was European art being copied without skill or intelligence, rendering the works merely "faddish" or worse, "no longer a liberating force."[31] Members of the circle could not dismiss this new challenge to the transformative function of art, and they began to restructure the practice and theory of the cooperative gallery.

In this transitional period, the Stieglitz circle fashioned a new cultural identity for America—collaborative, craft-conscious, and emphasizing the vernacular and intimate—defined in relation not only to European but also to American artistic predecessors. Again, their theory referred back to the particular kind of American character forecast by Walt Whitman in "Democratic Vistas," which Waldo Frank called "clearly our greatest book of social criticism as 'Leaves of Grass' is our greatest poem."[32] In this role as American social philosopher, Whitman presented a democratic ideology in which art makers were culture builders, transforming society through their constructions. Critical theorists and visual artists of the Stieglitz circle were also absorbing more contemporary influences from Sigmund Freud and Freud's dissenting disciple Carl Jung, whose theories of art led them to believe that imagery could affect the psyche as well as society. They collaborated to invent images and symbols thought to have healing power. The artists, especially in their landscapes, ranged from loose appropriations to near illustration in expressing the ideas of Whitman, Freud, and Jung. Conversely, the theorists translated visual symbols and motifs into words. The texts and images are interdependent and therefore ontologically equivalent.

Like Van Wyck Brooks earlier, the Stieglitz circle drew from Whitman not only aesthetic and social ideals but also their concept of the ideal artist. Whitman's call for new images and new role models for image makers was heeded by Paul Rosenfeld in *Port of New York*, which provided New York's visual artists with an ideology and ex-

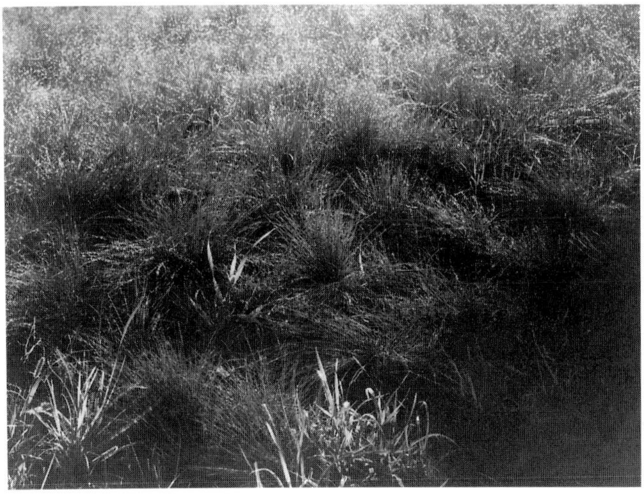

3. Alfred Stieglitz, *Lake George (Grasses)*, 1933 or 1934, gelatin silver photograph, 7 ¼ × 9 5⁄16 in. Gift of Georgia O'Keeffe, The Museum of Modern Art, New York, The Alfred Stieglitz Collection.

emplars both in his essays on "fourteen moderns" and in Stieglitz's famed photo-portraits that accompanied his text. That ideology was rooted in "Democratic Vistas," where Whitman prophesied the emergence of a "Third stage" of American intellectual, cultural, and social development, a stage beyond the hegemony of business and the corporate structure that even in the nineteenth century was felt by some to encroach on the liberties of individual citizens. He "announc[ed]" it as

> a native expression-spirit, getting into form, adult, and through mentality, for these States, self-contain'd, different from others, more expansive, more rich and free, to be evidenced by original authors and poets to come, by American personalities, plenty of them, male and female, traversing the States, none excepted—and by native superber tableaux and growths of language, songs, operas, orations, lectures, architecture—and by a sublime and serious Religious Democracy sternly taking command, dissolving the old, sloughing off surfaces, and from its own interior and vital principles, reconstructing, democratizing society. (p. 977)

In addition to this general, hortative recipe for a genuine American art, Whitman prescribed how future painters might interpret experience, and the visual artists of the group paid close attention.

Certain images created by the group refer directly to the most familiar writings of the poet. One literal reference to Whitman's work is Stieglitz's photograph alternately titled *Lake George* or *Grasses*, of 1933 or 1934 (figure 3). Not a landscape photograph in any traditional sense, the image is instead an extremely close-up view of long, curving grasses. The subject matter deftly pushes a viewer to invoke the title of Whitman's most popular collection of poems, *Leaves of Grass*. In this way Stieglitz wittily

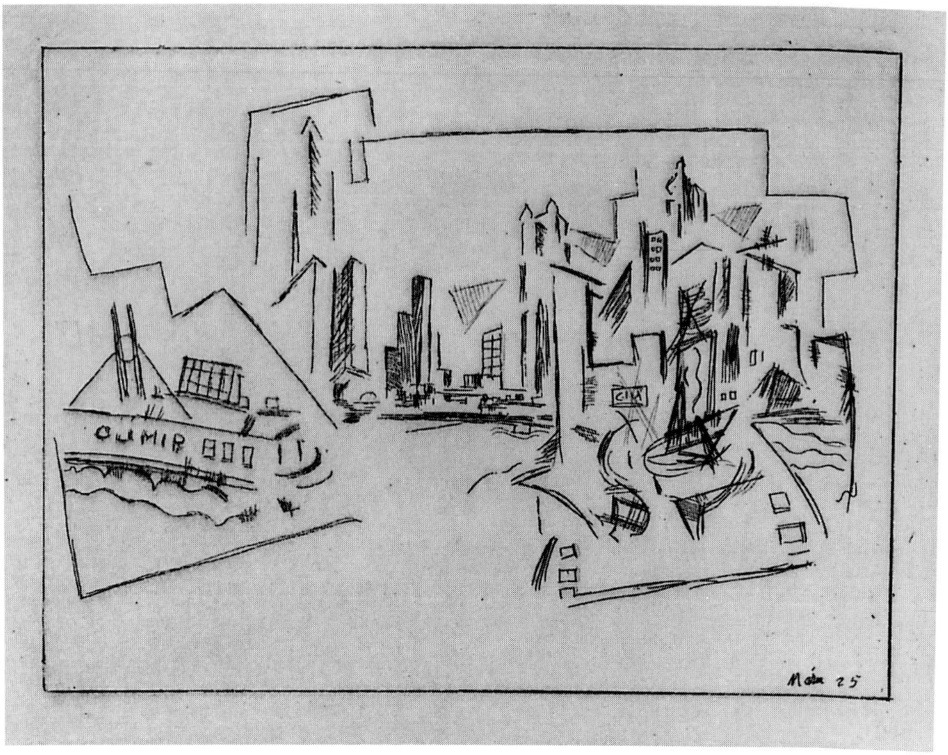

4. John Marin, *New York from the River (River Movement)*, 1925, etching printed in grayish black, plate: 7 ¾ × 9 9/16 in. Purchase, The Museum of Modern Art, New York.

appropriates one of Whitman's central images of nature. The upper section of the photograph depicts glistening, dew-drenched blades of grass; the droplets are sharply defined, capturing and reflecting an immense quantity of light. Three dramatic foci—three brightly lit patches of coarse grass in the lower left foreground—proclaim that the humble shall be exalted. The artist repeats Whitman's exhortation: nature is beautiful, observe it closely, celebrate it! Both the magnification of vision (employed in many of his own earlier works and those of Strand and O'Keeffe) and the attention to intimate detail encourage viewers to appreciate the particular form of each swatch of grass and to judge it breathtaking. The work argues that no artificial arrangement of flowers could compete with the assortment and variety that grasses present to the human eye. At the same time, the medium and the method deliberately flatten the natural objects into a Morrisian pattern and distinguish the work of photographic art from nature.

John Marin's *New York from the River,* also called *River Movement* (1925; figure 4), evoked the poetry and prose of Whitman with similar directness. The etching presents a strikingly novel view of a traditional subject, the river. The tone is lyrical, conveyed by an expansive lightness of touch; although composed of grays and bits of black, the work seems simple and fresh, not somber. The composition imparts an overwhelming sense of space and air. One suspects a subtext here, and Marin's clever device of frames within frames (adopted from the idol of his early career, James McNeill Whistler) heightens the sense that he is doing much more than simply recording a river's contours. Indeed, the artist positions us as viewers squarely on the waves. We immediately fill in the blanks in the artist's sketchlike notations and assume ourselves to be passengers on a boat or ferry. Any viewer familiar with Whitman could infer that Marin has paraphrased Whitman's powerful poem "Crossing Brooklyn Ferry." Instead of his usual playfulness, here the artist expresses a passion that mirrors Whitman's:

> Flow on, river! flow with the flood-tide, and ebb with the ebb-tide!
> Frolic on, crested and scallop-edg'd waves!
> Gorgeous clouds of the sunset! drench with your splendor me, or the men and women generations after me!
> Cross from shore to shore, countless crowds of passengers!
> Stand up, tall masts of Mannahatta! stand up, beautiful hills of Brooklyn!
> . . . .
> We fathom you not—we love you—there is perfection in you also,
> You furnish your parts toward eternity.
> Great or small, you furnish your parts toward the soul.[33]

Like this poem, the etching expresses not only the wondrous human-made sights beheld during the voyage through life but also a belief in the indestructibility of the human spirit. In "Crossing Brooklyn Ferry," the human psyche appears much as it does in "Democratic Vistas": "the soul, buoyant, indestructible, sailing space forever, visiting every region, as a ship the sea. And again lo! the pulsations of all matter, all spirit, throbbing forever—the eternal beats, eternal systole and diastole of life in things—wherefrom I feel and know that death is not the ending" (p. 988). Marin's work offers a sober reconsideration of Whitman's philosophy. *New York from the River* is a meditation on the meaning of human life and death, with no resolution provided; it is also a passionate tribute to an artistic predecessor who insisted that the artist has a duty to address such difficult subjects. The traditional image of the human soul as a "ship," often used by Whitman, also appears in many of Marin's seascapes. In addition, this etching recalls the many artworks, literary and visual, that revivify the classical myths of the river Styx. In this way artists of the Stieglitz circle both worked to promote the indigenous tradition they recognized in Whitman and presented multidimensional patterns of meaning—the traditional hallmark of significant works of art.

Out of Whitman's celebration of nature and notion of rootedness, the circle for-

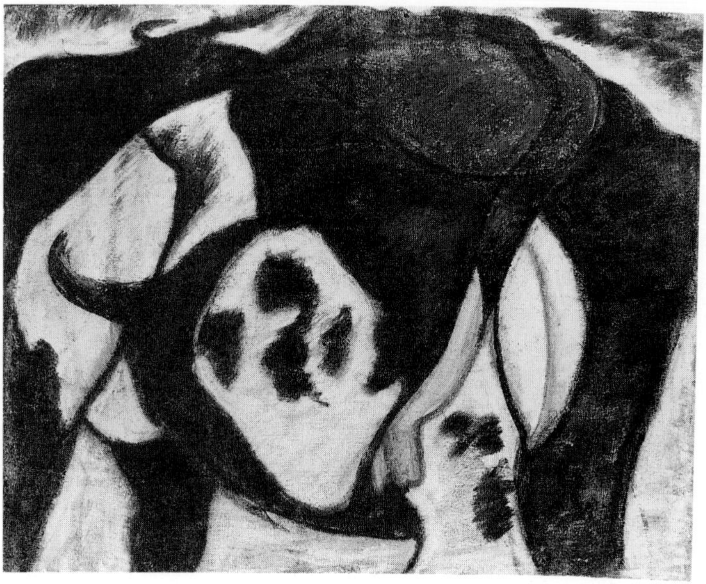

5. Arthur Dove, *Cow,* 1912–13, pastel on linen, 17 ¾ × 21 ½ in. Acquired 1949, The Metropolitan Museum of Art, Alfred Stieglitz Collection.

mulated a communal mythos and recast themselves to fit it. For example, Paul Rosenfeld took liberties with the facts of Arthur Dove's biography to portray him as a farmer-painter, with Jeffersonian resonance. Thus Dove's representation of domestic animals, especially cows and calves in his early experiments with pastel on linen (figure 5), "[b]rings us, with a queer thrill, close up to the gross and earthy substances. We lay our hands upon animal hides, rub them over rough stubby ground, pass good, gritty, soil through our fingers. Dove paintings bring to the nostrils the healthy pungence of pastures and barn-lofts. . . . [W]e are never left without the gratification of some solid feeling of native soil. Dove begins a sort of 'Leaves of Grass' through pigment."[34]

Significantly, Rosenfeld praises not just the artist's Whitmanian sensuousness but his ability to perform a kind of transubstantiation through works of art. By identifying or empathizing (like Whitman) with the objects of his gaze, Dove actually expands his self in discovering their properties and qualities. Dove's style, a New Realism, is here portrayed as nonegocentric, even nonanthropocentric, a subversion of the perspectival tradition inherited from Renaissance Europe: Rosenfeld celebrates this invention of a wholly new, nonhierarchical—that is, democratic—point of view.[35] He sees Dove not so much analyzing forms as expressing his own experience of and responses to his bovine models. The result thus offers an intimate view of the animal's sensory impact on the artist. Critics and visual artists of the circle agreed that to create a distinctive modern American worldview they must begin by addressing sense perception. In challenging the inherited Western tradition, the circle was more like the German expressionists than the French impressionists—hardly surprising, given Stieglitz's overt Germanophilia and the direct participation of a senior member, Marsden Hartley, in the Blue Rider group.

To understand the circle's relationship to Whitman, we must examine how acting out the prophecies of an artistic precursor is tied to a mythopoetic model of history, accepted by the Stieglitz circle in general but espoused with particular force by the social historian and cultural critic Waldo Frank. Frank saw in historical events not a linear pattern of cause and effect but a much more complex, mysterious set of relations. His mythos-history was borrowed from Whitman—who had himself appropriated it—and was embellished by twentieth-century knowledge of Eastern philosophies and religious beliefs. Paradoxically, it was also from Whitman that Frank inherited the traditional European notion of history as the acts of "great" individuals. Frank's revisionist history was a hybrid containing acknowledged internal conflicts and deliberately unresolved tensions, not unlike the historical paradigms proposed by theorists of the 1990s.

Of particular interest to us is how visual artists transmuted these appropriations from Whitman. The poet envisioned "a copious race of superb American men and women, cheerful, religious, ahead of any yet known," who must create themselves in the New World: "the models of persons, books, manners, &c., appropriate for former conditions and for European lands, are but exiles and exotics here" (p. 961). Thus he sought models not only for art but also for human personality. In addition to accepting Whitman's call for bands of "achievers," members of the circle assumed that role models were crucial to America's social and cultural progress. Consequently, they did their utmost to act as the societal transformers the poet described.

Although Whitman portrayed direct intervention in political affairs as a righteous act, he condemned as corrupt and corrupting the political intrigues he had observed when he worked as a minor government official in Washington, D.C. The terms of a radical democracy should instead take shape on the writing tables of poets and the drawing boards of artists. His emphasis on the moral function of the artist helps us understand Stieglitz's comment to Rosenfeld about a draft of *Port of New York:* "It struck me during the day that you say about me that I'm the greatest artist in America. Maybe, maybe not. I feel it's an unnecessary challenge and emphasizes something you really don't care to sacrifice at the expense of possibly your whole 'statement' about me. So I'd change that. Georgia agrees with me. I'm not sure about being as much an artist as one of the leading spiritual forces in this country."[36] In downplaying (but never denying) the cultural importance of those who make art, Stieglitz attempted to reestablish their moral importance in American society. He also saw visual artists as equal to, if not more important than, Whitman's "great literatus" (p. 932).

Some members of the circle stretched these notions of prophetic history and of the artists' spiritual leadership to the extreme. Waldo Frank was especially prone to hyperbole. Frank's personal acceptance of Whitman's challenge inspired him to search the contemporary literary scene for representations and authors to serve as models, and he found his ideal type in Sherwood Anderson, whose novels he praised extravagantly. "We shall create a Scripture in our own land," Frank wrote in *In the American Jungle,* "And of the stuff of Scripture are the glowing songs of 'Winesburg, Ohio' and 'A Story Teller's Story.'"[37] Indeed Frank's reviews were instrumental in winning Anderson's tales a popular audience. In his own assessment of Anderson, Paul Rosenfeld stressed the author's rural, untutored background and his closeness to nature. Such closeness underlies the prose that both Rosenfeld and Frank characterized as "truthful": that is, uncontaminated by the influences of urban culture.

Though they knew that their friend had for many years been a successful businessman in Elyria, Ohio, the pair of New York critics willfully obscured the facts that might weaken the mythopoetic model. The desire for an indigenous mythos—for the American "Scripture" that Frank located in Anderson's work—drove many members of the circle. They celebrated and even invented signs of it in their own manuscripts (like Anderson's *Winesburg, Ohio*), in manifestations of human personality that fit Whitman's criteria, and in their biographies. That Anderson had been born in the Midwest (unlike any other member of the circle except Georgia O'Keeffe) made him especially powerful mythopoetic material. Whitman's great spiritual men and women were quite deliberately conjured up in the prose reviews and critical essays of Frank, Rosenfeld, and Anderson himself.

Although they appropriated Whitman's democratic ethos of reform, members of the Stieglitz group recognized that American society had changed greatly since Whitman delivered his jeremiad. In Whitman's day, the poets' most formidable competitors for moral leadership were Protestant clerics; by the early twentieth century, the clerics had lost their sway and it was business leaders (in their advertising campaigns) who controlled the American imagination. Members of the circle did not find business per se offensive but thought odious the increasing impersonality with which modern business was transacted. In particular, the circle took issue with the separation of art from its maker and of the maker from the public—a public whose ethnic makeup was rapidly changing. In their private correspondence, members of the Stieglitz circle demonstrate a warmth and intimacy that contrast starkly with the impersonality of business dealings, including those of contemporary art dealers. In sustaining personal bonds in a community of makers who shared interests and goals, they practiced a form of social relations that no longer had currency in American society.

Artist-intellectuals and theorists of the 1920s who reached similar conclusions generated a body of literature designed to help educate their public, especially in understanding works in relatively inaccessible avant-garde styles. The Stieglitz circle authors exemplify a collective purposiveness and clarity. They often drew their vocabulary of art from popular images, familiar craft-based aesthetics, and literary works that were widely circulated to engage the broadest possible audience. These critics, inspired by Brooks's interpretation of Whitman's lyrical social theory and attack on Eurocentrism, addressed the concerns of all Americans, including the newest immigrants, who were attempting to make sense of a unique sociocultural experience. They urged art makers to foster communitarian values by forging strong local connections—social, cultural, and ecological.

From the late 1980s on, critics have tended to emphasize separation, difference, and otherness.[38] At the same time, some artists (e.g., Julian Schnabel and Jeff Koons) have turned to corporate-style strategies to market both their art and themselves as cultural personalities, a trend decried by popular art critics such as Robert Hughes.[39] Socially engaged theorists, who began in the 1970s to supplant the formalist critics long dominant in the United States, face a formidable challenge in their efforts to incorporate social, cultural, and political context into their writings—and necessarily take into account the role of the public, in the broadest sense. But they can find predecessors and a usable past in the alternative tradition of the Stieglitz group, which was also concerned with the role played by ideologies in the production of culture. Indeed, the circle's deep interest in all the circumstances of the crafting of objects, in the roles that these objects play in the community, and in the collective nature of the processes of reception can provide a model for contemporary artists.

2

RECYCLING WHITMAN

WALT WHITMAN WAS IDOLIZED not just by the Stieglitz circle but by all America in the early twentieth century; between 1900 and 1920 nineteen biographies and full-length studies of the poet were published, one of which won a Pulitzer Prize. A critically acclaimed volume of Whitman's prose works was published in 1914 by Mitchell Kennerly, Stieglitz's close friend and associate who was the director of the Anderson Galleries. Marsden Hartley wrote "Peter Doyle and the Whitman Group," an unpublished essay about Whitman's influence on a younger generation of art makers, and also created two visual homages to the poet: realist depictions of Whitman's Camden, New Jersey, home.[1]

Whitman's prose was also analyzed and celebrated in Paris by critics searching for insights into the democratic hybrid that had developed in America and the nature of the consciousness it had shaped.[2] His radical democratic ideology, created in the wreckage of the Civil War, appealed to Europeans and Americans who had been shocked by the carnage of World War I. Whitman's faith in and emphasis on the inevitability of a constructive American future too was heartening and inspiring. In 1923 Waldo Frank wrote: "I look on Whitman today not so much as a cultural possession of America . . . we have not yet won him . . . but rather as a Challenge. He is a challenge to our literature, to our criticism, to our institutions, to our entire social policy, to grow up to his own universal Norm. The prophets were such a challenge to the Hebrews . . . and they accepted it. Let us do likewise."[3]

Whitman believed that to fulfill America's promise, men and women would have to work collaboratively, in groups:

> I have dream'd . . . [of] a little or a larger band— . . . the members separated, it may be . . . —but always one, compact in soul, conscience-conserving, God-inculcating, inspired achievers, not only in literature, the greatest art, but achievers in all art—a new, undying order, dynasty, from age to age transmitted—a band, a class, at least as fit to cope with current years, our dangers, needs, as those who, for their times, so long, so well, in armor or in cowl, upheld and made illustrious, that far-back feudal, priestly world.[4]

His program provided ideological fuel for both communitarian ideals and visionary fervor. That members of the Stieglitz circle based their program specifically on Whitman's notion of a "band" as effective as medieval crusaders or clergy is doubly significant. To look back on the Middle Ages is to recall (as did the circle's other main guides, the reformist artists and critics William Morris and John Ruskin) a time when artists' guilds thrived and when collaborative craft created magnificent work in all forms of the fine and minor arts.

Artists in the circle, who saw themselves as the band of inspired achievers who could fulfill America's promise, altered Whitman's vision to include themselves. For while the poet did not overlook the social role of visual artists in "Democratic Vistas"—he included them in his rhetorical question, "Do you term that perpetual, pistareen, paste-pot work, American art, American drama, taste, verse?" (p. 955)—literature was primary for him. Indeed, Whitman replaced Plato's philosopher-king with the poet; because literature was "the greatest art," the poet can hold the greatest sway over the popular imagination, and thereby bears the greatest social responsibility and enjoys the highest prestige. The Stieglitz group appropriated the poet's role for visual artists.

For Whitman, a hierarchic organization of "inspired achievers" was a given of both the natural and social orders. By the eighteenth century, there were five fine arts whose ranking varied at different times;[5] modernism directly and repeatedly challenged the hierarchic schema. The invention of photography and its widespread dissemination made change more urgent. The struggle to validate photography as a form of fine art drove Alfred Stieglitz throughout his life. It was unquestionably a major factor in his involvement with the Photo-Secession (originally called the Camera Club of New York) and in his orchestration of the very first U.S. photographic show, held in the Albright Art Gallery (now the Albright-Knox Art Gallery) in Buffalo, New York, in 1910. Stieglitz also promoted modernist painting at the Photo-Secession's gallery, 291, welcoming both American and European works beginning in 1907. Such efforts demonstrate his ambitions, shared by his colleagues, to revise and then realize Whitman's vision of art as a cultural force.

The circle's attempts to raise the professional status of artists working in the newest visual media, photography and film, were part of a broader change taking place in American society. In the early twentieth century, the professional classes weathered an upheaval in relative status as new patterns of deference and power were formed. The rapid development of large cities, the emergence of great industrial plants, and the growth of corporations led to historic shifts, transforming forever the nineteenth-century social order. Americans increasingly began to seek prestige, as well as commercial markets, internationally.

The connection between prestige and the market is critical. American artists found the American art market expanding at a tremendous rate and suddenly becoming international following the Armory Show of 1913: as the competition for notoriety and power became fiercer, so did the struggle to exhibit and distribute their works. Artists were battling against not just economic disenfranchisement but also the loss of their hard-won position as communicators of ethical values. Those who shared Whitman's ideals and believed that the ultimate goal of the artist was to "morally influenc[e] the world" ("Democratic Vistas," p. 934) were particularly eager to apply that global dictum on the widening cultural stage.

Whitman, by grounding the transformative power of art in an American ideology, helped legitimize similar ideas more recently proposed by Europeans. All the modernists were spurred by the knowledge that visual artists in the past had won more prestige and power than seemed available to their twentieth-century descendants; those in the Stieglitz circle were driven by their conviction that that status was linked to the artist's imaginative power to transform other members of their society. They substituted the visual artist for Whitman's poet who gave birth to "the fervid and tremendous IDEA, melting everything else with resistless heat, and solving all lesser and definite distinctions in vast, indefinite, spiritual, emotional power" (p. 936).

These efforts to change the old hierarchy and gain influence became more explicit in 1919 when Waldo Frank published *Our America*. Written at the request of French intellectuals visiting New York who wanted to know the postwar "state of the arts" in America, the book contains a socially engaged writing unique to America at the time. Facts, mythopoetic fictions, and artistic and sociocultural criticism are interlaced throughout. While the first chapter presents *Our America* as a history of American civilization, drawing explicitly on the theories of the then-controversial historian Charles Beard to explore the economic underpinnings of American society, the introduction focuses on the political arena. Here Frank lambastes Progressivism (identified with the "decadent" Roosevelt administration) and its ideological ancestor, pragmatism (figured as the modern academic type).[6] Frank, like Van Wyck Brooks, distrusted Progressivism both because of its links with American business and because business, pursuing its own self-interest, was responsible for the ills of industrialism. Like Whitman and Brooks, Frank sought to replace the ideologies he claimed were outdated with a reformed, democratic realism (p. 8). His introduction ends memorably: "We go forth all to seek America. And in the seeking we create her.

In the quality of our search shall be the nature of the America that we create" (p. 10). Frank sought to compose not an economic history but an American mythos—specifically, a modern creation myth that would give Americans a new cultural identity. He and his colleagues were quite conscious that they were inventing an image: they believed that if America continued to be identified exclusively with commercial and military prowess, the careers and ambitions of the country's artists—and society as a whole—would suffer.

One hub of American creativity already familiar to Frank's international readers was 291. In *Our America* Frank describes his circle's first cooperative gallery as "a religious fact," a "refuge, certain and solitary, from the tearing grip of industrial disorder." Even more, "No place could be so holy as this place, for no place could be less holy than the world around it. New York was a lying destroying storm: '291' was a candle that did not go out, since it alone was the truth" (p. 184). Frank's image represented 291 as a new church, a communal gathering place constructed to produce and disseminate both a modern ethos and its accompanying mythos. As Whitman had predicted, visual artists and theorists were laying claim to the former prerogatives of religious institutions. Note, too, Frank's contention that the work of 291 had not ended though the gallery had closed. Continuing the religious metaphor, Frank insists that Stieglitz "is the prophet . . . the true Apostle of self-liberation in a destructive land. . . . Stieglitz is primarily the Jewish mystic" (p. 186). The French, like artists and critics around the world, were fully aware of Stieglitz's talents; he was inarguably the premier American photographer of the time. But with this loaded biblical imagery and hyperbolic praise, Frank tried to secure for the photographer a different kind of recognition: as a leader with remarkable spiritual qualities who could, as Whitman insisted, be the moral leader of his society. This is a kind of wish fulfillment that only image making permits—and satisfies. Whether the French accepted Frank's representation of the Stieglitz circle (and whether that matters) is outside the scope of my argument.[7] It was only one part of Frank's message.

Another important goal was to draw readers' attention to the issue of artists' groups in general. *Our America* ends with a leftist analysis of the contemporary political scene, which Frank found overrun with materialists and "shallow" liberals: "Everywhere it is clear that America is still in the chaotic stage of individual effort. The individualism of the unintegrated herd as contradistinguished from that of the social unit[.] . . . [O]nly the Opposition is close-knit. Millionaire and journalist and politician . . . each know each other's mind, corroborate each other's word" (p. 200). Not simply interest groups but classes are clashing as they refuse to compromise in pursuit of self-serving ends. As a remedy, Frank proposes the broadening and strengthening of the bases of support for American cultural "workers." Frank assures his European audience that "[i]n the scattered corners of the great Darkness, many men light many fitful fires. . . . We must begin to generate within ourselves the energy which is love of life. For that energy to whatever form the mind consigns it, is religious. Its act is creation. And in a dying world, creation is revolution" (p. 201). Only artists united in collaborative effort would have the creative energy to transform society. Frank thus proclaims his belief in the possibility of reform and his collaborative role in constructing a revolutionary democratic mythos for the still-scattered arts community.

Frank was not alone in attempting to update the French image of America. So did Marsden Hartley in *Adventures in the Arts* (1921), a series of essays dedicated to Alfred Stieglitz and also grounded in Whitmanian ethics. Frank had a hand in producing Hartley's treatise and wrote its introduction. There Frank presents a fictionalized portrait of Hartley, identifying him with the archetypal American artist: "Hartley is in some ways a continuance of Ryder." Albert Pinkham Ryder was an artistic progenitor revered almost as much as Whitman by the Stieglitz circle. (Hartley devotes an entire chapter to Ryder, as Paul Rosenfeld does later in *Port of New York*.) "One stage is Ryder, the solitary who remained one," Frank continued; "A second stage is Hartley, the solitary who stands against the more aggressive, more interested marketplace."[8] Frank's brief history tries to account for the dramatic changes in the socioeconomic context for making art in America. Indeed, in articles of the early 1920s, he often expressed his concern about what he ironically termed the "prosperity" of the American artist in the contemporary American art market (virtually synonymous with the New York art market). The remainder of the book suggests that Hartley closely shared Frank's interests.

After setting up Ryder as a model, Hartley writes a prescription for the type of artist that America needed: "The real art of America . . . will be headed by the imaginative artists . . . in point of their value as indigenous creators, having worked out their artistic destinies on home soil with all the virility of creators in the finer sense of the term."[9] Hartley himself could not meet this ideal. Critics have often blamed his international wanderings for his less successful works. Had Hartley chosen to remain a New Englander, they suggest, his work would certainly be more uniform in quality. Such an argument tells us little about Hartley's paintings and drawings but a great deal about the power of his own mythmaking.

As in his articles in the magazine *El Palacio*,[10] Hartley, in *Adventures in the Arts*, attributes the changes he perceived in the international artistic community to World War I: "Art in general is more national or local than it has ever been, due mostly to the recent upheaval, which has been of great service to the re-establishment of art interest and art appreciation everywhere in the modern world. Art, like life, has had to begin all over again, for the very end of the world had been made visible at last" (pp. 57–58). The war and its aftershocks, still felt in ongoing social and economic changes in the early twenties, were responsible for the international trend he observed toward native or local expression.[11] Most important, it is specifically the artist in the imaginative mode who must rise, phoenix-like, to resume an essential function that had been eclipsed during the war years.

In a chapter titled "Modern Art in America," Hartley turns to the subject of artists' cooperative groups, which he sees as the means by which artists will gain social ascendancy. He examines collaborative groups, such as the Stieglitz circle (whose members he carefully lists), and exhibition societies, such as the Society of Independent Artists and the Société Anonyme (pp. 62–63). These societies, like 291 (to which he compares them), functioned primarily not to sell works of art but to provide broader public exposure for them. Although Hartley was not naive about economics, in the early twenties he still clearly shared the priorities of his mentor and patron, Stieglitz. Status and prestige were the key issues, as is underscored by Hartley's comment on the circle members: "There may be no questioning as to how much success all of these artists would have in their respective ways in the various groupings that prevail in Europe at this time." And his definition of "success" follows Brooks's: "They would be recognized at once for the authenticity of their experience and for their integrity as artists gifted with international intelligence" (pp. 62–63). It is just this kind of success—the recognition of their talents and accomplishments as creative intellects by an international public—that Hartley and his colleagues desired most. We should remember that when he wrote *Adventures in the Arts,* Hartley had already exhibited abroad with the Blue Rider, a highly innovative German exhibition society, as well as at 291. At that time, banding together to work cooperatively seemed to him the only means for artists to achieve worldwide renown.

The early-twentieth-century modernist could choose to compete for fame in a variety of ways. In the early 1920s, for Hartley as for other circle members, to consign one's work to "middlemen" (a type of American dealer, following the European model, that had suddenly proliferated on the New York scene) seemed to compromise one's values. Moreover, as Hartley points out, it harms one's art: "There is no reason whatever for believing that America cannot have as many good artists as any other country. It simply does not have them because the integrity of the artist is trifled with by the intriguing agencies of materialism" (p. 61). One could value either reputation or economic gain as paramount; no middle path was envisioned, no negotiation acceptable.

American artists in the early decades of the twentieth century, especially those in New York's Greenwich Village, often saw themselves as bohemians, alienated from middle-class communities—a persona actually imported from Europe, where it was directly tied to rapid industrialization. It can be traced back to Henri Murger's romantic novel of life on the economic fringes of Paris, *Scènes de la Vie de Bohème* (1848), which became what Malcolm Cowley called "the bible of a veritable cult of bohemianism" that spread through Europe and reached New York City late in the 1850s, its popularity cresting again in the 1890s, when dozens of bohemian circles formed and little magazines were published in New York.[12]

Americans inherited another equally powerful European image of the modern artist: Charles Baudelaire's. American intellectuals belatedly familiarized themselves with the mysterious, shadowed new world that the French poet and art critic had depicted in the mid–nineteenth century. Like Murger, Baudelaire addressed the artist's social alienation and glorified it. His writings turned the traditional value-system of the middle classes on its head. At a time when capitalism was destroying the existing social order, his work completely rejected the long-accepted bases of social relationships. Raymond Williams notes that in Baudelaire, "Isolation and loss of connection were the conditions of a new and lively perception. . . . Into the twentieth century this was to become a major response. This social character of the city—its transitoriness, its unexpectedness, its essential and exciting isolation and procession of men and events—was seen as the reality of all human life."[13] Without doubt Baudelaire's *Fleurs du Mal* was found on shelves in Greenwich Village in the 1910s and 1920s as often as *Scènes de la Vie de Bohème*.

American writers, both influenced by the French authors and beginning to experience the social disruptions of their own rapidly industrializing state, documented their acute feelings of alienation during the prewar decades. Malcolm Cowley, in reminiscences published in 1934, assumed the role of spokesperson for his colleagues: "Their real exile was from society itself, from any society with purposes they could share, toward which they could honestly contribute and from which they could draw new strength. . . . But not many of them recognized the nature of their disease. Feeling oppressed by the society that existed, most of them proposed to cure themselves by withdrawing from it still further into a world of their own."[14] Most in the American literary community saw such a withdrawal as the appropriate response to changes generated by industrial capitalism, but some visual artists chose engagement, even at the risk of being viewed as *retardataire*—or worse, complicit with the dominant power interests.

In the 1920s and 1930s, the artists and critics of the Stieglitz circle were among those who chose social and cultural engagement. The novels of Sherwood Anderson, for example, depicted alienation as the most undesirable human condition, as devastating intellectually as it is physically. Waldo Frank stated the circle's position in *The Re-discovery of America* (1929): "the true way of the artist is neither to reflect nor to reject the world, but to accept and transform it."[15] Their belief that artists' physical environment markedly influenced their work assumes a connectedness to social as well as natural surroundings. This assumption also shaped the sociocultural art criticism produced by the circle's authors. Had he not believed that works of art can change society, a historian and social critic like Waldo Frank would probably not have been concerned with art criticism or the production of art.

The strong resolve of the circle's members to combat alienation suggests that they themselves felt it; several letters attest to their fear of becoming disconnected from society at large.[16] Publicly they decried postwar America for alienating its creative talent. That idea sets the tone in the first paragraph of Frank's 1926 review of an exhibition of Arthur Dove's work: "A woman does not know her unborn child, yet she is aware and concerned that it is quick within her. A woman is a more conscious creature than our old America which carries her pregnancy about, unknowing and denying. Were this not so of our land, a painter like Arthur Dove would not reach fifty years in an obscurity so little lighted."[17]

"The Alienation of the Artist: Alfred Stieglitz" by Joseph Shiffman, a classic work of scholarship that, perhaps inadvertently, leads a reader to imagine that alienation was a problem for Stieglitz alone, nevertheless accurately documents the photographer's continuous struggle to bridge the distance between himself and the American public.[18] However, treating his battle with alienation as an isolated case obscures the true nature of the problem, which is not exclusively social but rather (as Murger's *La Vie de Bohème* suggests) has an economic dimension. In a letter to Sherwood Anderson written at Lake George in 1925, Stieglitz confided:

> Last night as Georgia & I were admiring a few of my prints . . . I remarked to Georgia that it was quite wonderful that nobody seemed to want any of them. . . . [E]xperience has taught me that even if I let the prints go for $15–$20 each—I doubt if 50 prints would be sold a year—& those would primarily go to friends.—Of course I couldn't dream of working at such figures. The trouble is there is no public in America for such things as there is really no public for Marin, Hartley or Dove. For what real artist is there a public? . . . So when your letter came this morning I wasn't a bit surprised that you should feel you wish you could afford to write for yourself.[19]

Although group members had creative problems intermittently, they worried constantly about disseminating their work. Stieglitz sold no more than a handful of prints during his lifetime, partly because he wished to play the role of "amateur"—so that he would be linked to indigenous, folk, and noncommercial artists. But because he had a steady income from an inheritance, Stieglitz suffered less than other members of the circle from the conflict between the need to survive economically and the desire to avoid the compromises forced by involvement in the art market.

In a series of private letters and a sequence of articles published in the *New Republic* during the 1920s Frank criticized America's imposition of economic marginality on its artists. Stieglitz's response to Frank reflects his several decades of grappling with "the situation," the circle's shorthand for

> Money!—More money! And anything that will bring that—& ever more of that—Don't I know?—Isn't it the cry I've heard the last thirty years. . . . If you know your work—your contributions—to be something positive—I know it must hurt one constituted like yourself . . . to feel that true understanding of that work is lacking—that even your closest friends seem incapable of realizing its worth—you feel alone—I wonder if not every real Creator feels very alone. . . . [T]hese are very hard days for the true artist—May be the days were ever hard for all true Artists.[20]

By the mid-1920s critical writers associated with the Stieglitz circle, especially Anderson and Frank, had become more actively involved in the American socialist movement, often supporting its tenets publicly. They hoped, like many contemporary artists, that political engagement would give them a voice against the commercial interests they felt were corrupting their work. Privately, Sherwood Anderson aired his views on artists' activism: "I would like to see artists in America become a bit more class-conscious. I would like to see them quit kneeling down before money and middle-class standards."[21] Had Anderson's call been more persistent and found a wider audience, the issue of class difference might not have remained a blind spot of socially engaged American artists well into the 1990s.[22] Yet by following the native poetic tradition and spurning that of Baudelaire, the circle deliberately continued the chain of social involvement preached by Whitman in "Democratic Vistas." The ideal artist is not simply liberated but a leader who liberates others. The ethos transmitted by Whitman left the group facing an important question: if the artist—the rightful cultural-spiritual leader of America—succumbed to crass capitalism, what would happen to society as a whole?

By the twenties, acutely aware of extensive borrowings from Europe (influencing art, art marketing, and even the artists' self-image), the Stieglitz circle made a concerted effort to redirect American artists' interests and to forge relationships with a culturally minded community and society in general. In place of the "alienated" artist, circle members envisioned and practiced an active role in society. Their model artist remained skeptical not of politics or society but of the corrupting money and power interests attached to those domains.[23] Contemporaries recognized in the published writings of the circle the kind of ideological transformation they too were attempting to enact. Praising the criticism of Paul Rosenfeld, Robert Lovett wrote in the *Dial:* "The art which he envisages is thus at once personal and communal; it implies mastery of material by craftsmanship and enlargement of spirit by co-operation."[24]

In "Emerging Greatness," published first in the *Seven Arts* and reprinted in his 1924 collection of essays titled *Salvos,* Waldo Frank appropriated both Van Wyck Brooks's issues and his persuasive tone. Finding fault with James McNeill Whistler and Henry James for their rejection of American popular culture, Frank claimed that "the clear subtlety of these men was achieved by a rigorous avoidance of native stuff and native issues. Literally, they escaped America." He condemned American expatriates more generally: "Artist-senses have gone out, felt the raw of us, been repulsed by it, and so withdrawn to a magnificent introversion."[25]

Frank's debt to Brooks was also clear in the brief address he prepared for the annual Walt Whitman Celebration in 1923 (though he did not attend). This apotheosis of the poet echoed Brooks's assessment of Whitman's meaning for American cultural life. Frank fully accepted Whitman's view of the social function of the poet-leader, as expounded by Brooks; to raise contemporary writing to meet those moral and aesthetic standards was an enormous task, as he warned: "We shall then see in our possession of Walt Whitman a responsibility rather than a flattering boast: a responsibility that is very grim and very hard, indeed."[26] By intimating that his own prose showed the terrific strain, he demonstrated his seriousness of purpose—and, by extension, that of other socially engaged writers in the circle. The young critics whose reputations were intertwined with those of visual artists in the Stieglitz circle were (on the model of Whitman's notorious self-publicizing) fast becoming their own best public advocates.

In 1924 Frank produced the manifesto "For a Declaration of War," which appeared as the introduction to *Salvos*. In it he dispensed advice directly to visual artists, not prescriptively but hypothetically, by imagining a transformed future. In this respect, Frank's essay (like Paul Rosenfeld's *Port of New York*, published the same year) imitates another, with which it should be seen as in dialogue: André Breton's *Manifeste du Surréalisme* of 1924. By privileging the imagination and the unconscious, Frank shows himself a proponent of key Continental tenets. Moreover, he insists that cultural transformation must be based on an ethos: "The roots of culture are philosophical; religious, ethical, aesthetic. There can be no criticism for our modern world until there is a modern philosophical synthesis."[27] The purpose of his tract was to hasten the development of this needed synthesis, whose shape is familiar not from European theory but from Whitman and Brooks. Art will be crucial in this process, primarily because of its moral function: "The great work of art invests the individual with the ecstasy of participation in the Whole. This function is not kin to the religious, it is one with it. The great primal artists were creators, prophets, and sustainers of religion" (p. 17). "Religion" was valued by the circle mainly for fostering community cohesion.

Art, Frank points out—following Brooks—tends similarly to work as a binding social force in a community; it should—as Whitman declared—also serve a spiritual function. Frank, like Brooks, offers a version of the past that will provide a precedent, real or imagined, for a value structure that grants artistic creations and their makers high prestige. But to gain (or regain) that structure requires a war against "the mediocre minds . . . which control our universities and schools and churches, make our laws, rule our states and write almost all our books" (p. 23). Like Brooks, Frank takes to task an entire generation of Progressives, the thinkers in whose hands the interests of the country had rested for a generation.

Frank's rhetorical questions in "For a Declaration of War" are plain enough: Who interprets experience? Who mediates experience for the community? Frank (again like Brooks before him) named those who should, as well as those who should not. This essay, very much like the manifesto of French surrealists, is a war whoop of nondoctrinaire leftist thinkers fighting conservative intellectuals. Frank's opposition to logic and system parallels that of his French contemporaries. But while theorists such as André Breton and Paul Eluard looked to Marxian ideology for social solutions, Frank and his circle turned to Whitman's reform-minded democratic ethos and Morris's social and aesthetic thought. The American thinkers were concerned about who would ultimately control all representational media (of art as well as news) in their society. At stake, then as now, were power and prestige.

Circle authors attempted to reach a wider public by avoiding abstruse theorizing. That this was a deliberate choice is clear from Paul Rosenfeld's *Port of New York,* which defined the circle's notion of the role of artist leaders: to clarify and demarcate the common ground they shared with their audience, the American public at large. The desire to move beyond simply discussing ideals derived as much from a radical democratic ideology as from hostility toward French methods of art making and marketing. As Sherwood Anderson put it, urging his fellow artists to move "with greater daring into life": "We shall have to begin to write out of the people and not for the people."[28] The artist as observer must give way to the actively engaged artist participant. This idea of art "from down under" (to borrow a phrase from revisionist historians) underlies the 1960s phenomenon of pop art.

Port of New York was particularly instrumental in the circle's struggle toward a democratic art. Rosenfeld intended it to provide New York's community of visual artists with both an ideological base and exemplary models. Each of the fourteen critical essays that constitute the book takes as its subject an American of creative talent: painter, poet, musician, or political essayist. Included in these prose portraits are five visual artists of the Stieglitz circle: Marsden Hartley, John Marin, Arthur Dove, Georgia O'Keeffe, and Alfred Stieglitz. Others featured include Van Wyck Brooks, Sherwood Anderson, and Albert Pinkham Ryder. While most essays focus on contemporaries, others (like that of Ryder) are commemorative—tributes of the type Hartley praised in celebrating the style and content of American folk art.

Rosenfeld sets out his method plainly in his foreword. His selection of the fourteen characters portrayed was based not on rational criteria but on intuition: "all of them had given me the sensation one has when, at the close of a prolonged journey by boat, the watergate comes by, and one steps forth and stands with solid under foot."[29] In a single paragraph Rosenfeld both supports and demonstrates the antirational, mythopoetic mode of historical narrative prescribed earlier by Hartley and Frank. And he deploys imagery grounded in Whitman's nativist prose and Brooks's call for indigenous expression.

The "solid" under Rosenfeld's foot was the soil of Manhattan Island—the place he believed held the promise of America's postwar rejuvenation. The cultural products fashioned by the fourteen individuals chosen had given him "the happy sense of a new spirit dawning in American life, and awakened a sense of wealth, and of power which was not there before" (p. vi). Rosenfeld commends the wealth and power of a nation rich in high-quality cultural wares. Such an appraisal calls into question the dominant values of the time. In effect, Rosenfeld uses the prose portraits—and, more particularly, the works created by these Americans—to present his alternative to the middle-class business-centered priorities of a rapidly industrializing society.

He also tries to show that a democratic ethos, the sole source of America's real prosperity, had survived the war.

Rosenfeld's description of the nineteenth-century American painter Ryder praises the power of artistic imagination, thereby contradicting the claims of contemporary French purists, who argued for the supremacy of reason in art: "He worked from feeling. Life at length had brought forth in the West a painter able to work from what he perceived upon his eyelids when his eyes were shut" (p. 15). This revisionist history places Ryder at the very center of Western painterly tradition—not in the peripheral or eccentric position to which he, along with American artists in general, is customarily assigned. Rosenfeld is in part answering Breton's first *Surrealist Manifesto*. Where the Europeans claimed Giorgio de Chirico as forebear and model, Rosenfeld attempts to establish Ryder, an indigenous American painter, as a primary inventor of the modern imaginative mode in the visual arts. His homage to Ryder's ability to paint an inner vision, legitimizing the modernists' preference for nonmimetic paintings, echoes Whitman, who pronounced the act of the subjective imagination superior to objective, rational analysis. By engaging in this transatlantic conversation, Rosenfeld's *Port of New York,* like Frank's *Our America,* helped inform the critical reception in Europe of the next generation of American visual artists. And its effects have been lasting: three-quarters of a century later, we tend to agree with Rosenfeld that a Eurocentric canon of Western art history that heroizes de Chirico but ignores Ryder leaves itself open to question, at the very least.

In his treatment of Van Wyck Brooks, Rosenfeld sketches the vision he shares with the elder critic, stressing their mutual reliance on Whitman and skepticism about pragmatic thinking. He asks rhetorically: "Does not pragmatism therefore turn the natural order of things inside out when it accepts the intelligence instead of the imagination as the value-creating entity?" Rosenfeld answers his own question immediately: "It does, virtually if not absolutely. . . . It makes its bed where the winged horse of poetry ought to lie" (p. 40). With Brooks, Rosenfeld joins in the search for the poet-hero who will liberate contemporary American society from the grip of materialism. In subsequent chapters the mythic poet-hero does in fact appear, in the person of Carl Sandburg as well as William Carlos Williams. But in Rosenfeld's view, as his selection of subjects in *Port of New York* makes obvious, the true hero is not the poet but the visual artist.

Rosenfeld begins to make his case for the important cultural role of painters and photographers in his essay on Marsden Hartley, a longtime member of the Stieglitz circle. Tellingly, he says nothing about Hartley's role as writer and critic, concentrating on him solely as visual artist. Like Ryder, Hartley is praised for his imagination: "On the materials of the exterior cosmos he establishes a little sealed world declarative of his own inward human order" (p. 86). For Rosenfeld, the artist becomes a "creator" not by reproducing visible appearances but by inventing a distinct and personal view. Rosenfeld cleverly draws on Hartley's earlier assessment of American folk art to evaluate the painter's own works. And he argues that Hartley's New England heritage makes him the literal, legitimate heir of the values and (purported) social stature of early folk artists.

In Rosenfeld's *Port of New York* as in the *Surrealist Manifesto,* logic has no place: in its stead is an American mythos, which is consciously fabricated. In fact, Hartley's family moved from Maine to Ohio when he was quite young. And by casting Hartley as the descendant of folk artists, Rosenfeld glosses over Hartley's many years of study in the United States and abroad. Like virtually all members of the Stieglitz circle, including the Yale-educated Frank and Rosenfeld, Hartley received academic training that was both thorough and traditional. Their attempts to cultivate the modes and expressiveness of the untutored in fact demonstrated their sophistication of taste, not naïveté.

Noting Hartley's and Frank's calls for ultrarealism, Rosenfeld praises Hartley in particular for impressing his own vision so powerfully on those who view his works that "To go to New England mountain country in fall-time is to see early Hartleys strewn up every furry hillside and 'round every blue-black lake" (p. 92). Because the artist's memorable representations of land are indelibly etched in viewers' minds, they can no longer innocently perceive raw landscape. And it is Hartley's art that makes landscape valuable to behold. By implication, cultural authority and power accrue to visual artists on the basis of their extraordinary power to shape the beholder's view.

The essay on John Marin begins: "Marin is fast in American life like a tough and fibrous apple tree lodged and rooted in good ground" (p. 153).[30] Rosenfeld is clearly recalling Brooks's notion of "rootedness," which was itself an elucidation of Whitman's call for an indigenous artistic tradition. Rosenfeld's debt to both authors is evident throughout the essay, and his oblique references both affirm the vitality of their theories and lend weight to his approval of the painter. In particular, he applauds Marin's balance: "Feeling and thought are one in him inseparably" (p. 158). For Rosenfeld, by seeming to resolve the split between hand and brain that Brooks had seen as a pathological American condition, Marin has become the prototype of a new, more "healthy" American. Rosenfeld sees Marin as belonging to the new class of cultural achievers prophesied by Whitman (and links him to his environment as "the Ancient Mariner").[31] He goes further: "None but one American-born could have rubbed this pigment and made it into the peculiarly tempered color it is," Rosenfeld claims. "It strikes a western dominant with its salt and slap. Something Walt Whitmanish abides in its essence" (p. 162). In Rosenfeld's story the prophecy had been fulfilled with the appearance of a visual artist whose imaginative powers and sensuous and idiosyncratic expression rival those of Whitman himself. This written appreciation of Marin's talents celebrated an individual; more important, however, it constituted a seminal moment in the history of American art and art theory and criticism, for it went beyond reflecting culture to create culture.

Whitman has other rivals. The works of Arthur Dove are, for Rosenfeld, "a sort of

'Leaves of Grass' through pigment" (p. 169). In discussing Dove and Dove's works Rosenfeld continues to build his case against pragmatic thinking, insisting that imagination is harnessed through the senses:

> When [Dove] paints, the pressure on the brush in his hand carries the weight of the body as a whole, and the life of the body as a whole. He has always a fund of robust and delicate animalism to express. He has dark, pungent, gritty hues in his palette; dark subtle silences and delicate gradations of earth-brown and dull shadowy greens and dirt-grays and interesting whites that seem to flow from the body's fearless complete acceptance of itself. (p. 169)

Besides Whitman's sensuousness, Dove is said to achieve in his paintings the inclusiveness characteristic of the poet. Rosenfeld claims that like Whitman, Dove, through an act of empathy, becomes one with the object beheld: "Objects do not bring him consciousness of his own person. Rather, they make him lose it in the discovery of the qualities and identities of the object. The center of life comes to exist for him outside himself, in the thing, tree or lamp or woman, opposite him. He has moved himself out into the object" (p. 171). Like the poet, a visual artist can enable the public to participate in an expansive psychological experience. For Rosenfeld, the ability he finds in Dove is valuable not only because of its novel, ostensibly democratic qualities but also because it accommodates both Hartley's and Frank's theories.

As we have already seen in his treatment of Hartley and Marin, Rosenfeld refashions Dove into a mythopoetic figure. In *Port of New York* and other writings, he pictures Dove as the reincarnation of the type of American farmer who is the mainstay of Jeffersonian democracy. The critic declares: "He was a farmer when he painted most of his pieces, and cows and calves and growing plants were in his mind" (p. 173). It is a strong and durable American image, but Rosenfeld weaves in a story of even greater age and resonance: Dove, the overseer of the untouched acres of rural America, is also caretaker of Eden—the new Adam. "Dove comes out of a culture commencing to base itself upon the whole personality," Rosenfeld affirms. "In Ryder the old Puritan dividedness still obtained; the fugitive state from body and earth; the duality of body and soul. That is passed in the New Man" (p. 173). By implication, the visual artist will effect the reformation of American society that Rosenfeld and his circle desire. This claim for the power of visual artists and art itself is both lofty and staggering.

Given the major role that Rosenfeld accords to the visual artists, we might well wonder what he finds praiseworthy in an author. He writes of Sherwood Anderson: "He has taken the words surely, has set them firmly end to end, and underneath his hand there has come to be a surface as clean and fragrant as that of joyously made things in a fresh young country. The vocabulary of the simplest folk; words of a primer, a copy-book quotidianness, form a surface as hard as that of pungent fresh-planed boards of pine and oak" (p. 176). Rosenfeld sees Anderson's prose, like Hartley's paintings, as resembling well-crafted folk art. He values Anderson's concreteness, the ability to use vernacular constructions to conjure sensuous images. More important than Anderson's prose are his methods, which Rosenfeld compares to those of folk craftworkers of America's past—makers whose attitude toward their work, we are told, was joyous. In addition, Rosenfeld is captivated by Anderson's realism. "For the business of seeing people without romanticizing them, of drawing them without putting himself below or above them" (p. 194), he congratulates Anderson and credits him for democratizing his point of view and thereby inventing a new realistic mode—one predicted by both Hartley and Frank.[32]

In *Port of New York* Rosenfeld shapes Sherwood Anderson's image as deliberately as he had those of other members of the circle. For the rest of his career Anderson would be figured as a convert, like the apostle Paul. Rosenfeld tells the reader: "Towards his thirty-fifth year he became sick of soul. He commenced to feel the state in which he was living was filthy. . . . Business began to become a bore. Businessmen, with their self-importance and goshing simplicity, began to become ludicrous" (p. 193). Anderson had been a successful Illinois businessman. And he had chosen to leave his business, his wife, and his children to pursue his hobby—writing. Rosenfeld fictionalizes Anderson as a reformed man of commerce whose psyche was healed through his transformation into amateur author. Beyond defining the image of each artist in the group, Rosenfeld was concerned with how they meshed together. Indeed, the Stieglitz circle was intent on creating a collective identity. Who was the artist in modern American society? Who was he or she permitted to be? By forming such a communal group, the artists attempted to protect their powers of self-representation—from dealers, from the press, and from the rising American bourgeoisie.

Rosenfeld's treatment in *Port of New York* of Georgia O'Keeffe, who fit uneasily into this collective identity, is both dated and unsettling. While the purple prose may strike us as amusing, the assumptions behind his portrait now seem insidious. The essay, though no doubt intended as a respectful salute to O'Keeffe (who was a good friend), is in fact an exercise in sexual division. Rosenfeld begins by praising her art for the same qualities that in his view distinguished the work of the male members of the circle: imaginativeness, invention, feeling, expressiveness. In addition, he commended her sensuous line and torrid color. But in the same breath he claimed that her uniqueness and value rested in her sex rather than in her trained talents, judging that "Her concepts are not half in man's tradition" (p. 204). In essence, O'Keeffe's ideas are viewed as "other"; she cannot be compared with her male colleagues, for her art must be set apart. O'Keeffe, irritated throughout her professional career by being marked as "different" and by her isolation from the male members of the circle, at the same time was spurred by such treatment to compete more vigorously.

To create O'Keeffe's public image, Rosenfeld combined a number of late-nineteenth-century symbolist stereotypes of women. Since there were few strong female prototypes on which to draw—ancient mariners, Jeffersonian farmers, and converted apostles were an exclusively male lot—Rosenfeld depicted O'Keeffe as "the little girl and the sybil, the wild, mysterious, long haired one and the great calm rooted tree" (p. 204). This sexualized image dogged O'Keeffe into her ninetieth year, when she was rumored to have captivated the affections of a young potter—a protégé fifty years her junior.

The image of O'Keeffe as seductress and of her works as charged with an electric eroticism had at least Stieglitz's imprimatur. Indeed, he capitalized on it in 1921, publicly displaying part of his serial portrait of her, begun during the first year of their relationship. Some of the photographs in this formally innovative series are strikingly sexual, even by late-twentieth-century standards. The early-twentieth-century press gave the nude portrayals top billing, and crowds of titillated spectators thronged the exhibition. Moreover, Rosenfeld revised part of *Port of New York* while a guest in the summer home of Stieglitz's family at Lake George, New York. Without question, Rosenfeld would have excised any representation of O'Keeffe Stieglitz found unacceptable. It is equally clear that O'Keeffe was not sold on this public image; as early as 1922 she tried (with little success) to create an alternative that emphasized her professional accomplishments.[33] In their attempts to model O'Keeffe's image after the eternal feminine, an image given new currency by psychoanalytic theory, both Stieglitz and Rosenfeld also commercialized it, manipulating prurient public interest to broaden their audience and further the circle's renown. Contemporary French surrealists, too, commodified the female body in depicting the female "muse": if the lover-companions of the male artists more often than not were artists in their own right, the males did not represent this more public and social role in their images. This was one ancient trope that modernists on both sides of the Atlantic continued to employ.

The final prose portrait in Rosenfeld's book, and thus in a sense his last word on the theories he is offering, is of his friend and patron, Alfred Stieglitz. Before launching into a lengthy panegyric on the photographer, his art, and his gallery activities, Rosenfeld—doubtless at Stieglitz's prompting—sets the record straight on the history of 291. "It was not because of the public's attitude that the gallery closed," Rosenfeld assures us. "It was because of the smallness of the artists that it had to be destroyed." This is indeed a provocative claim. Is Rosenfeld about to chastise his fellow circle members? No, they are not guilty of violating the cooperative spirit of the first gallery. He elaborates: "Stieglitz had imported modern French painting for the sake of an idea; and the French painters and their friends seemed incapable of understanding that '291' was anything but a salesroom" (p. 266). The accuracy of this account is less important than its status: it was the view favored by Stieglitz, and through his influence it had become the authorized version of history. The corrosive commercialism that reared its (Gallic) head threatened cooperative and democratic American ideals: "the artists insisted on considering Stieglitz a man overflowing with cash and full of an inexhaustible power of procuring the same for them. They seemed to have lost all sense of the idea . . . [that] the little place was never a business" (p. 266).

Here, too, Rosenfeld was engaged in creating an image: Stieglitz's mythos was comprehensive and formidable, and tailor-made by his supporters. Though the claim that Stieglitz was never a dealer stretches the definition of the word, it was hotly defended by the photographer himself as well as other group members. His lack of financial interest helped provide the basis for his ethical and cultural leadership, both within the circle and more broadly. Stieglitz is depicted by Rosenfeld as "the man who believed that a spiritual America existed somewhere, that America was not the grave of the Occident; and [the man who] had been making it possible with nourishment spiritual and physical for artists to bring out of the soil the human values of the land" (p. 268). This portrayal was everything that Stieglitz could have wished. Here he is the magnetic spiritual leader whose own creative potency draws forth the talents of others, sparking them into life like the hand of the Creator touching Adam. Rosenfeld continues in this vein, claiming, "The shows of 1921 and of 1923 [that Stieglitz orchestrated at the Anderson Galleries] were religious demonstrations" (pp. 268–69).

The critic stacks metaphor on metaphor, the same technique he uses in arguing for Hartley's and Dove's artistic prowess, to make his image of the photographer unassailable. Rosenfeld alludes to common Western religious imagery to show Stieglitz's spiritual nature (unlike Frank, who, as noted above, had called Stieglitz a Jewish mystic) and evokes as well pagan skills: "Before the lens of Stieglitz' camera, the moveless heavy woman, American life, has thrilled as from the touch of a wizard's wand" (p. 269). Stieglitz's photographic art, that is, metamorphosed America's culture—the "moveless heavy woman, American life"—so that it became vital. Rosenfeld's image evokes Stieglitz's subject in *The Last Days of "291"* (1917): the motionless, heavy folk carving of a warrior-woman, changed by the photograph into a symbol of the little gallery that had breathed life into American society. Rosenfeld may in fact have drawn his image from that photograph; in his writings he often used the figure of an unresponsive or inanimate woman to represent the spiritless America of the past and the seductive body of a female nude to image the salubrious and beautiful landscape of America in the future. By a further extension of this metaphor, O'Keeffe and the sensual photographs of her nude torso taken by Stieglitz become "equivalents"—in the rhetoric of the circle—representing America's potential and its cultural promise.

In his epilogue to *Port of New York* Rosenfeld wrote, "Somewhere in one always there had been the will to take root in New York; to come into relation with the things and the people, not in the insane self-abnegation of current patriotism and nationalism, but in the form of one's utmost self." And by the mid-twenties this desire came to pass: "A kind of strong, hearty daylight has come upon the port. Once, thought of it filled us with nostalgia and wander-dreams. Today, it brings a wash of strength and power over us. Sudden, at the foot of a street, the vague wandering eye perceives with a joyous shock a loading steamer carrying high its mast as a child carries a cross in an all-saints procession" (p. 291). At first, Rosenfeld appears to be praising the resumption of international business-as-usual after the end of the war. But his steamer is not packed with objects of trade. The change he sees as having overtaken America "is that the values have come to stand among us[;] . . . they may have stood before, in earlier American days. But in our time they were gone" (p. 295). America now is exchanging its indigenous cultural products on the international market. And for Rosenfeld and other members of the Stieglitz circle, these alone bore and imparted value. Rosenfeld sought to replace the narrow patriotic and nationalistic ideals he decried in the book with the Whitman-inflected democratic values he had carefully woven into his portraits of early-twentieth-century American visual artists. In his view, the figures represented in his text were responsible for beginning the sociocultural transformation of American society that he points to in his epilogue: "For, if to-day, the values stand aloft; if to-day the commencement of a religious sense is here; if to-day men on American land are commencing to come into relationship with one another and with the places in which they dwell, it is through the labor of some dozens of artist hands" (p. 295).

Port of New York is intended to perform multiple functions. In arguing that Whitman's "class" of artist-achievers has begun to fulfill America's promise as prophesied, Rosenfeld not only depends on and underscores the authority of Whitman's ethos, but also provides a pedigree for the artists he has selected and the ideals they represent—in their personalities as well as in their works. By creating for them an interlocking collective mythos, he also lays the groundwork for restoring to American artists the privileged social status they had enjoyed. Because they put into practice the highly valued democratic ethos, the critic feels he can ascribe to them the moral superiority that will secure their professional ascendancy. Rosenfeld specifically identifies a code of ethics with the artistic caste. This critical propaganda bound the circle in closer intimate collaboration; at the same time, it created an audience primed to appreciate their works, to develop a taste for their cultural products. Interest in and support of visual artists are made to appear not simply patriotic (as late-nineteenth-century art critics had held) but ethically imperative. Implicitly Rosenfeld promises newly converted viewers—who, like him, recognize the value of artworks—a share in the spirituality inherent in the artists' creativity.

In *Port of New York,* as elsewhere in his writings, Rosenfeld specifically links and compares the visual artists John Marin and Arthur Dove to Walt Whitman, finding them equal to the poet. His claim for Stieglitz's art, however, is that it will ultimately supplant Whitman's. Because of his expertise in the ultramodern technology of the camera, Stieglitz can mediate modern experience more effectively than his painter protégés. Today such an argument is familiar. And indeed, media based on new technologies are becoming more accessible, effective, and popular than the traditional ones; new forms of imagery are gaining dominance. In the mid-1920s Paul Rosenfeld suggested that the inherent intelligibility of photographs ensured the kind of widespread and lasting interest enjoyed by popular publications (especially those by Whitman) of the prior generation. Now computer-literate artists in new genres, whose work is featured on the Internet and the Web and increasingly shown in exhibitions devoted to the digital, are attempting to surpass older forms. Perhaps what we most need now is a renewed awareness of the important role of aesthetics in the communication system of the visual arts. In the Italian Renaissance, makers and theorists created styles that were intelligible to a broad audience and relied on their appeal to perceptual responses; during the American Renaissance of the early twentieth century, artists in both white and black communities remembered well the lessons of that earlier Renaissance and profited from them. Ultimately they arrived at a deep understanding and reevaluation of the popular and persistent appeal and diverse pleasures that a cunning aesthetics provides.

3

"A DIRECT POINT OF CONTACT"

The Intimate Gallery and An American Place

IN THE SAME SPIRIT OF TURNING TO THE PAST for visual models, the Stieglitz circle also looked for models of associating with other artists and with the public—alternatives, that is, to marketing art through dealers. The group set up a modern version of a medieval guild, the artist's cooperative, onto which they grafted contemporary practices such as the credit and installment plan. They sought not just Morrisian aesthetic reform but a thoroughgoing reconsideration of society, including its economic structure. And their desire to recapture the balance between independence and intimate relations that fortunate nineteenth-century artists had enjoyed with patrons led them to experiment with methods of display and self-representation that eliminated the need for dealers.

To appreciate the innovations of the Stieglitz circle's profit-sharing alternative, we must consider its context—the traditional ways in which art had been handled in New York City. In the 1870s, New York's National Academy of Design provided American visual artists with virtually the only sustained and consistent opportunities to exhibit and sell their work. Artists met patrons at the academy's annual exhibition and reception at the Studio Building on Tenth Street. No middlemen were involved in these interactions; dealers were almost unknown.

Besides providing a forum in which artists might meet patrons, the academy's exhibition, like its European model, the French Salon, could ensure critical notice in newspapers or art journals with an advantageous hanging. As the largest and most powerful institution in the American art market, the academy had enormous influence over the prestige and careers of its artist participants. Such control led to rebellion; by the end of the decade William Merritt Chase, a competent painter and talented teacher much favored by middle-class patrons, assumed the leadership of the Society of American Artists, a faction that split from the National Academy of Design. One of the society's main concerns was the low sales of most practicing American visual artists. The academy had managed to create only a handful of celebrities who enjoyed regular sales and good prices. As early as February 1878, members of the society were meeting to discuss how to enhance their reputations and expand the market. As the power of the academy faded during the 1870s, so too did that of the older generation of American collectors.

In the first half of the nineteenth century, American "aristocrats" (upper-class white men) had sponsored selected artists, with whom they enjoyed personal relationships. These patrons followed their chosen artists' careers closely and purchased from them regularly, even providing additional financial assistance when necessary. But by 1900 American artists found themselves in a dramatically different marketplace. A new figure had entered the scene: the dealer. Influenced by dealers, a younger generation of collectors—self-made merchants, manufacturers, and bankers—began to view artworks as a form of investment. Members of this new breed of art buyer rarely had any contact with the object's maker. (A similar shift in patronage styles recurred in America in the 1970s among purchasers of pop and superrealist art.)

The dealers did more than change how art was sold: by promoting a new taste for European works, they changed what art was sold. From the 1880s well into the twentieth century, their profits came mainly from the sales of old master and contemporary European works. American collectors found foreign works not only more desirable but more readily available, and these works commanded higher prices than comparable American works. The result was an unprecedented economic crisis for American artists. Many left the National Academy of Design, whose leaders had responded to the shift in taste by adopting French styles; ironically, the most vocal supporters of indigenous art were paying the highest prices for American works that looked most French. Frustrated artists turned to the Society of American Artists and other groups to devise new strategies for increasing their sales.

In 1892 the American Fine Arts Society, a professional organization made up of several groups opposed to the policies of the National Academy of Design, realized the hopes voiced by visual artists for two decades: it incorporated and established a permanent exhibition space in New York on Fifty-seventh Street, between Broadway and Seventh Avenue. The building gave physical form to both the society's opposition to the older institution at Tenth Street and the general uptown movement of New York's art community. It housed almost every major exhibit in New York for more than a decade, facilitating the critical appraisal of new works, if not increasing their sale.

The year 1892 was a watershed in the distribution of American art. That year Macbeth's, the first commercial gallery in New York City to succeed by dealing exclusively in American art, was established. Its success spurred others to finance similar ventures. As the number of dealerships willing to speculate in American cultural products slowly increased, so did the number of exhibitions, the number of sales, and (aided by the new Society of American Artists) the amount of press coverage they received. All factors indicate burgeoning public interest in American artworks and American art makers. But the dealers, like the society, could provide American artists with only one component of success: public recognition. Money was still hard to come by. Indeed, artists in the early twentieth century often complained that they did not receive a fair share when dealers sold their works. Customarily, artists received slightly over half the sale price of a work, while dealers often enjoyed a 100 percent profit. These commissions played a large part in the artists' dissatisfaction with the marketing of their works in New York, America's art capital in the early twentieth century.

American art collectors in the late nineteenth and early twentieth century, moreover, spent the greatest portion of their money not on American but on European art. Even the expansion of the New York art market worked against living American artists, as Linda Skalet explains:

> What had formerly been a matter of artists and patrons dealing on a one-to-one basis, had grown to include many other organizations and individuals whose sole purpose was the sale of works of art: dealers, auction houses, artists societies, etc. The nature of the relationship between artist and patron became depersonalized to a large degree[, and] . . . the economic situation for the artist without a dealer to represent him had become precarious[;] . . . he had to sell his work in an art market which was becoming more and more commercial.[1]

Painters were especially hard-pressed. What had been a secure and established career in America in the mid–nineteenth century became in the twentieth, as E. P. Richardson aptly puts it, "a poverty-stricken and insecure pursuit—as it has remained since."[2]

Such was the situation of the American artist in 1905, when members of the Stieglitz group opened their first little co-op gallery, 291. It was precisely this lack of money and status that the circle's cooperatively run galleries sought to redress, by reestablishing direct and personal relations between art maker and cultural consumer and seeking an audience larger than the one addressed by nineteenth-century artists. Members hoped to model democratized methods of operations, particularly in the two later galleries, the Intimate Gallery and An American Place, which (unlike 291) were surrounded by commercial dealers.

Of course, the transformation and expansion of American markets affected not merely cultural products but the entire system of production and consumption; the art market, bound up with changing tastes and habits of collecting, was exceptionally responsive to these developments. One conspicuous, and seemingly permanent, change in the marketing of American-made goods first appeared at this time. America's traditional method of business transaction, cash-and-carry, was gradually replaced by the credit and installment plan.[3] The new system was so well received and so widely practiced that by the end of the 1920s more than half of all major purchases were bought "on installment."

The new pattern of American buying held in all arenas. The increased number of art dealerships in New York City during the 1910s made cultural products more widely available to consumers who had more spending power than ever. The dealers embraced new methods of distribution borrowed from business as eagerly as they did the new European styles of painting and sculpture. Following the example that had brought wealth to the new class of patrons, New York dealers of the period made credit readily available and payment by installment became common. An art object in the hands of even the best-intentioned dealer who subscribed to these new sales tactics necessarily lost its former status. Now permanently separated from its maker's character and personality, a canvas or photograph became a commodity no different from all other consumables. In the name of democracy—of increasing the availability of American products and broadening the market for even cultural salables—the notion that art has an intrinsic moral and spiritual value was easily discarded. Once the public began to equate paintings and refrigerators, the meanings that early-twentieth-century American modernists wished to assign to cultural products were lost.

When art dealers of the twenties, like manufacturers, reorganized the display of goods to satisfy their customers they also began to predict more accurately and even to shape the demand for their wares. Like producers of durable goods, art dealers heightened demand by introducing rapid changes in style, promoted by advertising. The techniques of advertising became crucial for distributors and art intermediaries as competition became more intense. Although painting, sculpture, and music benefited from the increased patronage they attracted as the media disseminated more information about them, the gains were relative. American dollars were invested mainly in industrial design, the burgeoning motion picture industry, and architecture.

This context suggests why 291 closed its doors in 1917. The official version blames the marketplace. As we saw in chapter 2, for Paul Rosenfeld in *Port of New York* the problem was that "the French painters and their friends seemed incapable of understanding that '291' was anything but a salesroom."[4] With the benefit of seven years' hindsight, Rosenfeld blamed the demise of the first gallery on the conflict between capitalism and the co-op structure. Stieglitz clearly shared Rosenfeld's view. In a letter to Charles Demuth written in January 1930, he lamented his inability to get what he considered a fair price for a Demuth still life. Stieglitz blamed the competition, complaining that none of the Americans he had backed "have become rich like the French artists so lovingly supported by art loving America! Why arent [*sic*] you and Marin and O'Keeffe and Dove Frenchmen? And I at least a Man Ray in Paris? . . . Dear France! Priceless France—where would America be without its art dealers—and its hosts of great artists ('its' meaning France's)."[5]

The reasons for Stieglitz's anger are complex. He was responding not merely to the commercial practices of the French dealers (practices widely adopted by American dealers after World War I). French artists, aided by advertising and promotion, were setting the styles and attracting most of the media attention as the American market expanded. As Rosenfeld commented, looking back at the years immediately after the war: "The smart world had said 'tag' to Cézanne and he was IT. A new academy was commencing to form under his sign; and Stieglitz . . . wished he could place his foot squarely through every one of the beatified canvases of the beatified painter."[6] Indeed, a certain envy seems only appropriate. The American market for art that Stieglitz had nurtured through 291 and through the Armory Show of 1913, which he had helped stage, had taken an unforeseen shape. The growing interest in culture after the war meant a wider range of art consumers who had more money to spend than ever before. Much to the chagrin of American artists, this new audience preferred European art, whose pedigree made it seem most worthy of attention and the safest investment.

The notion of an artists' cooperative had occurred to Stieglitz at least as early as his founding of the Photo-Secession in 1902. Others in America largely ignored it during the first two decades of the twentieth century, however, and 291 remained unique in its collective approach. As we have seen, as late as 1919 Waldo Frank claimed in *Our America* that individualism still reigned—but it was "the individualism of the unintegrated herd. . . . To step out from the Lump means to find ourselves alone. Group life on the level of young America still fails."[7] The image of the "Lump" is taken directly from Whitman and refers to the American community, in which the visual artist or writer appropriately participates and finds support. But Frank predicted a change in the current state, heralded by the emergence of circles such as his: "Slowly, painfully, America moves toward the period where artists converge into groups. Loose groups, as a rule, the best of which protest they are no groups at all: but generative of the sort of energy that prods the half-awakened intellectual classes of our cities."[8] Frank's concern for the artists' economic marginality, voiced in articles in the *Seven Arts,* called attention to group cohesion as benefiting the artist participants economically as well as psychologically.

Artists of the early decades of the twentieth century were hardly alone in their sense of isolation and displacement. Rapid social and economic changes in America before and during World War I spread such feelings widely, though the awareness or concern of particular groups with the changes wrought by industrialization varied.

Manufacturers, merchants, farmers, and workers were most troubled by the shift to a price-driven market economy. Religious leaders, women reformers affiliated with the National American Women's Suffrage Association, and the rising clique of metropolitan intellectuals were horrified by the materialism of industrializing society and by the inhospitable environment it created for the human mind and body. The worries of American artists in general and the Stieglitz group in particular intersected both sets of concerns, and their responses were distinguished by their tendency not simply to experience and fight against but to thematize their sense of alienation. That sense of alienation from modern American society and from its newly imposed materialistic values in the early twentieth century drove some of them into American socialist groups that aimed to supplant materialism and competition with cooperation.[9] Members of the Stieglitz group, reacting in part to the self-interested American individualism Whitman's essays had attacked, believed that group identity and collective activity would ensure individual self-expression.

A social movement influenced by the ideas of the designer and social activist William Morris that had taken hold in America was flourishing as World War I began. Nationwide, Arts and Crafts societies were formed in an attempt to revive traditional craft industries that had been replaced by mass production. The new techniques and standards had disrupted not only preindustrial guilds and a long-standing system of apprenticeship but also the communal spirit: the feelings of social and psychological interrelatedness that handicraft activities engender. The workplace had suffered badly, and the need to regroup was pressing. New communities of craftworkers appeared in upstate New York, in rural New England, and in Appalachia.[10] And just as the 291 gallery produced its own magazine, *Camera Work,* to provide a model of craft in photography and graphic design, so the American Arts and Crafts movement published the *Craftsman,* a magazine distributed nationally between 1901 and 1916. As we saw in chapter 1, the ideology of the *Craftsman* (like that of the later literary magazine the *Seven Arts,* produced by circle advocates) was based on the theories of Morris and of the British art and architectural critic John Ruskin. Following Morris, the *Craftsman* had an agrarian bias: a concern for protecting and preserving the natural world and a skepticism about the modern locus of social life, the city.[11]

The craft ideal propounded by American Arts and Craft societies and the *Craftsman* counterbalanced the harmful effects of unregulated industry and inferior machine-made products. By asserting that the maker is the focus of the production-consumption relation, Morris and his followers restated, in concrete terms, a labor theory of value compatible with the American tradition of equal rights. The ideal artist-craftworker alone controlled his or her labor, creative work that was itself a social activity that both set and upheld standards of quality in production. The colonies of artists and craftworkers in America that emerged at the beginning of the twentieth century attempted to remove the workplace from the capitalist system. Embracing the same radical notion, Stieglitz and his colleagues banded together in New York City to maintain an exhibition space outside current art-marketing practices. Both efforts, rural and urban, achieved a degree of critical distance and independence from the capitalist marketplace.

From the first, the Stieglitz circle's galleries followed a socialist model. Stieglitz would pay part of the profits from each sale to the artist-maker, applying a percentage to the rent and miscellaneous costs of gallery operation. Theoretically, all members would benefit equally from the profit-sharing scheme. Especially during the 1924–34 period that is our concern, all had the same number of exhibitions in the gallery spaces. All the visual artists contributed to the costs of retaining and maintaining the exhibition rooms. Authors associated with the circle gave money—sometimes receiving works in return, often not. No one profited directly but the maker, and there were no "losses" as customarily defined. Above all there were none of the written contracts usual in Western business practice, but oral, personal agreements backed by friendship and mutual commitment. Flexible arrangements were key, as Stieglitz reiterated in a letter to Arthur Dove in March 1936: "The original idea was, you know, that when I bought something from you & any one was ready to pay more that I'd reimburse myself with the original outlay & the surplus after that would be divided between you & The Place."[12] The standard practice at the circle's later galleries is exemplified in a detailed, handwritten letter by Stieglitz to the buyer of a Marin oil painting: "When convenient to you, send a check for $1,500 to Alfred Stieglitz (John Marin Fund). It will interest you to know that of this money $1125 will go to Marin, and 375 will go to the Dorothy Norman Rent Fund for The Place."[13] Usually one-quarter of the profit on a single work went to the rent fund, less than most commercial art dealers of the period took for a commission. While the eventual use of the moneys held back—to pay rent, for example—might in some cases have been the same in a commercial operation, the group personalized all transactions. In the same spirit, the handwritten correspondence that recorded arrangements was purposefully crafted. Only in the last years of Stieglitz's control over gallery operations, when illness forced the change on him, did he employ secretaries to type these letters. All this is quite distinct from the practices of art cooperatives in America in the 1990s, where a forty-sixty split is standard (with the maker taking the smaller portion) and e-mail the common means of communication.

Yet another cooperative gesture that required much time and effort was made by O'Keeffe, who designed and directed the hanging of exhibitions for all group members. As the artist herself admitted,[14] this uncompensated labor was not exactly the proverbial labor of love but a form of "dues paying." It was one way a woman artist of the period could ensure continued acceptance within an all-male group in a predominantly male field of endeavor.

Ironically, members of the Stieglitz circle and other twentieth-century American artists were compelled by their social and economic situation to work collectively in order to maintain independence and individuality of creation. Just as ironically, the industrialization that forced them to band together also thrust them headlong onto the world scene, securing them a place in the international art market. The industrialization that intensified Americans' desire for material success had an even greater effect on the work environment and the natural landscape. The landscape paintings and photographs that constitute most of the circle's output eloquently address both areas. They implicitly criticize the methods and motives of those engaged in modern industry and celebrate the natural processes in which human beings can participate through unhampered creativity. The high-quality craft of these works itself embodies an ethics of production and consumption grounded in the notion of independence. The postwar paintings and photographs of the circle provided alternatives to the waste and fragmentation of industrialized society, showing America and its artists the way to a new, collaborative (not corporate) cultural identity. Through their works of literary and visual art, through the very act of production, group members achieved what commercial manufacture fails to offer: culture and its principles of cohesion.

Circle operations always relied heavily on private support, though only in the later years of the third gallery, An American Place, were large subscription drives undertaken (largely at the instigation of Dorothy Norman, Stieglitz's photographer protégée, the wife of the Sears Company heir, who began to assist in operating and fundraising for the galleries in the mid-1920s). Like the "little magazines" of the period that were subsidized by individual patrons rather than commercial advertisers, the little galleries had a well-choreographed system of self-support. A 1923 call for funds to support John Marin is typical. Titled "An Invitation to the Friends of John Marin," it pleads for the American watercolorist: "To relieve him from yearly exhibitions and from endless financial worries, a group of his friends are undertaking to guarantee 3000 dollars a year for three years, that he may work unhampered, knowing his wife and eight year old son will be cared for." The "Invitation" further asserts that Marin's artistic achievements fully merit such a "guarantee of freedom to produce."[15]

This kind of independence was the dream of artists in and outside the group, and Stieglitz always sought to procure for his colleagues an economic stability comparable to his own. Arrangements such as Marin's usually depended on the artist's knowing those willing to pledge support, for only a personal bond between artist and patron ensured security. In fact, a "membership list" of 1924 shows that one-third of the members of the "Friends of Marin" were circle intimates—among them Stieglitz himself, Georgia O'Keeffe, Paul Strand, and Paul Rosenfeld.[16] Friends did not always contribute solely from philanthropic motives or a sense of obligation to the artist or to art in general. The "Invitation" (like other solicitations) offered an enticement: "This Group of Friends is limited to twenty persons, each pledged to pay 600 dollars, the entire sum upon admission, or in three yearly instalments of 200 dollars due on or before April 15 of 1923, 1924 and 1925. This fee entitles the subscriber to double its value in Marin watercolors. It is applicable to purchases of Marin's work at the price regularly made to dealers, namely one-half the price fixed to the public." Buying on credit and in installments had by 1923 become part of the artists' cooperative plan. To underline his own position as a "disinterested" gallerist, Stieglitz closed the "Invitation" with a reminder: "All moneys received will go to John Marin without deduction."

If making money in itself (however pressing a concern) was not conceived as the final end of art making, what was the point of the circle's self-promotion? The most immediate goal was clearly control of their own image. For the group, this was to be a broader-minded, socially oriented self like that sketched by Whitman in "Democratic Vistas," a self that was accepting of difference.[17] In oral, textual, and visual presentations, they attempted, as representatives of the American public, to define and celebrate the dignity of the American cultural experience. While striving to speak for the public at large, they also worked to create a different kind of reception for cultural goods. The efforts of the Stieglitz group were part of a more comprehensive American interest in understanding, critiquing, and defining their own culture that fostered the serious study of folk culture and the cultures of marginalized groups in- and outside American society, as well as inquiries into regional behavior, values, and symbols of country dwellers—undertaken not in the name of nationalism but rather in the spirit of a common quest for a new identity, a new self-definition, a new self-image for America and Americans.

Nor was prestige among their contemporaries, though they certainly sought it, the ultimate aim. Their long-term goal, like that of Western artists since the fourteenth century, was fame. In a poignantly self-revealing letter, Stieglitz confided to Frank: "The new little prints are 'additions' so I'll appear eventually not entirely empty-handed—But think of it. I know I have achieved something worth while with these little prints—yet I also know that their span of life is about 30 years in spite of all my supreme care in making them[.] . . . [T]he paper your book is printed on may last a bit longer but its [*sic*] also doomed. Still your book can be reprinted. But my little prints—well—[.]"[18] Fortunately Stieglitz's worst fears, expressed in repeated diatribes against the Kodak Company and its "inferior" papers, were unfounded.

The Stieglitz circle attempted to win for makers, not buyers, a monopoly on the ability to set tastes in reputedly classless America. To gain cultural power, status, and economic independence, the artists had to educate the swelling and culturally uninformed American middle classes. Prosperity encouraged a more democratic and extensive audience for creative work—a fact that Marcel Duchamp, Francis Picabia, and other cultural émigrés recognized and used to their advantage after World War I.

In his role as representative of six visual artists, Stieglitz had in effect (but not in writing) an exclusive contract for their work: that is, he had an agreement covering the total production of each member of the circle. Such plans became widespread in galleries both in the United States and in France during the period. Stieglitz kept control of the market for each artist he represented, an arrangement that gave him a great deal of power over their careers. The use of such contracts is in itself a significant development in the way art is disseminated. Stieglitz used the exclusivity to create a demand for the works of his colleagues, always within the scope of a broader concern for preserving artistic independence. The artist-run cooperative system worked, for all the circle artists (except Arthur Dove) prospered during the economically unstable years before and after the Depression.

Stieglitz's unique role as unpaid gallerist assumed mythic proportions in the written tributes of circle advocates, but it had practical dimensions as well. When the operations of the Intimate Gallery were questioned by the State Tax Commission in 1928, Stieglitz replied from his family home at Lake George: "I am not in business either here or in N.Y. City—Room 303, 489 Park Ave., N.Y. City—belongs to artists—a loose group—& each one makes his individual tax report. I receive no remuneration in any shape directly or indirectly for the role I play."[19] The continuing desire of artists to support themselves was a major spur to reorganizing gallery operations, which culminated in the opening of the Intimate Gallery in 1925. Two successful auctions, one of Hartley's work in 1921 and a second in 1922 that included works of most members of the Stieglitz circle (plus those of some notable contemporaries, such as Thomas Hart Benton, Charles Sheeler, and Morton Schamberg), had been staged by Stieglitz at the Anderson Galleries building at Fifth Avenue and Fifty-ninth Street under the aegis of Mitchell Kennerly, president of the galleries. Both were held because the artists needed money. A letter from Stieglitz to Charles Demuth makes clear their financial concerns:

> *Dear Demuth:*
>
> *I've been thinking an awful lot about the whole situation. That is, the situation of the, what I call, A-1 men. And amongst the A-1 men of course is the woman, O'Keeffe. I feel more and more that the so-called dealers have no idea of handling the situation. . . . If I were only young enough I'd really finally hang out my shingle, not to make money, but just to show these wise men called art dealers what rotten business men they are.*[20]

Complaints about "the situation" run throughout Stieglitz's correspondence, underscoring his continued dissatisfaction with the economic lot of American artists in general and his worries about the hardships of his intimates in particular.

In addition to auctions, Stieglitz arranged with Kennerly for exhibitions of his own work in February 1921, April 1923, and March 1924. The latter two were joint shows with Georgia O'Keeffe, whom he married in 1924.[21] Each of the three shows was accompanied by a brief essay. Taken together, they point to a new direction in the ideology of the Stieglitz circle. And the change in rhetoric accompanied a heightened clarity in Stieglitz's photographic imagery. Through his collaboration with a younger generation of American sociocultural critics, Stieglitz was becoming engrossed in a different set of issues and developing new ways to define the values in the art created and exhibited by the circle.

The final paragraph of the 1921 essay sweeps away the critical terminology used in *Camera Work,* the periodical published by 291, urging viewers to discard the vocabulary of European theory and criticism:

> PLEASE NOTE: In the above STATEMENT, the following, fast becoming "obsolete," terms do not appear: ART, SCIENCE, BEAUTY, RELIGION, every ISM, ABSTRACTION, FORM, PLASTICITY, OBJECTIVITY, SUBJECTIVITY, OLD MASTERS, MODERN ART, PSYCHOANALYSIS, AESTHETICS, PICTORIAL PHOTOGRAPHY, DEMOCRACY, CEZANNE, "291," PROHIBITION. The term TRUTH did creep in but may be kicked out by anyone.[22]

With this declaration, Stieglitz publicly aligned himself with the antirationalist stance of the "Young Intellectuals"—Waldo Frank, Paul Rosenfeld, and Sherwood Anderson. He also identified himself with the dadaists, praised by Marsden Hartley in *Adventures in the Arts* (1921), who advocated rejecting prior modes of representation and destroying hierarchies in art.[23] Despite the circle's emphasis on indigenous art, this shift effectively brought its aesthetic in line with contemporary European surrealist thinking. By abandoning older critical "isms," the circle acceded to Hartley's demand for a New Realism (discussed below and in chapter 4) to replace the nineteenth-century American version. And in pointing to the need to reclassify art objects, Stieglitz opened the way for a critical reinterpretation of his own works and those of his co-exhibitor, O'Keeffe. The catalogue essay challenges the growing art audience and professional reviewers to receive their art in a new, informed way.

The important essay also prefigures the tone and emphasis of the 1925 exhibition *Seven Americans,* which introduced the newly regrouped coterie by displaying "159 Paintings Photographs and Things recent and never before publicly shown" by Arthur Dove, Marsden Hartley, John Marin, Charles Demuth, Paul Strand, Georgia O'Keeffe, and Alfred Stieglitz. This crucial inaugural show of the Intimate Gallery, which was also presented at the Anderson Galleries, tested the public's response to the circle's reestablishing a permanent exhibition space. The addition of Demuth to the co-op is especially telling. His work was the painterly equivalent of Stieglitz's and Strand's sharp-focused depictions. Some of Demuth's paintings in fact mimic "straight" photographs, in homage to his colleagues.

In addition to alerting the American public that artists were reassembling under the Stieglitz circle banner, the show also established the group's primary identity. Its title, *Seven Americans,* underscores the new indigenous accent, and in the 1925 catalogue Stieglitz also stressed this change:

> The pictures are an integral part of their makers.
> That I know.
> Are the pictures or their makers an integral part of America of to-day?
> That I am endeavoring to know.
> Because of that—the inevitability of this
> Exhibition—American.[24]

Equally important, though less emphasized, was the participants' assumed relation to European artistic tradition. The inclusion in the short catalogue of a full page in which the European sculptor Arnold Rönnebeck recorded his impressions of his association with members of the group and speculated on the meaning of the phrase "essentially American" betrays a lingering concern with the judgments of a contemporary European audience—significantly, of artistic peers, not critics or connoisseurs. Both of the group's identities—as rooted Americans and as participants in the forward march of Western culture—placed them in the international art scene. By emphatically classifying themselves as *American* artists, they in fact defined themselves *in relation to* an international cultural milieu.

The art and social critics aligned with the Stieglitz group also accentuated the group members' identification of themselves as "Americans." After the war their theoretical writings, along with the ideologies expressed by the paintings and photographs, set the works of the artists apart from those of both contemporary American artists and European competitors. As they once again put together exhibitions, the Stieglitz group introduced what they called "New Realism," a self-consciously democratic mode of visual representation. Imagistic, it was characterized by a return to traditional American subjects, such as still lifes and landscapes—but treated in a different way. The circle meant to popularize it as a style intelligible to a rapidly expanding audience that included immigrants newly arrived in America, an intent first propounded in the writings of the painter Marsden Hartley.[25] The New Realism was one of the diverse styles created by circle artists that reaffirmed traditional American ideals of plurality and tolerance.[26]

The new approach to visual representation was quite pointedly part of the search for an American cultural identity. When Waldo Frank wrote in *Our America*, "We go forth all to seek America. And in the seeking we create her,"[27] he was articulating the group's desire for a new American cultural image while at the same time implying that the American visual artist has tremendous power and influence. The Stieglitz circle defined their new approach in contradistinction to contemporary European movements. Writers and painters of the group opposed French purism, a style conceived and developed after the war by the artists Amédée Ozenfant and Charles-Edouard Jeanneret (better known as Le Corbusier). Purist still lifes routinely emphasized the universal and rational properties of objects in order to celebrate ideals of balance and order.[28] In deliberate contrast, works by the Stieglitz group accented the intimate and subjective. They opposed purism's measured forms and subdued color with irregular natural forms and torrid colors. By the mid-1920s, however, the circle had begun to create in a manner quite intentionally equivalent to and indeed competitive with French surrealism. For evidence we have not only the paintings—compare O'Keeffe's visionary desertscapes with Dalí's dream landscapes—but also the testimony of Paul Rosenfeld's *Port of New York* (1924), published, as noted in chapter 2, the same year that André Breton's first *Surrealist Manifesto* appeared in print. By the late twenties, Stieglitz could ask Charles Demuth rhetorically, "Why arent you and Marin and O'Keeffe and Dove Frenchmen? And I at least a Man Ray in Paris?" with confidence that his group's paintings and photographs presented a view of the transformed postwar world just as innovative and timely as that of the French.[29]

As gallery operator, however, Stieglitz was acutely aware of the crucial difference between America and Europe. The democratic New Realism grew out of the economic straits of American visual artists, which had become even worse after 1913, when the success of the landmark Armory Show encouraged the rapid proliferation of American art dealerships. The expanded marketplace in America, and internationally, however, continued to favor European, particularly French, art, both old master and modern.[30] As troubling as the American dollars that flowed to France was what the French were sending to America: impersonal, commercial practices in selling art. One of the things "new" about the New Realism was its production, presentation, and distribution through the circle's cooperative galleries, the nonprofit and mutually supportive exhibition space that deliberately challenged entrenched practices of patronage.[31]

Of course, the trouble was not just the American dollars exported or the objectionable means by which they were extracted but France's monopoly over that treasured but intangible commodity, fame. After almost two hundred years of Parisian cultural hegemony, Paris-based artists could not easily share the New York group's ideal of profit and prestige democratically distributed. For, as already noted, members of the Stieglitz circle desired not American cultural dominance but a fair portion of the economic return, artistic power, and status that had belonged exclusively to the artists of Western Europe. Not until the thirties, when their program promoting native art was co-opted by a small group of painters known as the Regionalists (discussed in chapter 4), did narrow nationalistic sentiments and "nativism" in its more insidious sense became prominent in the American art world.

While the group claimed a place in the international art market, the catalogue accompanying the 1925 exhibition emphasized the "Americanness" of the works, both in its text and in the paintings it reproduced,[32] all landscapes selected from the works of Dove, Marin, O'Keeffe, and Hartley. A glance at the titles listed in the catalogue confirms that landscape was a privileged genre, one in which the members of the circle displayed the artist's rootedness in society and his or her function as recorder and conserver of the natural environment. Their approach was a reversal of the European landscape tradition: rather than treat landscape as property, as object, Stieglitz circle artists—partly in hopes of appealing to the émigrés they wished to win as viewers—represented it as homeland. In their art and theory, they inverted the usual relationship between the land and the people who belonged to it; moreover, such belonging was not a given but could only be established over time. The Stieglitz circle's obsession with exploring and exploiting this genre continued well into the forties.

The text of the *Seven Americans* catalogue, as well as the majority of the paintings displayed, also introduced the dialogue between rural and urban that would shape the artists' later works. "Seven Alive," Sherwood Anderson's contribution, a prose landscape of contemporary New York City, provides an entry into this new element of the circle's ideology:

> The city is very tired.
> The men and women of the city are very tired.
> When you have been a long time away from simple
> elemental things, from wind, clouds, rain, fire, the
> sea—these things become a little terrible.
>
> . . . .
>
> Here are seven artists bringing to you city dwellers their moments of life.
> They also are tired as you are tired; life presses down upon them as it presses down upon you.
> See them here in their moments of life—
>
> . . . .
>
> When they were alive and conscious of all—everything—
> When they were conscious of clouds, horses, fields,
> winds, and water.
> This show is for me the distillation of the clean
> emotional life of seven real American artists.[33]

In addition to reiterating the nativist accent introduced by Stieglitz, Anderson's prose-poem sharply distinguishes urban life from nature—one physically oppressive, the other enlivening. This rhetorical opposition has a long history, but we need only consider its meanings in a specific social and historical context: the art-making community of New York City during the 1920s and early 1930s.

Anderson's notion of nature, one shared by circle members, derived in large part from the ideas of Walt Whitman. In pressing for artistic reform in "Democratic Vistas," Whitman represents nature as the catalyst for the necessary changes:

> Present literature, while magnificently fulfilling certain popular demands, with plenteous knowledge and verbal smartness, is profoundly sophisticated, insane, and its very joy is morbid. It needs tally and express Nature, and the spirit of Nature, and to know and obey the standards. I say the question of Nature, largely consider'd, involves the questions of the esthetic, the emotional, and the religious—and involves happiness. A fitly born and bred race, growing up in right conditions of out-door as much as in-door harmony, activity and development, would probably, from and in those conditions, find it enough merely *to live*—and would, in their relations to the sky, air, water, trees, &c., and to the countless common shows, and in the fact of life itself, discover and achieve happiness—with Being suffused night and day by wholesome extasy[.][34]

Here Whitman attaches a traditional notion first recorded by the ancient Greeks—achieving physical and psychological health by engaging vigorously with nature—to an ideology of image making. He goes on to strengthen the conceptual link between art and nature: "Nature, true Nature, and the true idea of Nature, long absent, must, above all, become fully restored, enlarged, and must furnish the pervading atmosphere to poems, and the test of all high literary and esthetic compositions" (p. 984). The poet also spells out the function of the effective work of art in society; what is to be achieved are works that are "worthy the immortal soul of man, and which, while absorbing materials, and, in their own sense, the shows of Nature, will, above all, have, both directly and indirectly, a freeing, fluidizing, expanding, religious character, exulting with science, fructifying the moral elements, and stimulating aspirations, and meditations on the unknown" (p. 986). This spiritually liberating art might translate into the terminology of the late twentieth century as "consciousness-raising"; whatever we call it, the ideal art clearly has transformative and even healing power.

Significantly, Whitman's remarks on nature's role in art making preface, in each case, an argument against "realistic" (i.e., literally mimetic) representation. In their quest for a new and indigenous ultrarealism, visual artists and literati of the Stieglitz circle could depend on the high regard in which an international public held Whitman's ideas to provide a kind of ideological validation. While mimesis was no longer an option for those making pictures, the poet recommended "meditations on the unknown" and thereby reinforced the circle's propensity for imaginative, expressive imagery. And Whitman's description of the kind of nature he wished to see reproduced in art must have seemed prophetically crafted to suit the special interests of the group. "I do not mean the smooth walks, trimm'd hedges, poseys and nightingales of the English poets," he asserted, "but the whole orb, with its geologic history, the kosmos, carrying fire and snow, that rolls through the illimitable areas, light as a feather, though weighing billions of tons" (p. 984). "Democratic Vistas" demanded a celebration of the sublime aspects of nature, its awesome and mysterious sides—rough and untrimmed, in an untouched, primitive state.

Whitman's sketch for a new way of reproducing in art a specifically American landscape (for what other vast continent could claim such crudity and geologic splendor?) became a crucial element in the theory of the Stieglitz circle. His notion that works of art can—indeed must—borrow from nature's power to transform and edify the American public was already a core belief of circle members at least as early as Anderson's evocation of it in "Seven Alive." Indeed, images of nature and details of natural landscapes run through all of Anderson's fiction, and nature (figured as the rural landscape) is often depicted in his writing as the agent responsible for dramatic transformations in the characters portrayed. When his characters are grotesques, it is because their true "natures" are repressed. Their moments of truth are customarily played out against a living, natural environment.[35]

Personification and the pathetic fallacy—that is, displacing human attributes and attitudes onto external nature—are ancient devices. The central concerns of a culture make their way into its fictions, in both text and paint. For example, in the seventeenth and eighteenth centuries still lifes were a primary means of presenting the moral and practical issues of the painter's society. The landscape painters of the nineteenth century, Continental and American, used allegory to represent values to imitate and debate. Inspired by Whitman, the Stieglitz circle artists attempted to define and encode in depictions of the American landscape their interpretations of the most important contemporary issues.

To convey their point of view, group members first needed to refocus their audience's attention, a task they undertook by redefining form, technique, and medium. The Stieglitz circle adopted an active, sympathetic, Whitmanian stance toward nature during the 1920s—a decade when Americans were transforming land, water, and raw minerals on a massive scale. Viewed against the historical backdrop of spreading industrialism, their position clearly shows a nascent ecological consciousness, which was faintly echoed in the contemporary academic community. The antagonist implicit in all their works was more often than not industrialized society. The circle frequently expressed its social critique in the image of the city, specifically New York City.

Their rhetorical opposition of city and country was not simple. In a *New York Times* review of a John Marin exhibition held at the Kennedy Galleries in New York in the fall of 1981, the art critic Hilton Kramer summarized the sociohistorical influences on Stieglitz circle members and their contemporaries:

> The American artists who came of age in the last years of the 19th century and the early years of the 20th often found themselves inhabiting two very different worlds. One was dominated by the life of small towns, rural landscapes and comfortable, middle-size cities that were only just awakening to the problems and promises of the industrial era, but were not yet overwhelmed by them. The other was the world of modern engineering and the kind of fast-paced technological change that was quickly altering the very look and rhythm of life in the main metropolitan centers.
>
> The contrasts of feeling that separated these worlds often set the terms that would continue to haunt this generation of artists—the first generation of modernists—in their most characteristic work. Even when they eagerly embraced the imagery and dynamism of the new technological era, their outlook remained deeply attached to the simpler and more innocent world that had shaped them.[36]

For the Stieglitz circle, the city-country dialogue was situated in a feeling that emerged not from a romantic attachment to a lost past and its presumed "innocence" but from a real set of small-town values and ideals familiar from the artists' own pasts—values and ideals that seemed irrelevant in the metropolitan centers rising across America. They responded to the clash of communal values and the new social codes of urban life with an acute self-consciousness that, in turn, led to the struggles and reevaluation evident in their postwar critical and theoretical writings and in their visual products.

Contemporary commentators on the Stieglitz galleries—even 291—recognized them as updated cooperatives designed with broad social aspirations, seeking in particular to educate a wider public about modern art. In a volume of essays assembled in 1934 to acknowledge the circle's contributions to American culture, Harold Clurman, director of an experimental performance troop called the Group Theatre, pointedly titled his contribution "Alfred Stieglitz and the Group Ideal."[37] Part of the circle's appeal to a younger generation of American critics and authors (who found themselves trying to make sense of socialist and communist theories flooding in from Europe) was the unique attempt of a small group of "workers" to cooperate and create a different relation to the art market. To date, the aims of the Stieglitz circle have not been adequately analyzed. What compelled photographers and painters to gather in mutual support with writers on art, society, and culture? Certainly Stieglitz himself was not motivated by hopes of greater recognition; he already had an international reputation when he took up the editorship of Photo-Secession's *Camera Notes* (the precursor of *Camera Work*). Instead, social pressures shaped his attitudes and actions and those of other early modernists.

In the early decades of the twentieth century the new structures of industrialism changed the lives of all Americans. Businessmen, farmers, and industrial workers realized that only by banding together as discrete interest groups could they effectively wield power. And although they often viewed themselves as outsiders, artists too were forced to come to terms with shifting social conditions and the economic issues that were central to the circle's existence.

But economic issues were not decisive in their cooperative activities: there were higher stakes involved, which their theoretical platform emphasized. As a rare place where American modernists could argue and discuss critical contemporary issues, 291 had a function perhaps more important to the production of art than simply offering walls on which to display the finished works. Later, the Intimate Gallery and An American Place were similar havens for artists in New York City, places where modernists could seek the company of other artists—and find a floor to sleep on when money was scarce. Doors were always left unlocked as an invitation to the public.

Circle members saw art dealers, who routinely acted the role of interested intermediary that Stieglitz shunned, as businessmen with no real understanding or appreciation of intellectual or cultural work. Artists attacked modern dealers not only for profiteering but for failing (like the popular press) to create an audience and a market for art by informing the public about it. Stieglitz, wrongly termed an elitist by Regionalists in the 1930s and formalists in the 1940s, joined Sherwood Anderson, Van Wyck Brooks, Waldo Frank, Lewis Mumford, and Paul Rosenfeld in believing that a broad-based audience for art existed in America. On one occasion he wrote to Anderson, "Yes, the people would respond if given half a chance. They might not make the artist rich but they'd give them a chance to work. I'm sure of it."[38] The seemingly uninformed methods of selection and distribution of the numerous competitive little galleries that sprang up in New York City after the war challenged circle members' high professional standards of craft and of display. What linked these craft practices to the economy was the issue of value. According to their theory, if creative artists could fully control production and consumption, then they could likewise control quality and the value of their work.

Craft is crucial to a discussion of the audience for visual art during the early decades of the twentieth century. With the high quality of their works exhibited in the Stieglitz galleries (a level of craft on which much of the effect of the artwork depended), the artists made a statement about the value of manual production and the role of the maker in American society. Nor did their paintings and photographs provide the only evidence of such claims. Films (products of collaborative art) in the 1920s also consciously aspired to both mass appreciation and high quality. Indeed, the universal American appetite for the newest art form was a taste that bound together the nation's intellectual and cultural elite with a popular audience. The sophistication of the audience for film reveals how the appreciation of quality craftwork and considerable visual literacy permeated American society during the period.

By 1930 the search for a new American cultural identity that the Stieglitz circle had undertaken in the wake of Brooks's urgings had become more than a national preoccupation. Comprehensive national and (more to the point) international exhibitions of American art in that decade were dominated by American subject matter and uniquely American modes of representation. These large shows, for example, the 1931 Carnegie International at Pittsburgh (unlike the blockbusters of the 1980s), clearly indicated the interests of both the artists themselves and the general public. At the moment when the search for identity reached its height, reactionary Regionalist painters and hostile critics of the 1930s tried to exclude the Stieglitz circle—the actual founders of this important movement for sociocultural liberation.

Despite the flourishing of such exhibitions, the Stieglitz galleries were nearly alone among exhibitors of modern art in New York City in concentrating on American art. Between the little postwar galleries of the circle and the few other contemporary sponsors of American art, there were important differences as well as similarities. The Frank Rehn gallery, which supported Edward Hopper and Charles Burchfield throughout the twenties, appealed to a more conservative audience. And in 1924, the German émigré J. B. Newmann opened a print room and bookshop on Fifty-seventh Street; there, until the Depression, the circle enjoyed an alternative space for exhibiting works on paper. After the Armory Show in 1913, the Montross Gallery featured both American and European moderns; like most contemporary dealers who handled both, its owner exhibited artist groups and media together unsystematically. Only at the Stieglitz galleries were one-person shows the norm; even thematically organized shows featuring different artists were rare. Stephan Bourgeois, however, had a gallery very much like and indeed modeled on the circle's galleries, exhibiting works by artists he considered in sympathy with his personal philosophy: an antirational worldview influenced by Asian thought. Additionally, three well-established New York galleries featured early modern American works during the twenties: Knoedler and Company, Kranshaar Galleries, and, with a distinctively French accent, Wildenstein and Company.

The most commercially successful alternative to the later Stieglitz circle cooperatives was that run by Charles Daniel, a former restaurateur. Inspired by 291, but with exclusively commercial motives, he opened a showroom for modern art in 1913. Until the Depression, the Daniel Gallery prospered; in 1924 it moved to the new, more chic, uptown gallery district on Madison Avenue. Much has been made of the relationship between Daniel and Stieglitz, which is often cast as a bad-natured rivalry from the twenties on. It has even been suggested that Daniel's business was hurt by Stieglitz's decision to reopen an exhibition space in 1925, since the Intimate Gallery attracted Charles Demuth and John Marin away from Daniel's.[39] Because Daniel had launched Demuth's career, we might well wonder what convinced the artist to switch his allegiance.[40] As for Marin, Daniel had "discovered" the watercolorist at 291 where, in 1910, he had bought two of Marin's studies of Paris.

Although Elizabeth McCausland, an art critic and historian, claimed in the 1950s that all the records of the Daniel Gallery were lost when it closed, some of its exhibition brochures have been preserved in the Smithsonian's Archives of American Art.[41] Daniel took no intellectual stance regarding the artworks, providing neither analytic catalogue essays nor even brief interpretive notes to accompany exhibitions (such as the handwritten notices that the Stieglitz galleries consistently offered). Instead he merely supplied typeset checklists, in small format and unillustrated, naming the title and maker of each work.[42] No ideology was implied—social, cultural, or political—just a straightforward business transaction.

As noted earlier in this chapter, the most powerful tool of the industrial complex was introduced into these new impersonal, mediated, and commercial relations between artists and patrons: advertising techniques. The circle saw modern advertising, like the new (largely imported) methods of selling, as yet another corruption of human relations fostered by the capitalist system. Herbert Seligmann, an aspiring artist associated with the circle during the years of the later galleries, remembered Stieglitz saying, "The basis of all business . . . was the creation in people of a desire for things that advertising had persuaded them they wanted. The public was constantly fooled and duped. The basis of it all, of American business, was hypocrisy."[43]

Just as farmers around the world had been forced to adopt modern technology and methods inspired by industry, so American artists were driven to adopt modern advertising practices (which became an increasingly important part of American life in the late 1910s and 1920s) to have a chance of succeeding in an unfavorable market. Advertising ensured native artists access to buyers and established the pedigree of European work in America. Auction houses advertised European cultural goods in print, while agents for wealthy collectors publicized by word of mouth. Press releases for exhibitions in New York's little postwar galleries often imitated advertisements, and critical reviews used the new jargon. New York art circles adopted the powerful and manipulative rhetoric of advertising companies to increase sales even as the ad industry appropriated for its purposes what was useful in "high" culture. Though an aim of the Stieglitz circle was wider distribution of artwork, members vehemently opposed the manipulative element of advertising. The artists became angry as businesses took possession of the prerogatives of high culture—setting and popularizing styles, and determining public taste. Modern advertising could perform such functions efficiently and on a vast scale. A number of American modernists understandably felt that their independence and their purpose were being eroded.

The Intimate Gallery was an attempt to fight back, announcing its aim of reaching a broader audience; as "a Direct Point of Contact between Artist and Public," it would function differently from competitive galleries, with their nonartist managers. The announcement explains further, "Intimacy and Concentration, we believe, in this instance, will breed a broader appreciation. This may lead to a wider distribution of the work."[44] Invoking older values and practices, the "Intimacy and Concentration" of first-person relationships with patrons recall art market practices of the recent past with a certain nostalgia. Clearly the older system had its drawbacks. But in the capitalist marketplace, the American artist suffered economic insecurity. As Thomas Cochran and William Miller report in their history of this period, which they call "the age of enterprise," "Collecting was entrusted to agents or dealers who, like the shrewd businessmen they were, sought maximum commissions by handling only the most reliable goods at the highest possible prices. Comparatively unknown American artists, therefore, had little chance to sell their works for they had scant access to the market."[45] Moreover, members of the circle realized that when these third parties came between artist and patron, the maker of art lost not only money but status.

Ironically, advertisers borrowed ideas from the 291 cooperative gallery, whose innovative displays had set new standards while drawing a large audience.[46] American commercial artists, eager to rank with practitioners of the "fine" arts, mimicked the gallery's look and sought by implication to elevate their own practices. As early as the mid-1920s large New York City advertising agencies were creating their own "galleries," where advertisements by commercial artists were regularly exhibited.[47] N. W. Ayer and Son, for example, emulated the decor that the photographer-painter Edward Steichen had invented for 291, linking advertising and artistic professionalism.[48] The artists who had invented this modern gallery aesthetic found such an appropriation of status worrisome, for it forced them to vie for social status and credibility not only internationally, with other artists, but also domestically, with the advertising business. Modernists somehow had to establish their position, not merely as style setters and tastemakers, but—more important—as the culture's truth tellers.

In both the United States and Europe, new cultural tastes were promulgated largely through manifestos and exhibition catalogues. In Paris, the art historian Malcolm Gee informs us, "If books played a specific role in the creation of concepts about modern art at this time, it was a conservative one."[49] There were few books on the avant-garde, and no French critics analyzed and supported contemporary art and related sociocultural issues as Waldo Frank and Paul Rosenfeld did. However, more Parisian than American art dealers produced their own periodicals—small-scale but important texts focused on various media. An example is Léonce Rosenberg's *Bulletin de l'Effort Moderne,* which bears comparison with Stieglitz gallery catalogues of the postwar period.[50] Like the circle's exhibition catalogues, the *Bulletin* featured articles by artists and critics associated with a particular gallery. In both quality and seriousness, Rosenberg's and the Stieglitz group's gallery releases matched specialized publications that had solid financial backing, such as the famous *L'Esprit Moderne* and *Cahiers d'Art.*[51] However, unlike similar circle publications, the *Bulletin* generally contained illustrations unrelated to the subject of the text, using them as advertisements to serve commerce rather than ideology or instruction.

With the global economic strain caused by World War I the market for art suffered, forcing many New York galleries to close or, at best, to abbreviate their exhibition schedules. By 1923 the economies of both New York and Paris had strengthened and a new interest in art (particularly modern painting) was evident. Yet while modernism was viewed more favorably in these major cultural markets after the war, cutting-edge avant-garde art received little support. Paris, often associated with innovation and novelty, was just as conservative in this regard as contemporary New York. The typical Parisian art gallery of the time rarely speculated in unknowns but instead concentrated on selling orthodox modern figurative paintings.[52] Between 1910 and 1930, the little gallery, which was a new method of selling art, had replaced the official salons as the focal point of interest for the Western art market. It was intended to support continuing stylistic innovation and experiment, but the operators of these galleries failed to educate and challenge the public, motivating (and justifying) the Stieglitz group's criticism. Joining in the attack across the Atlantic was Léonce Rosenberg, the only established Parisian gallerist who throughout the twenties and thirties handled artists whose innovations were not salable.[53] Because the rise of the little gallery marked a decisive change in the market for cultural goods, the selective support given to artists had a particularly telling effect.

In Paris during the first half of the twentieth century, the young aristocrats, with their influence rooted in inherited status and wealth, continued to be the arbiters of taste and strengthened the market for avant-garde works. The high prices paid by prestigious collectors heightened the efforts of dealers to establish a clientele for innovative art. In the United States, in contrast, newly rich professionals seem to have been the typical collectors of avant-garde art (more research is needed in this area).

The Stieglitz circle sought both a different public and a different relationship with the public; the artist's cooperative, in its American variant, reflected a specifically democratic approach to making and distributing art.

The cooperative form took art making out of the capitalist marketplace and out of the hierarchies structured by the academy and by dealerships on the French model. The diverse individual artistic productions the co-op exhibited and distributed were emblematic of the pluralism the Stieglitz group sought in American culture. With hindsight, we might wish that other racial groups had been represented among those makers and critics; at the time, however, the inclusion of Jews and women in a cultural sphere that had been exclusively patrician and patriarchal was radical. The ideology of separate spheres—differentiated by both sex and race—was pervasive before World War II.

The Stieglitz circle cooperative set out to provide America with a concrete precapitalist model of community: the joining of individuals not just for leisure and consumption but also for work and production. The astonishing private aggrandizement of a small class that had followed rapid industrialization had obscured the complex interdependence of individuals in earlier American society. The cooperative form was meant to reveal and reinstate these connections, while exemplifying what American society could become. As Frank reminded Stieglitz in a letter of 1927, the circle was held together by the idea that the economic independence of artists was the surest guarantee that their artistic work would be ethical and truthful.[54] Once artists were freed from economic constraints, the cooperative galleries would demonstrate that profit need not be the basis of human relations. Stieglitz indicated the enormity of the effort involved when he wrote to the collector Duncan Phillips in 1943: "It has been a terrific struggle for 54 years to keep the 'WALLS WHITE' I think you will understand the significance of that. And by 'WALLS' I mean the basis of all relationships."[55] What threatened to sully the walls—and weaken the basis of cooperative relations—was the crass capitalist marketplace.

The image of "white walls" is a typical example of how the circle used material reality figuratively. The design of the Intimate Gallery and An American Place makes clear that the exhibition spaces were conceived as palpable metonyms of America at large, representing the country to itself in miniature. The point is underscored by the name of the last Stieglitz gallery: An American Place. Extremely useful descriptions are provided by Sue Davidson Lowe, Stieglitz's niece and biographer as well as a frequent visitor to both later galleries. When the Intimate Gallery was initially rented, its high walls were overlaid with black velour, the traditional background on which gilt-framed works of the academy or old masters were hung. Before the public was admitted, Georgia O'Keeffe covered the walls from picture rail to wainscot with white cloth. In this way the gallery space was symbolically cut off from the Victorian past: its early modernist white, the color of canvas and of photographic paper, announced the anti-academic present. At An American Place as well, O'Keeffe selected the color scheme, supervising the painting of the walls and ceilings of the gallery's two smaller rooms in pure white. The third and largest room was painted a pearl gray tone she mixed herself.[56]

The ascetic design of the galleries was intended not only to highlight the art on their walls but also to present a dramatic contrast with their ancestral form: the artist's studio. Before the opening of 291, the only permanent spaces in America where artists encountered the public were their private studios, which (unlike the later little galleries) only collectors and patrons entered. The most famous of these was the studio of the painter William Merritt Chase, opulent and exotic, decorated with an extensive collection of European and Oriental objects. And though the studios of American artists of the Gilded Age displayed a wide range of styles, most copied the ornamentation used in the studios of successful European artists, just as the artists copied European styles of painting.

Studio spaces were extensions and elaborations of artists' self-image. They combined two different impulses. The cluttered and histrionic studio decor pronounced, to a limited and elite group, the artist's identity as creative "genius," a distinctly European type. At the same time, artists' studios of the late nineteenth century mirrored the homes of wealthy patrons—typically, American businessmen who were too conservative in their tastes and lifestyles to accept anything truly bohemian. Thus standard studio decor was in fact a sanitized middle-class interpretation of the exotic. The clean white walls of the Stieglitz galleries tacitly protested against this inauthenticity, especially when it was inauthentically European. To define a new American artist's self, and to broaden and democratize relations with the American public, the members of the Stieglitz circle demanded aesthetic reform.

The most telling description of any of the co-op spaces is by Dorothy Norman, the photographer, gallery assistant, and fund-raiser who virtually took over the administration of circle galleries in the late thirties. Norman's essay, "An American Place," appeared in *America and Alfred Stieglitz,* the celebratory collection published in 1934. In it she imaginatively escorts the reader through the gallery, showing how its carefully chosen form and spatial organization reflected the circle's belief in the relation of diverse parts to a whole: through fluid communication, they can create unity. Again, we see that An American Place was to be taken as a metonym for America; the gallery should be interpreted as "[s]imply a place in America: An American Place, not only as a living cell out of the body entire, but as a laboratory in which to study the cell itself and by means of which to create the body entire anew." According to this view, shared by other members of the circle and here urged on the reader, the Stieglitz galleries represented not simply America but America's transformation. Norman elaborates: "There is the door open to all. . . . There is the democracy of taking any space, whether a garret or a loft in an office building and through respect for one's materials . . . transforming the materials of the marketplace into a veritable shrine."[57]

In the course of her essay, Norman casts the Stieglitz gallery as a specifically public space, variously comparing it to a cathedral, a museum, an educational institution, and finally a shrine. She thereby invites the reader to understand and celebrate the group's conception of a new collective and communal artists' space that affirms the shared ideas, beliefs, and history of the American public. Her tribute underscores how the free, accessible spaces of the cooperative galleries in which the Stieglitz circle's exhibitions were held constituted a kind of address: a public one. Moreover, like the galleries that housed them, the works of art engaged the visitor not as private individual but as American citizen. In this way, both white walls and multicolored works contrived to reinstate the American notion that real freedom and happiness are to be found in the public realm. The Jeffersonian definition of value revitalized by the circle opposed the assumption of twentieth-century capitalism that private consumerism and the individual pursuit of happiness offer freedom and satisfaction.

Beyond providing public access to art, the space of the Stieglitz circle galleries, like their changing contents, made a clear ideological statement. It described and defined the American social and cultural self to viewers experiencing the free voices of a democratic American community. That self and that community opposed alternatives offered by both the past—what Whitman had decried as perverted individualism—and the present, the modern individual constructed by advertising, who found "freedom" only in the marketplace. Whereas advertisements treat their viewers exclusively as consumers, the little galleries, in both their cultural context and content, promoted the American self as a producer or worker. In the manner and content of their work, members of the circle refused to accept the artist as just another alienated laborer in industrial capitalism.

Drawing on the models of Morrisian artist-run co-ops in Europe that featured both new and traditional media and of contemporaneous experiments such as Germany's Bridge and Blue Rider groups, the Stieglitz circle effectively ran cooperative galleries in New York from 1905 until the photographer's death in 1946. That their three galleries remained relatively separate from the dominant marketplace helps explain their success not only during the economically prosperous 1920s but also, as noted above, during the Great Depression, when most artists were forced to turn to New Deal programs for their survival. It also explains why the cooperative became popular in the 1960s, when those favoring a radical participatory tradition attacked liberal democracy. Demanding new freedoms, including freedom from the marketplace, American activist artists sought alternative spaces and returned to artists' cooperatives. The complex history of that flourishing movement—which included A.I.R., the collective of women artists founded in New York City in 1972, and Kate Millett's co-op, Noho, founded by the sculptor-writer in 1975—is just beginning to receive serious scrutiny from art historians.[58]

Examining the theories of the Stieglitz circle, at a remove of eight decades from the historical circumstances of their production, we can see that they were inadequately developed, in large part because the writers simply chose to avoid amplification. Additionally, in acting as if historical conditions had already been transformed—operating as if their cooperative idea had already overturned the capitalist market for art—members of the group favored wishful thinking over effective struggle toward their goals. For although their own perspective and their lives appear to have been altered in the process of creating the art for a future society (as Marx had predicted), neither their art nor their ideas were ultimately disseminated broadly enough to change others. Their reluctance to allow their images to be reproduced—still the bane of scholars researching them—ironically works against their stated desire for democratic accessibility. And such research is essential. As the problems inherent in New York's system for marketing art become ever more apparent, careful analysis of earlier American experiments may suggest to today's art makers, theorists, and critics the workable possibilities for the future.

4

RECONFIGURING REALISM

THE CARNAGE OF WORLD WAR I led people everywhere—especially artists and writers—to reevaluate all realms of human endeavor. What had been taken for "reality," as encompassed by commonly held and trusted human values and beliefs, had vanished, and nothing had yet taken its place. Similarly, realism, as nineteenth-century artists had invented and understood it, no longer seemed able to express twentieth-century experiences, and many found pure abstraction, the brainchild of the early 1910s, equally inadequate. Visual artists with a theoretical bent began to seek new modes of representation that would help fill the void.

While some Europeans called on art makers to turn inward and examine their private psyches, the impulse of many American artists was to first reassess their collective history. Inspired by Van Wyck Brooks's search for a usable literary past, visual artists like Marsden Hartley of the Stieglitz circle searched the roots of a democratic artistic tradition both for a vocabulary of forms and for meaningful content that could be reconfigured for current use. One result was "New Realism," which Hartley outlined in "Aesthetic Sincerity" in the December 1918 issue of *El Palacio,* a magazine jointly sponsored by the Art Museum and the Archaeological Society of Santa Fe, New Mexico. Hartley formulated this approach during his stay in New Mexico, after the war forced his return to the United States from Europe; it clearly reflects a knowledge and appreciation of Brooks's criticism. In "America as Landscape," which appeared in the same issue, Hartley further underscored his reliance on both Brooks and Walt Whitman.

In "Aesthetic Sincerity" Hartley claims to have discovered that the land of the American Southwest itself clearly defined how it should be represented, contending that "there is no sensation of rococo applicable to this land."[1] This argument is no surprise, for it closely follows Whitman's recipe for depicting landscapes. The painter attacked realism, a historical style of representation he thought no longer effective. In suggesting a remedy, he leans heavily on Whitman, adopting not only the poet's image of an active earth but also his tone of exhortation: "We as painters will have to get 'on the ground' and 'into' the subject. There is necessity for a definite reaction from the soil itself" (p. 322). Hartley might have felt an especially strong tie to Whitman, since he too worked in multiple genres; his own prose writings, critical theories, and lyric poems formed a body of work nearly as extensive as his paintings. Other members of the Stieglitz circle saw Hartley as an exemplary figure of artistic prowess, powerfully wielding both pen and brush.

This dual power was an important part of Hartley's public self, which he used to put his theory into a historical context: "The war has accomplished this for the painter, it has demanded originality of him. It has sent him back to his own soil to ponder and readjust himself to a conviction of his own and an esthetics of his own." As in the writings of French purists, war is the catalyst for a new view. Hartley presents his specific situation as a generic condition of creative American minds, if not of all of humanity. What was American creative talent to do under these pressing circumstances? Hartley is firm: "We are now finished with 'à la mode' esthetics. There is among the sincerer types of ultramodernists a conviction toward the essential reality. This is the next step to follow cubism and futurism" (p. 333). Hartley had probably collaborated with European artists in beginning to formulate a notion of New Realism before returning to the United States. His theory represents a very early call for an end to the rapid stylistic changes encouraged by the art market (which was increasingly slipping from the control of professional artists), as well as a challenge to the modernist idea of progress in the history of art practices.

In several letters to Stieglitz, Waldo Frank sketches the efforts he was making during the early twenties to help Hartley edit and restructure his arguments. In fact, in *Our America* (1919), Frank adopts Hartley's call for a reconfigured realistic mode, wedding that "essential vision" with Whitmanian idealism. The New Realism, informed by a democratic idealism deeply rooted in Whitman's ethos, was presented first by Hartley as an artistic imperative and subsequently by Frank as the ideological weapon to combat pragmatism's recent offspring, Progressivism. Frank in effect adopted Hartley's cultural concerns and politicized them.

For Frank, as for Brooks, pragmatism was a threat because it relied on capitalism's definition of success. In his attack, he clearly and deliberately echoes the words of Whitman: "The pragmatic measure of value is utility . . . [A]ccording to its pattern, the world is the paradigm of 'getting on,' of success. The values of life lose their inherency, become subordinate to the abstract conception of Progress. . . . Value, therefore, does not implicitly inhere in being."[2] Against this measure, he sets Whitman's essentially non-Western perspective. Other writers affiliated with the circle would later join him in insisting that "being" is the ultimate aim of existence. They took that position in deliberate opposition to John Dewey who, in advocating "doing" as the reason for living, seemed to some to conspire with capitalists who emphasized progress and functional relations. The Stieglitz group's advocacy of being effectively continued the attempts by American transcendentalist philosophers to decenter Western rationalism by drawing on Eastern thought and experience.

In a chapter titled "New York," Frank salutes Brooks's greatest feat: the reinjection of Whitman into the American psyche (p. 195). And in the next chapter, "The Multitudes in Whitman," Frank adds his own critical assessment of the poet's role in contemporary society, pointing specifically to "Democratic Vistas" and proclaiming it America's greatest work of social criticism (p. 205). Whitman's compelling utterances, potently overlaid with the early modern socialist interpretations of Van Wyck Brooks, remained the bedrock of the circle's social ethic and aesthetic philosophy until the circle's slow, inevitable disbanding after Stieglitz's death in 1946.

In a particularly ardent passage of *Our America* Frank sings an ode to place: "America is vivid and vibrant beyond the scales of temperate Europe. The Southwest throbs with shrill reds and golds of earth and blues of sky. Rocky New England swoons every summer in a purple verdure that cries against the browns and blacks of the soil" (p. 6). He described the American landscape in glowing terms. But even a reader barely familiar with the works of Hartley, Marin, or O'Keeffe would recognize that Frank refers to that land only indirectly, through paintings he had seen in the circle's galleries. If for Whitman, the land imprinted the citizen, for Frank, with his eye on a group of landscape paintings, the imprint of land, the literal landscape on canvas, could serve as an index of identity. He treats these Stieglitz circle icons as cultural products in the broad sense—representations of America by America's image makers—and also (as in Paul Rosenfeld's *Port of New York*) more narrowly as the work of model American craftworkers. Both treatments suit Frank's purpose in this book: to convince the French, who were providing the stiffest economic and aesthetic competition, of the high quality of American artistic wares.

Significantly, Hartley's other article published in the December 1918 *El Palacio* informed Waldo Frank's thinking about the meaning of Whitman's sense of geography for contemporary culture. The title alone, "America as Landscape," is revealing. Hartley's intended audience, unlike Frank's, was a community of visual artists that had been congregating in Santa Fe and Taos since before the turn of the century. He accuses them of treating the unique American landscape negligently, applying French styles and thereby thwarting the establishment of an American cultural identity.

Hartley sees some promising signs that "the fetish of Paris, for [the] painter at least, has been destroyed by the war." "America as Landscape" extended the main theme of "Aesthetic Sincerity," arguing that the turn to a reconstituted realism was immanent, "a sturdy kind of realism, a mode that can approach the solidity of landscape itself and for the American painter the reality of his own American landscape." Hartley also invokes Whitman, calling him the "precipitant" (thus acknowledging Brooks's assessment of Whitman's role in "precipitating" the American character) and claims that contemporary poets taking Whitman's cue had already made a "comfortable attempt at radical and geographical sincerity."[3] Hartley's purpose was to push himself and other visual artists to break with the imported stylistic "isms" of the 1910s. Frank's purpose in *Our America,* in which he depends heavily on Hartley as artist informant, was to persuade the French that members of the Stieglitz circle were already showing examples of indigenous forms and methods.

Hartley's and Frank's interest in the American past was (like Brooks's) in important ways an outgrowth of America's romance with the Arts and Crafts movement, which peaked in the decade before World War I. The movement, reacting against socioeconomic conditions that had disrupted the craft tradition as well as the communal spirit it engendered, showed the American public good craftwork as a potent social force and fostered an aesthetic reform that spilled over into the next decades. By the mid-twenties, the taste for folk arts and craft objects had become sufficiently strong—at least among contemporary artists, buyers, sellers, and others in New York interested in art—to support exhibitions of indigenous crafts.

While contemporary French purists suppressed the memories of their immediate art-historical past in constructing a new identity and new values for modern French society, members of the Stieglitz circle (like Picasso) reassessed the past and conserved what seemed valuable, consciously following in the footsteps of Van Wyck Brooks. Marsden Hartley's only book, *Adventures in the Arts* (1921), can help us understand how the group's interests were reframed after World War I. Although the entire book offers valuable clues, the chapter titled "The Virtues of Amateur Painting" conveys most usefully the values Hartley ascribed to his subject: "amateur" pictures of the mid-Victorian era.

His detailed descriptions (Hartley cites examples in the Maine Historical Society in Portland and the Marine Museum in Salem, Massachusetts) make plain that these are works now commonly called folk art.[4] He brings into the discussion the French painter Henri Rousseau, whose greatest claim to contemporary renown was his "naïveté," highly prized by the Parisian critical community since Baudelaire's famous redefinition of the term. Hartley saw in Rousseau, whose American premiere had been at 291 in 1910, the same values he promoted in American folk painting. It is also important to remember in this regard that artists of the German exhibition society with which Hartley had shown in the late 1910s, the Blue Rider (Der

Blaue Reiter), had extolled the value of European folk art and used it as a model of "the primitive."[5]

What Hartley valued in the American folk works was "the most admirably sincere qualities of painting as well as singularly enchanting gifts for simplification." On closer examination he discovered a discrete elegiac mode, praising "the richness of memory and the sentimental aspects of bereavement" (pp. 135, 135–36).[6] He also applauds the "painted memories of life" of American folk artists, who were able to commemorate the past and address the difficult subject of human mortality. Their powerful expression belied the need for academic training and for learning a set of artistic conventions, two traditional prerequisites already challenged by most European practitioners of early modernism. To artists around the world, such folk art seemed to legitimate their protests against the academy.

Focusing on a particular amateur painter, Jennie Vanvleet Cowdery, Hartley named inventiveness and imaginativeness among the assets of the folk style, summing up his appreciation by commending its practitioners: "They remain always charming painters of personal visionary experience, and as such are entitled to praise for their genuine gifts in rendering, as well as for a natural genius for interpretation" (p. 143). Hartley compliments these artists both for their vision (what he so admired in the American painter Albert Pinkham Ryder) and for their untutored drawing ability and idiosyncratic modes of expression.

The qualities Hartley approved in American folk art are those he later attempted to inject into his own works, with varying success. Other Stieglitz circle members also strove to incorporate and cultivate the values Hartley's theories had delineated. American folk painters provided for the group (as for a whole generation of American artists a decade later) a usable, accessible visual past. And for the group, as for artists of the 1930s, folk works embodied both aesthetic and social imperatives. With "The Virtues of Amateur Painting," Hartley's theories helped not only the circle but the broader New York art community develop a taste for outsider or marginalized art—a taste that the Stieglitz co-op galleries had been instrumental in fostering. In addition to showing paintings and drawings by Henri Rousseau in November 1910, the 291 gallery had staged three successive exhibitions of work by children. It was first in the United States to display (in December 1915) the work of Eli Nadelman, a naturalized American sculptor whose early interest in, and collecting of, American folk art is especially relevant to us.[7]

The standard account dates the discovery of American folk art to an exhibition held in 1924 at the Whitney Studio Club, but in so doing privileges the tastes of patrons and collectors and neglects an earlier discovery and appreciation by visual artists.[8] For Nadelman, according to Lincoln Kirstein, immediately became interested in American folk arts and crafts when he arrived from France in 1914.[9] Indeed, it seems likely that a foreign artist would be highly sensitive to the various forms of art or craft available in his newly adopted homeland. One thing is certain: by 1919 Nadelman and his American wife had already amassed a vast collection of American folk arts and crafts; it was eventually stored and exhibited in a purpose-built structure on their estate in Riverdale-on-Hudson.[10] Nadelman had also established close relations with several members of the Stieglitz circle by the time he first exhibited at 291. We may safely assume that the sculptor entertained his artist friends on his estate, inviting them to study and enjoy his impressive collection.

As Marsden Hartley's appreciative remarks in *Adventures in the Arts* make plain, the appeal of folk art lay principally not in its form or subject matter but in what it shared with goals of early modernists: independence from cosmopolitan or academic traditions, simplicity and nonsophistication of form and technique, and roots in the craft rather than the fine arts tradition. Perhaps of greatest importance for Hartley and his circle was folk art's historical association with America's nascent democracy, with what they believed to be a simpler and more moral preindustrial past. While boldness of style and invention were in themselves highly attractive, these formal characteristics were perceived as marks of a particular type of artist, one who worked under the influence of a morally sound social code.

The circle's appropriation of folk attributes was not simply an exercise in nostalgia. Hartley (and, through him and Nadelman, other group members) saw clearly that the amateur American artists whose works he praised in fact contributed greatly to the mainstream of American culture in the young democracy's formative years. This image of American folk artists gave the group's art critics the historical precedent they desired to support the social ascendancy of the contemporary American artist. As we have seen, members of the circle wished to replace the modern European image of the alienated artist with some precursor from the American past, and the folk artist became their main candidate. In an unpublished, unedited, and undated manuscript titled "American Primitives," Marsden Hartley notes with characteristic passion: "There are no amateurs today, everyone is a professional, no matter what the field of expression may be, and the ingratiating charm of amateurship is gone from our midst. . . . [I]n the 18th and 19th centuries there were plenty of amateurs, but it is certain that 20th century mechanism has destroyed all these simple impulses."[11] In the chapter titled "The Virtues of Amateur Painting" in *Adventures in the Arts* Hartley similarly praises amateurs and their motives: "Some of the finest instances of painting will be found not as might be imagined by the layman, among the professional artists, but among those amateurs whose chief occupation is amusing themselves first of all" (p. 134).

Hartley stresses that the American folk painter did not produce works for profit. This fiction (which may or may not have been a conscious construction) served to buttress the broader rewriting of history that Hartley undertakes. In the same chapter he raises the related issue of leisure—the leisure of the nonprofessional, the amateur's respite from the demands of modern, efficiency-conscious, profit-oriented industry. "These amateurs," Hartley assures us, "are never troubled with the 'how' of mediocre painting; neither are they troubled with the wiles of the outer world." He ends by cajoling early modernists: "I would recommend to those artists who are long since jaded with repetition and success . . . to refresh their eyes and their senses with the work of these outwardly unassuming but thoroughly convincing amateurs" (p. 143).

Hartley's theory is multivalent, following William Morris's blending of economic and aesthetic considerations. The amateur painters of the past were also distinguished from their modern successors by the primacy of nature in their works—a nature intimately seen or reenvisioned, as in the writings of Whitman. In "American Primitives" Hartley claims: "This primitive painting has nothing to do with intellectualized representation, it has but one concern, namely the desire of the simple mind to satisfy a deferred longing to create a comprehensible, and reasonable representation of nature such as the simple eye has seen or the simple imagination has conjured." And the manuscript points to what nature offers the artist: "None of these artists assumed anything but the desire to register in terms of the given medium a peculiar pleasure derived from nature, no one of them is trying to prove an esthetic case, and herein lies the very special pleasure of these primitive paintings."[12] The abundance and fecundity of visible nature, together with creativity of human nature brought to bear on the activity of painting, give pleasure to the maker and to viewers, who can realize their own creative potential in the image.

Returning once again to his call for New Realism, in *Adventures in the Arts* Hartley commends the experimental nature of the American works of prior centuries. Sounding (perhaps deliberately) like a reincarnation of the eighteenth-century critic Diderot, Hartley continues: "It is sensation at first hand with these charmingly amateur artists. They have been hampered in no way with the banality of school technique learned in the manner of the ever-present and unoriginal copyist. They literally invent expression out of a personally accumulated passion for beauty and they have become aware of it through their own intensely personalised contact with life" (p. 135). Like the theorists Paul Rosenfeld and Waldo Frank, Hartley considered life experience, whether received or transcribed through the senses, the fundamental basis of art. Not surprisingly, according to Hartley's historical account, only the unalienated art of the preindustrial era can successfully embody the relation of citizens to nature, of citizens to each other. Hartley writes, "What a relief it is for us who are tired of art as we have been forced [to view it] ever since impressionism took hold to go back for instance to the honest-to-God realization of an artist like Courbet."[13] His interpretation of impressionist painting, especially his realization of its tacit partnership with industrialization, is prescient, as is his naming of the pre-impressionist Courbet as a model for the independent, socially engaged landscape practices he was promoting in America.

For twentieth-century pioneers of American art such as Hartley and his colleagues, who were consciously attempting to compete with Europe, the idea of an indigenous art—first introduced by the painter-theorist Robert Henri—was paramount.[14] Hartley tackled the notion head-on in "American Primitives." Of eighteenth- and nineteenth-century untutored painters of nature Hartley states:

> As for the Americanism that exists in them, that takes care of itself. These pictures could have been done by no one else, for nothing exists in them but specialized, American sensitivity. The quality that makes Copley, Audubon, Earle and the other Americans what they are to us, is the same quality that tempers all these primitive pictures, they are essentially cool, restrained and brittle, and they are happily devoid of extraneous showmanship.[15]

The folk artists' emphasis on design over optical realism, or "copying," served Hartley's argument for an updated superrealism. Since the Armory Show of 1913, abstract art and a limited taste for abstraction, actively encouraged by 291 gallery, had taken root in the United States. And although there were competent American abstractionists, the upsurge of nationalistic tendencies after the war greatly lowered the prestige of abstraction, with its purportedly foreign origins. This suspicion lasted through the twenties. Unlike abstraction, New Realism was intended for a nonelite, nonspecialized audience. Like folk art, it drew on popular culture; and it was calculated to appeal to an international public's growing curiosity about American cultural wares.

Following Hartley's example, Arthur Dove was the next member of the Stieglitz circle to experiment with the new indigenous mode founded on folk art of the past. The similarities between Dove's assemblages, executed between 1924 and 1930, and Victorian mixed-media constructions have been noted,[16] although no one has yet attempted to establish their meanings within the context of either the Stieglitz circle or American material culture after World War I. Dove's two- and three-dimensional "things," as he named them, in which he experimented with a variety of materials, put into practice the theories of Hartley's *Adventures in the Arts.* Even in nonassemblage objects, he substituted glass or metal for canvas.[17] By using materials customarily segregated from the fine arts, as folk artists typically did, he also set the new forms further outside the academic tradition inherited from Europe.

Craft, technique, and design, rather than "imitation," are the core criteria of folk art. These same emphases are evident in Dove's works. His assemblages—particularly the portraits—demonstrate that it is not necessary to rely on conventions and copy appearances to produce representational "likenesses." Because these assemblages generated a great deal of press coverage in stories and reviews, they played an important role in the group's bid for international fame.

In his classic history of the time around World War I, *The End of American Innocence,* Henry May suggests one reason for such favorable attention: he argues that in 1917 the press was taken over by what he called the "Young Intellectuals." He also examines the birth of new styles of American writing and names Sherwood Anderson as the creator of a new prose style that was terse, sharp-focused, and deceptively simple.[18] May's description applies equally well to the photographic work of Alfred

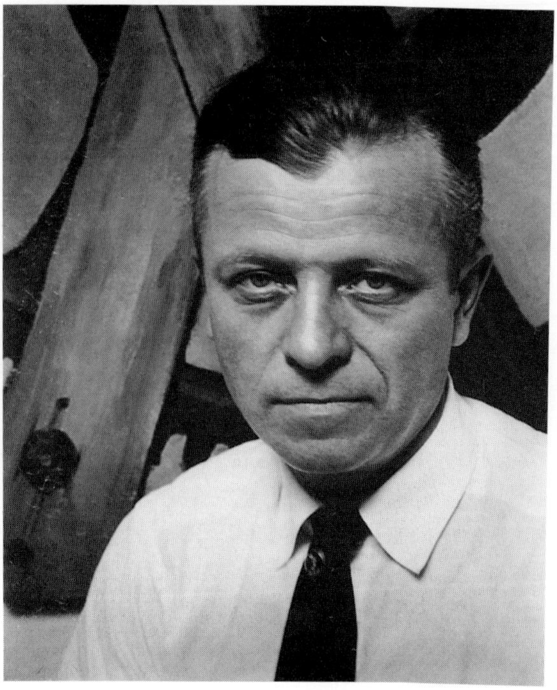

6. Alfred Stieglitz, *Portrait of Arthur Dove,* 1915, platinum photograph, 9 3/8 × 7 1/2 in. National Gallery of Art, Washington, D.C., Alfred Stieglitz Collection.

Stieglitz and Paul Strand after the war. Although Stieglitz had occasionally experimented with darkroom techniques in the early years of his career, in his postwar works he strictly avoids manipulation, producing works increasingly marked by acuteness of image and clarity of focus.

Stieglitz's probing photograph of Arthur Dove, *Portrait of Arthur Dove* (1915; figure 6), represents the painter as archetypal artist-craftsworker: a serious, committed maker of cultural objects, compelled by the mission of reforming the American cultural self. This view of Dove also implies a deep identification between artist and object, maker and material, for the photographer juxtaposes one of Dove's own images with Dove himself—like another Whitman, intimately identified with his own works. Moreover, in the photograph Dove is wearing on his tie a portrait miniature, an eighteenth- and nineteenth-century art form very popular in America and made primarily by amateurs. For their revised definition of American art maker, the group looked back not only to Whitman but also to America's folk artisans, popular artists practicing a popular art. If one accepted the premises of Marsden Hartley's theories of folk art, as Dove's assemblages suggest Dove himself did, then existing works by American folk practitioners provided a precedent for an indigenous tradition of visual art making.[19]

Dove's assemblages of the 1920s are outstanding examples of the Stieglitz group's very early appreciation and use of these folk art precedents. One well-known witty

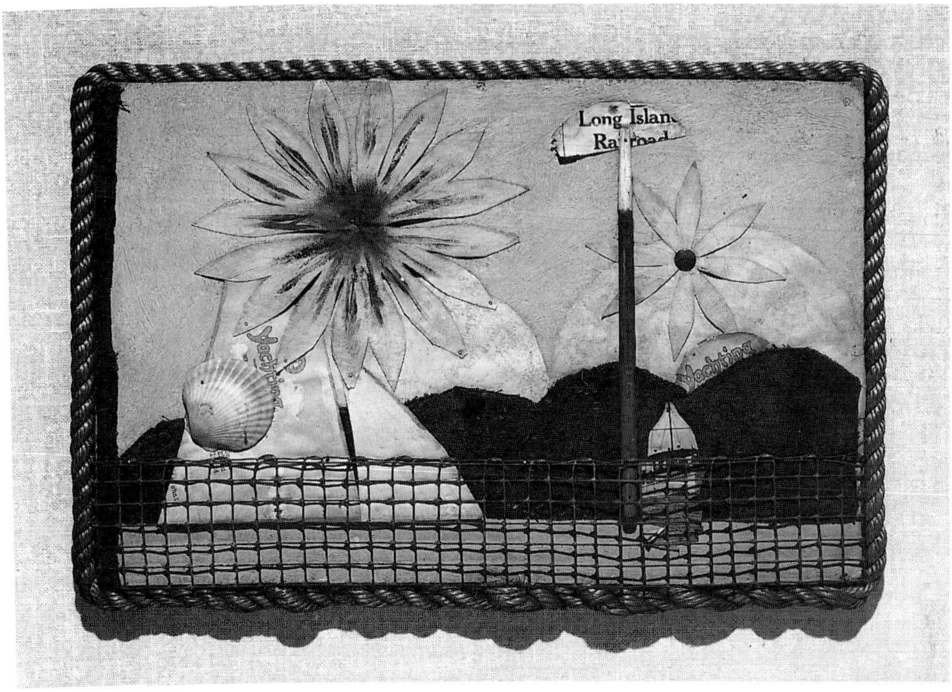

7. Arthur Dove, *Huntington Harbor,* 1924, oil, oil on paper, photomechanical reproductions, fabric, metal screening, seashell, wood, rope, and tacks on paperboard mounted on wood, 9 ¼ × 13 ⅛ in. Purchase, Hirshhorn Museum and Sculpture Garden, Smithsonian Institution, Washington, D.C.; photography by Lee Stalsworth.

example, *Grandmother* (1925, Museum of Modern Art, New York) quite deliberately recalls mid-Victorian collage. Dove's use of real objects (wood, needlepoint, leaves, a page from a Bible) responded as well to Hartley's call in 1918 for Americans to create a New Realism to supersede imported European isms: cubism, purism, futurism. In *Huntington Harbor,* the third in a series of assemblages of 1924 (figure 7), Dove produces a more sophisticated composition, in a more complex medium, than his earlier efforts. The image combines oil paint on paper, photomechanical reproduction, fabric, metal screening, wood, rope, tacks, and a seashell; all are mounted on a wooden panel. Beneath the real shell (midground left), the date of the painting, mechanically reproduced, is affixed to the panel surface. Also machine-rendered, the word "Yachting," apparently cut from some publication, is pasted at a jaunty angle just above the shell. The word's reproduced double is attached on the bias in the right midground. Just off-center to the right, in the portion of the landscape that depicts sky, is the name "Long Island Railroad"; printed on a fragment of what could be a train schedule, it haloes the top of a mastlike form. The printed fragment is a clear reference, at least to locals, to a transportation system linking New York City to Montauk Point at the far eastern tip of Long Island. Habitués of the train, and New York viewers in general, could plausibly interpret the mastlike form as the lighthouse at Montauk, a notable geographical marker.

In the work Dove presents with irony the "ideal" image of leisure. A small black-and-white reproduction of middle-class folks yachting, probably from a magazine advertisement, appears in the middle ground to the right, affixed to Dove's fabric mountains. A mast/lighthouse, actually the tapered end of an artist's paintbrush, stands beside a cutout that bears the word "Yachting." The stalwart mast-cum-beacon for souls lost at sea (which also literally represents an artist's tool) is mirrored by a calligraphic reproduction at left that forms the sail of a large yacht in the foreground. The sustained visual pun on the word *craft,* meaning both "boat" and "artistic knowledge," is only part of Dove's wry commentary in this assemblage. The image of middle-class leisure is undercut when one knows the context in which Dove made the work. He produced *Huntington Harbor* and most of his other twenty-five assemblages from 1924 to 1930 on board the *Mona,* a fishing yawl on which the artist and his second wife, the painter Helen Torr, lived and worked on Long Island Sound. While for well-to-do inhabitants and visitors a fishing excursion might suggest leisure, the artist's fishing boat was not recreational. The *Mona* provided a place, austere and cramped, for Dove and Torr to practice their craft; at the time, most of their small income came from fishing. Dove's calculated use of popular advertising can be taken as a pointed criticism not so much of its form as of the mythology, the shaping of the "American Dream," by such idealized renderings of "typical" American life.

As a potent social comment addressing the economic inequities in American life, particularly the life of the American artist, the work goes beyond the formalist concerns of many French cubists who often worked in collage. *Huntington Harbor* displays the satirical humor of the New York dadaists and draws on the surrealists' evocative world of multiple reference while recalling specific principles of construction from nineteenth-century American art. By using a length of real rope to frame the image, the work also recalls Picasso's well-known *Still Life with Chair Caning* (1912, Musée Picasso, Paris), an oil paint and oilcloth collage on canvas that is similarly surrounded with manufactured hemp rope. Though artists of the Stieglitz circle vigorously denied any relation with contemporary French surrealism and German New Realism—which also used found objects and socially engaged collage techniques—the influences are marked; ironically, the group assimilated foreign styles in the name of native production. The circle's long-established international networks linked the members to contemporary Italian and Soviet artistic endeavors as well. But while their European colleagues were largely content to transform the formal conventions of traditional systems of representation, Dove (and his circle) deployed art to transform their audience's view of social realities.

Not all commercially reproduced images were used for biting cultural criticism,

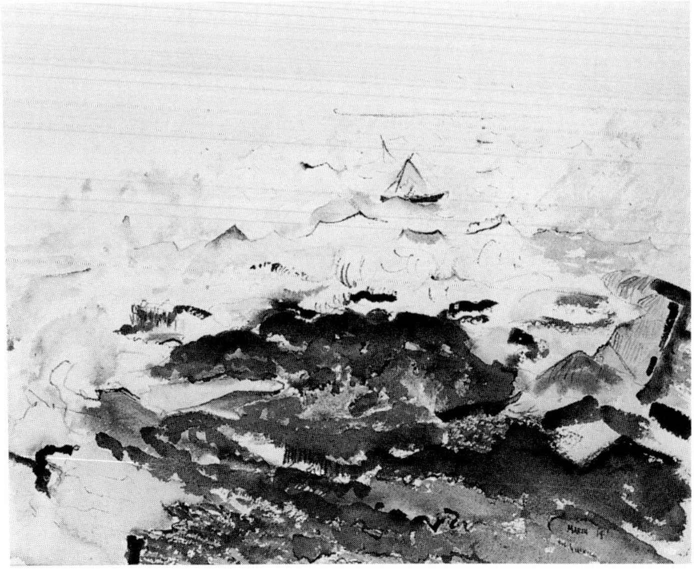

8. John Marin, *The Little Boat,* 1914, watercolor, 16 ¼ × 19 ⅜ in. Acquired 1949, The Metropolitan Museum of Art, Alfred Stieglitz Collection.

and Dove was not alone in his deep interest in the mechanical image. John Marin's scrapbooks are full of reproductions from magazines and newspapers, as well as post-card images of clippers, schooners, and all types of boats in full sail.[20] In addition to somber paintings of boats, Marin produced many in a lighter key. Perhaps one of the reproductions he had collected served as a guide to the completion of *The Little Boat* (1914; figure 8), a picture as clever as Dove's *Huntington Harbor* and equally dependent on the visual pun that suggestively equates "boat" with "craft." Marin's persona as "Ancient Mariner," promoted by Paul Rosenfeld in *Port of New York,* also comes readily to mind, adding a touch of humor to the work.

The Little Boat is representative of many other paintings by the Maine-based artist. Like Dove's assemblage, the work in part makes a statement about the artist's role in society. The entire palette is used in this small work, justifying the frequent and apt praise of the contemporary critic Henry McBride, who called Marin the "Beethoven of watercolorists" in creating painted symphonies. The painter's reproduced craft, the little boat, is deliberately diminished; in skillfully portraying the land and choppy sea, Marin effectively overwhelms the boat in color and size. The boat is "small," and the title calls attention to the maker's decision to dispense with the traditional use of perspective; he achieves a convincing illusion of space instead through form and color alone. The exuberance of color in the work—aquas, greens, violets, ochers, grays, reds, pinks, oranges, and blends of each—suggests to viewers that the picture's subject is craft itself. The small boat serves as a surrogate for the artist: Marin in particular and the American artist in general. The archetypal American artist remains afloat

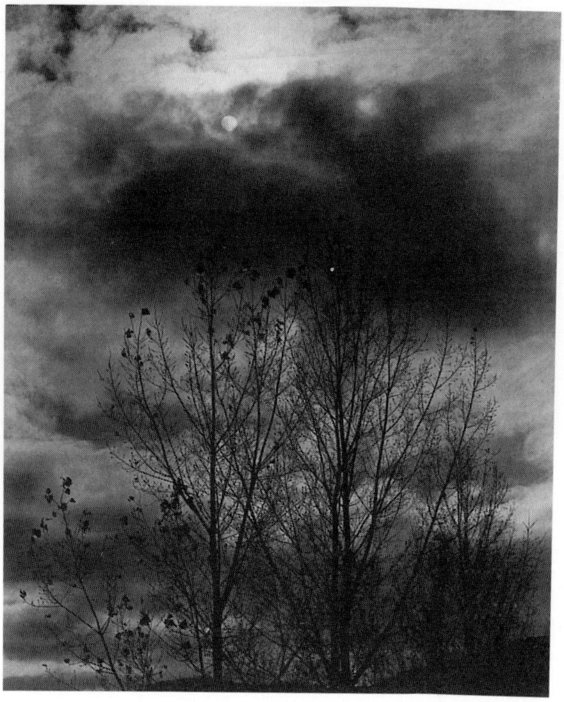

9. Arthur Stieglitz, *Trees and Clouds, Lake George,* ca. 1928, gelatin silver photograph. National Gallery of Art, Washington, D.C., Alfred Stieglitz Collection.

in postwar currents of extraordinary turbulence and change through his or her knowledge of craft.

What distinguishes the work of Marin and Dove from previous paintings on marine subjects is not the use of the boat to figure the soul or self of the artist (and sometimes of any individual) but the self-consciousness of the artists' gestures as they fashion their statements. Their use of various media and of technique itself to assert traditional myths and symbols declares their modernity.

While the circle's residual symbolism perpetuated fin-de-siècle spiritual concerns, other devices provided a modern psychological twist. Dove's animal pictures, for example, recall the works both of Picasso (who unquestionably influenced all members of the Stieglitz group from the time of his first American showing at 291) and of the German artist Franz Marc, who imbued animals with rare spiritual beauty and meaning. It was not only in their portrayals of animal life that Dove and other members of the circle captured a haunting sense of spirit or "animus." Many of Dove's semi-abstracted landscapes endow the land itself with a spirit that watches, sometimes not so benevolently, as humans mark its surface. And images by other circle members share the eerie beauty usually attributed exclusively to paintings by Charles Burchfield, without conjuring, as he did, nature's malevolent spirits.

One thinks especially of photographs by Stieglitz such as *Trees and Clouds, Lake*

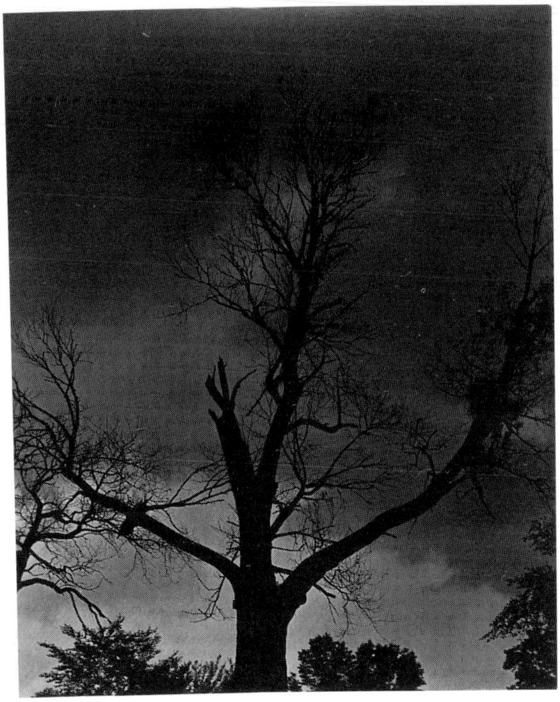

10. Arthur Stieglitz, *Tree Set*, ca. 1927, gelatin silver photograph. National Gallery of Art, Washington, D.C., Alfred Stieglitz Collection.

George or *Tree Set* (ca. 1928, ca. 1927; figures 9 and 10). *Trees and Clouds* is a hauntingly beautiful vertical landscape; though inescapably Burchfield-esque, with its prominent autumnal moon, it is somewhat softer in its poetic mood than comparable works by the midwesterner. A stunningly high contrast between the moonlit clouds and surrounding dark emphasizes the delicacy of the tree forms, making them look like a fine etching. Stieglitz often used this device to call attention to the processes that photography shares with printing—the older, better-established form. The artist's delight in knowing these underscores his similar pleasure in night's alchemical effect on the human psyche and in the transformative powers of human artistry. Like so much else in the art of the circle, Stieglitz's choice of the nighttime as subject invites comparison with the work of contemporary European surrealists as much as with American contemporaries such as Burchfield.

In contrast, Stieglitz's *Tree Set* is a daytime view; yet the interpretation of a dead tree in the backyard of his family's summer home at Lake George is no less dramatic. This particular work posits a spirit in nature and its forms similar to that portrayed in the work of American "naive" or "autodidact" painters, formerly called primitives. Very dark clouds, seeming to warn of an impending deluge, crown the image of the tree, which (because of the view selected) appears to be gesticulating. The silhouette of the tree—extremely crisp, clear, and saturated in its blackness—is the protagonist of the composition. Viewers are humbled by this object, which is made into a talisman by the deliberately low viewpoint, the time of day, and the weather. Through his artistry, the photographer contrives to suggest that even in the dead forms of nature there is a spirit that relates to and has meaning for the interior life of humans.

The relation of such anthropomorphizing works to contemporary European surrealism did not escape the notice of Paul Rosenfeld. In "The World of Arthur Dove" (1932), Rosenfeld attributed Dove's belated success to the current vogue for "subconscious" expression, particularly in surrealist painting. Rosenfeld's review went on to claim—not only for this artist but for the entire Stieglitz group—the territory of the unconscious mind as a source for American avant-gardists. In fact, according to Rosenfeld, "The entire Group of 291 with which he has long been associated is prolific of such expressions of the fixed and secret things which color their whole existences with anguish or with joy."[21] With hindsight, Rosenfeld's account in fact brings to mind the ways in which Max Ernst, Léonor Fini, Yves Tanguy (and their source, de Chirico) made inanimate objects into fascinatingly humanoid presences.

The circle chose to explore not just the unfamiliar zones of the mindscape but also novel external landscapes, particularly those of the Southwest. A Clason travel guide in 1920 extolled the superior riches of New Mexico, its abundant and untapped natural stores of minerals and ores. And it highlighted the indigenous architecture—the communal Indian dwellings called pueblos—that made the New Mexican landscape a veritable outdoor museum of social history. New Mexico is also described as a health resort, a land possessing restorative powers for both the body and the mind.[22] Although Taos had not yet won a place for itself on the guidebook map, Santa Fe had: "Where else can you, in a day's journey, reach Indian pueblos and Mexican villages, cliff dwellings and pre-historic ruins, the haunts of bear and mountain lion, snow-clad peaks and trout streams?"[23] Indeed, for the artists of the Stieglitz group, disenchanted as they were becoming with the urban scene and its clamoring, competitive marketplace, the lure of untouched, sparsely populated land proved irresistible. When they moved to or simply visited New Mexico, they could mix with an indigenous non-white cultural community whose arts, crafts, architecture, and cooperative social forms attracted their attention and praise as it had that of contemporary anthropologists.

Marsden Hartley (who was already using Native American design motifs in his artwork before the war, during his association with the Blue Rider group in Germany) was the first of the circle to be drawn to the Southwest. His immediate responses to the land and to the ancient and modern cultures of New Mexico were recorded in a series of four articles, two of which appeared in *El Palacio* and two in the periodical *Art and Archaeology.* In "America as Landscape" (whose appropriation of both Whitmanian ideas and the strategies of folk artworks was discussed at the beginning of this chapter) Hartley singles out issues that would shape his postwar arguments and those of other critics. He muses: "Races have always invented their own esthetics as a racial necessity. The redman has always made pots, danced, sung songs, woven blankets for himself because the need of self-expression was persistent. . . . We whites have had to borrow quickly because we have no tradition and no racial background."[24] The kind of "borrowing" Hartley had in mind was the imitation of European styles that he opposed; in contrast, Native Americans were driven by cultural necessity to invent their own aesthetics. The products of the Native American, unlike those of whites, are not hierarchically organized, and Hartley welcomes this democratization of the arts. In "Aesthetic Sincerity," which appeared in the same issue of *El Palacio,* Hartley praises indigenous architectural forms, claiming that "there is no place in the world where the architecture has been made to fit the scene more perfectly, no instance of where nature itself had so completely dictated the human habitation."[25] Hartley was, in fact, praising traditional and regional forms. As the modern visitor to the Southwest quickly realizes, the form and feeling of even the most recent buildings—public and private—derive largely from the idea of the Indian pueblo, both in their structural elements and in the use of natural, local materials. That the language spoken by the indigenous architecture is the language of nature, its curves and its sensuous elements, appealed to Hartley most.

In "Red Man Ceremonials: An American Plea for American Esthetics" (1920), Hartley codifies the impressions and ideas of his two-year experience in northern New Mexico into a practical theory of art. He depicts the Native American artist (as he had the folk artist) as an archetype of the image maker that he and his circle hoped would proliferate in modern American communities, a viable alternative to the contemporary white European model associated with the alienated and alienating. The American Indian "has shown us the significance of the poetic aspects of our original land. Without him we should still be unrepresented in the cultural development of the world." He names the Native American art maker "[t]he one truly indigenous religionist and esthete of America."[26] These craftworkers were also compared with African American artists:

> It is the buffalo, the eagle, and the deer dances that show you their essential greatness as artists. You find a species of rhythm so perfected in its relation to racial interpretation, as hardly to admit of witnessing ever again the copied varieties of dancing such as we whites of the present hour are familiar with. It is nothing short of captivating artistry of first excellence, and we are familiar with nothing that equals it outside of the negro syncopation which we now know so well, and from which we have borrowed all we have of native expression.
>
> If we had the redman sense of time in our system, we would be better able to express ourselves. (p. 8)

Hartley believed that this imputed ease of movement, an implied sensuousness and body consciousness, distinguished Native Americans and African Americans from whites and gave them a greater degree of self-expressiveness, to which he attributed high aesthetic value. The white majority must heed their example, which "would teach us to be ourselves in a still greater degree" (p. 8). The ultimate beauty of Native American objects rests in the evidence they gave of the maker's participation in a communal sense of self.[27]

Romantic notions of "primitiveness," which had captured the imagination of early modern artists in America at least as early as the Armory Show of 1913 and 291's groundbreaking exhibit of African tribal sculpture in 1914, underlay Hartley's appreciative claims. The taste for outsider art—the art of children, of illiterates, of autodidacts, of the mad—that had its roots in the eighteenth-century philosophy of Rousseau was still very much alive. It is important to recognize in Hartley's theory his attempt to create positive stereotypes of Native Americans and African Americans, as well as his vision of how outsider or marginalized art functions in Western society. The valued expressiveness of so-called primitives could (among other things) help undo the repression purportedly engendered by the white Puritan forefathers.

Hartley (too uncritically and somewhat patronizingly) represents the Native American as a "natural" voice of nature; his art is "of a piece with his conception of nature and the struggle for realism is not necessary, since he is at all times the natural actor, the natural expresser of the indications and suggestions derived from the great theme of nature which occupies his mind, and body, and soul" (p. 9). Pointing to his model's lack of formal, institutional training, Hartley underlines his own antimimetic stance. The Native American can show the early modern artist how to represent nature without veristic copying. Hartley's socioanthropological view of Native Americans is dramatically and categorically different from that of most earlier artists.

Hartley, like the anthropologists of his time, interpreted the Indian dance form as an analogue for indigenous communal relations, seeing each individual performer as "a powerful unit of the group in which he may be performing. He is esthetically a responsible factor, since it concerns him as part of the great idea" (p. 9). This insight was later borrowed and elaborated on by both Waldo Frank and Paul Rosenfeld. Frank never visited the Southwest but depended on the firsthand written reports of Hartley and Rosenfeld and on the paintings and photographs of Hartley, Marin, and Strand. All their accounts claim that the dance, and by extension art in general, has redeeming social value. It is the performative act, the act of representation itself, that defines and ensures human relationships.

In his conclusion to "Red Man Ceremonials," Hartley pleads for the preservation of Indian communities and their unique modes of artistic expression. He prods his white, middle-class audience, both flattering and chastening them as "the infant prodigy among races":

> there is much we could inherit from these people if we could prove ourselves more worthy and less egotistic. . . . We have nothing more native at our disposal than the beautiful creations of this people. . . . We need an esthetic concept of our own. . . . We need to admit, and speedily, the rare and excellent esthetics in our midst a[s] part of our own intimate

> scene. . . . It would help at least a little toward proving to the world around us that we are not so young a country as we might seem. (pp. 12–13)

This pointed condemnation of the chauvinistic Eurocentrism of white-dominated society was later effectively welded to an ethics of racial and ethnic tolerance in Rosenfeld's critical essays. Hartley's urgent call to recognize the contributions of Native Americans was echoed by contemporary anthropologists who contributed to the same periodicals that published his essays. In arguing for a particular model of indigenous American image maker, "Red Man Ceremonials" presented a concrete example of the kind of active social participation that Hartley recommended. These writings demonstrate that an artist could play as vital a role as an anthropologist in interpreting and preserving cultural forms.

Hartley's final article on the Southwest appeared in the September 1922 issue of *Art and Archaeology*. While describing the yearly fiesta at San Geronimo at Taos, Hartley added a few final strokes to his earlier observations on what Native American ceremonies mean for their culture and for modern American society. Aesthetics had been the focus of the 1920 essay, but spirituality was key in its sequel. To Hartley, the indigenous peoples of the Southwest were exemplary because, historically, "They had larger views to impose upon themselves, they had the sun to sign themselves to, and their ethics and morality as well as their spiritual conceptions have been too highly evolved to make compromises."[28] The "compromises" here were those imposed by the domination of whites; the "larger views" are contained in cosmic mythologies distinct from the anthropocentric religion of the Christian West. "The religion of confession and absolution is replaced," Hartley reports, "with a more convincing religion of the body." His equation of the athletic sensuosity and glowing health of tribesmen with a kind of primitive spirituality had its roots in Whitman. In their culture, Hartley locates a tradition as useful to American visual artists as that passed down in the West since the Renaissance. The Native American modes of art making are at least as old as the European ones; they are, as Hartley asserts, "the perpetuation of customs of two thousand years, and even more."[29]

Although Hartley's theories about New Mexico's Indian communities and the significance of their ritual activities were not fully developed until 1920, they were born during his 1918–19 visit to the state. His impressions are mirrored and reframed in Waldo Frank's *Our America* of 1919, which abounds with positive representations of Native American communities. Frank may have been influenced by conversations with Hartley. It is also possible that as he was writing his own book Frank had already begun editorial work on the 1921 compilation of Hartley's theoretical essays, *Adventures in the Arts,* which included a version of "Red Man Ceremonials" titled simply "The Red Man." Though he visited the Southwest only in his imagination, Frank set those distant communities of nonwhites within contemporary psychoanalytic theory. He joined Hartley in celebrating the unrepressed physical vitality that he interpreted as a sign of psychological balance. For both, the spirituality of tribal members is grounded in physical health: the Native American "prays for harmony between himself and the mysterious forces that surround him, for he has learned that from this harmony comes health." The vitality and awareness of the Indian is the "outward mark of that harmony which the race has won."[30]

Frank also reiterates Hartley's plea that whites engaged with their own society and culture must help the valuable ancient culture survive. Like his colleague, he based his petition on the notion that the expressive capacity of the white majority could be expanded by embracing indigenous Indian values. "There is in us all," Frank asserts in 1929 in *The Re-discovery of America,* "the dark conscience of our murder of the primeval forests—of something in their depth which is deep in us; of our refusal of their value, of our disdain of the red man who was the spirit of those forests and who is yet, beneath the layers of law and memory, the spirit of ourselves. For our root is the red man; our true building must arise from recognition of his base in our heart; and our denial of this is a disease within us."[31] Unlike the postmodernist theorists of the 1990s, Frank argued that we must recognize commonality rather than emphasize difference. And the uses to which the new stereotype of the Native American was put by reform-minded artists and social critics in the 1930s were strongly influenced by the particular social and economic pressures in America felt by what had been—before the stock market crash of 1929—the upper middle classes.

In the early twenties Hartley found in the Native American community a model that would enable early modern American art makers to reform their own self-image and to realign their practices with sociocultural needs. At the end of the decade Frank represented Native Americans as a group with a remarkable ability to remain sane despite social oppression. The crucial psychological journey toward discovering an authentic American self begins, according to Frank, when the dominant white majority recognizes its spiritual ancestor in the instinctual, expressive self personified by the Native American. Theorists of the group were not simply using the indigenous peoples as a handy vehicle to express their ideas; they apparently believed that they were bound to Native Americans—not through blood ties, of course, but through spiritual ties, relations based "in the heart," as Frank wrote.[32] This psychological kinship, which was grounded in common values and beliefs, such as reverence for the natural world and a related commitment to conserve natural resources, followed from one of the circle's primary assumptions. It is not blood lines or pedigree that makes one "American": the land itself is the dominant and determining force that shapes the psyche and social behavior. Immigrants to the country are shaped, over time, by their interactions with soil and geography and are thereby transformed into something else: Americans.

Frank's most interesting rhetorical use of the affirmative image of Native Americans appears in "Straight Streets," an essay written in 1925 and included in his 1937 compilation of articles and papers, *In the American Jungle.* Here, in a variant of the country-city opposition that was a major theme of the Stieglitz circle in the postwar years, Frank juxtaposes two images: white urban rigidity and rural Indian flexibility. The properties of regularity, conformity, and regimentation evidenced in the gridded structure of the city's plan are seen as a superimposed order not found in nature. The straight streets of the metropolis are in fact understood as a willed opposition to nature's principles. "What is the meaning of our cities of rectangular streets? What is their effect on our souls?" Frank asks rhetorically. "It is plain that Nature likes curves. . . . Our physical dynamo has not a straight line in it. And our mental digestion is tortuous as our intestines. Logic may proceed theoretically like a plummet, but there's nothing natural in such logic. Draconian justice might be called rectilinear, but it, too, does not exist in Nature."[33]

Frank is arguing once more against Dewey's philosophy, this time to suggest the Indian culture as the indigenous alternative to the pragmatic mind-set of the modern American. "The Indian culture began," he suggests, "when his innate spiritual and intellectual values formed a solution with the world about him; his culture was achieved when the responses between his soul and the world had rounded into a unified life which expressed both fully." Expanding Hartley's observations on the particular architectural environment, Frank shapes them into a more encompassing principle. And he invents an emblem to replace the grid plan he had condemned: "The Amerind was profoundly, beautifully adjusted to the land. If you study him in his demeanor, his dance, his music, his pyramiding pueblos or his simple tepees, in his flinted arrows, in his decorations, you will find that the general symbol of his expression is a curve so sharp and so severe that it barely escapes being an angle. The curve is the way of acceptance: the angle is the way of resistance" (p. 126).

Frank's valorization of this design principle found its way into Rosenfeld's theories of Native American culture. Whether the interpretation is valid anthropologically, or even constitutes good art criticism, is beside the point—which is that Frank uses the Indian community to present an alternative to modern American society's wrongheaded "self-assertion against a cosmic factor" (p. 127). In Frank, Hartley's moving petition for integrating Indian values into white culture takes the form of an imperative: "The Indian's culture is prophetic of what our culture must be. His nature is a guide to the understanding and achievement of our own" (p. 125). During his long literary career Frank proposed a number of models for an American society of the future. The socialist model prescribed by Van Wyck Brooks was especially appealing to him, as it was to Stieglitz and other members of the circle. Through the publications of Hartley, Frank, and Rosenfeld, members of the circle and a broader readership came to understand the tightly integrated communal forms of the Native American—given physical form in both ancient ruins and modern pueblos—as an early and workable (because enduring) form of socialist interrelation.

Rosenfeld, who like Frank was influenced by Hartley, focused in his published recollections of his trip to the Southwest on the art form of the Indian dance:

specifically, the Corn Dance. For him the performance is analogous to a poem by Whitman, and in fact he uses Whitman's philosophy to decode the dance. In this interpretive process, the poet's strong conceptions transform the critic's perceptions. In "Turning to America: The Corn Dance," Rosenfeld recalls experiencing a revelatory moment while he was actually viewing the dance in New Mexico:

> The abstract presence of America was plain. A moment, still, the blissful monotone of the related media, and the gratification of feeling a form, a rhythm, take up one's personal life and America, and hold and objectify them[.] . . . [F]eeling, about myself and my friends and the visageless undefined numberless throng of compatriots was curiously fluent. . . . It spread, America, no place of becoming. . . . Being, not becoming; pure timeless being, was the secret unifying principle of this continent as of all other dry and classic soils. The solid, long, level chant of Whitman knew it![34]

And the author's spiritual experience, triggered by the Indian art form, confirms his intuition that New Mexico itself is conducive to a harmony of environment that ultimately becomes social: "the red man's cognition of basal forces, and hymn and thanks to them, plainly communicated; timeless station and rejection of the lone-star, self-feeling individual" (p. 230).

In opposing American individualism, Rosenfeld draws a comparison similar to that offered by Frank in "Straight Streets"—a superbly superreal image that sustains the tone of revelation. He imagines the skyline of New York City from his position on the New Mexico plains: "To the east across the plains the tall New York shot up, turbid flames of self-assertion, towering ambition, ceaseless becoming. . . . [W]hat had once been cosmic yearning now expressed itself in senseless motion; and what had been the assertive romantic ego now lived on in the degenerate form of insatiable personal wishes" (pp. 230–31). The communal harmony of the Native American throws the avarice and competition of the white-dominated metropolitan marketplace into high relief. And, for a line or two, Rosenfeld loses hope that white America can integrate the example and customs of the native inhabitant into the larger class-bound, fragmented culture.

Rosenfeld's pessimism is quickly dispelled by his fervent belief in the inevitable triumph of the natural forces of human relations. Those intimately personal forces—in contrast to the impersonal ones of industrial productivity—would eventually motivate even city dwellers. A new sense of community would follow, though "[w]hat the new communism would resemble . . . could not be prophesied. But it was inevitable and welcome; since through it the intuition, the cognition that gave this serene, level, Indian dance of Kansas and New Mexico and the whole intra-oceanic stretch its form, would reappear, in the new white America" (pp. 234–35). The transformation he envisions and desires will happen by way of art, as the title of his essay predicts. For Rosenfeld, the visual arts alone, functioning like the Corn Dance, will bring to white urban America the social harmony it lacked. His reflections end on a characteristically optimistic note: "Yes," he professes, "when the soil and man and the machines were in relation . . . art would top man's day like a temple-dome" (p. 235). A socially engaged, powerful art could crown America with the kind of spirituality whose absence Rosenfeld and others of the Stieglitz circle felt so keenly.

The New Mexican landscape and lifestyle clearly inspired the circle's writers and visual artists to make major changes in both the emphases and motives of their work. It was during his 1918–19 visit that Hartley first wrote letters and essays calling for a New Realism in the arts and a decentering of recognizably European manners. And Hartley followed his own instructions closely in his pastels drawn from life. An early biographer, Elizabeth McCausland, noted that they were "remarkably free from influences," their scenes "recognizable without being representational."[35]

The quest for a native expression, spearheaded in the first decade of the twentieth century by Robert Henri and his Ashcan group in the visual arts, and supported in the twenties by the texts and pictures of the Stieglitz circle, took a different turn in the 1930s. Influenced by the writings of a new set of critics, it became a search for a nativist expression. The term *nationalistic* had been applied to works of art before the thirties, but its use increased and its connotations changed dramatically. The American art world had accepted the term, as the title of a highly publicized debate sponsored by the Whitney Museum of American Art in 1932 makes clear: "Nationalism in Art—Is It an Advantage?"[36] Around the same time, the editor of the *Arts,* in its final issue, denounced the methods of Parisian art dealers who had turned modern art into "a kind of international dressmaker-painting, spattering it with the spirit of their own cynicism."[37] A contemporary arts organization known as "An American Group" banded together to combat "the French art racket."[38] As familiar as this may sound after the discussion in earlier chapters of the Stieglitz circle's public and private attacks on Paris dealers, the anti-Parisian propaganda of the thirties is different, with new nativist overtones and broad public acceptance. The public interested in art was itself largely a creation of those who pioneered indigenous expression in the twenties.

Artists of the thirties also appropriated and altered the narrative of America's cultural renaissance, a historical account of the twenties disseminated by members of the Stieglitz group and their contemporaries. They believed that an American renaissance would not be led by Whitman's heroic visionary artists but would rather occur inevitably—and soon—as the result of collaborative efforts. We might think immediately of Waldo Frank's early calls for the unification of American artists in cooperative interest groups. We might also remember the African American artists and theorists of the twenties whose Harlem Renaissance challenged the glib predictions of the later artists.

In the thirties artists also commandeered and modified the environmental determinism on which the Stieglitz group relied to explain and justify a specifically "American" art. The geographical ideas of the French historian and critic Hippolyte Taine had inspired few Americans before the turn of the century, but as interpreted and disseminated by the staff of *Camera Work* between 1903 and 1917, they made their way into the mainstream of art discourse.[39] The Regionalist painters Thomas Hart Benton, Grant Wood, and John Steuart Curry were framed by their principal advocate, Thomas Craven, as opposing the Stieglitz group. At least one of these artists, Benton, considered this opposition more than merely rhetorical. Significantly, these four, unlike the Stieglitz circle, did not form a cohesive group. Their association was a literary fiction invented by contemporary critics; according to the art historian Matthew Baigell, Benton met Curry only in 1929 and Wood in 1934. And the rubric under which they were promoted—Regionalism—itself is highly problematic.[40]

Benton's work raises questions about the uses of realism, as does a large body of contemporary works—not only so-called fine art but also the more widely available periodical reproductions, which in large part imitated Benton. According to Baigell,

> One finds a great number of illustrations in magazines of the period depicting scenes that can only be described as bleak, ugly, commonplace, bare and crude. . . .
>
> Recognized as part of the emerging nativist school, perhaps even of the nascent American Renaissance, these artists recorded images that were more an indictment of America than a glory song.
>
> Their hard, gritty realism, acerbic and melancholy at the same time, had more in common with that line of novelists running from Hamlin Garland and Edgar W. Howe through Sinclair Lewis than with earlier realist painters such as Robert Henri and his circle. Qualities like joy and love of life do not resonate from their works as they did from the paintings of older men, nor can one read in their works a sense of energy or drive. They painted a tired America, one seemingly drained of all ebullient spirits, one afraid to continue existing. . . . They evoked a spirit of doubt, often stated and ever present after the Crash, concerning the future of America.[41]

Contemporary observers of the American cultural scene also commented on the gloomy tone of much of the art being produced, promoted, and disseminated. Marsden Hartley noted in an unpublished manuscript of the 1930s entitled "Is There an American Art?" the "melancholy attached to the chauvinism of certain painters of today [the Regionalists] and in the attitude of their defenders as well." He singled out the landscapes of Grant Wood to illustrate his point: "Anyone with half an imagination can project himself into any space—and since all that Western country is vast, open and supposedly free in spirit—there should be a convincing energy coming forth out of Mr. Wood's paintings which to many who are perfectly sincere—is not there."[42]

Another serious critic of the period, also a Stieglitz circle partisan, compared Wood's works unfavorably to those of Arthur Dove. Reviewing a Dove exhibition at An American Place for the *New Yorker,* Lewis Mumford praised this artist's greater imaginative power: "He is not without a certain kinship to Wood, in that he is tempted to transform the visual facts of the landscape into more abstract symbols, but whereas Wood is betrayed into turning trees into lesser objects like rubber balls, Dove goes the whole hog and creates complete abstractions."[43] Baigell's later appraisal of Wood suggests something more than mere rubber balls in his landscapes: "As one looks at his immaculately groomed, cartoonlike landscapes, one almost expects Porky Pig to bounce out of the shrubbery. Thus it is possible that Wood knowingly allowed his landscapes to accord with the Iowan image of the land."[44] Such deliberate manipulation in fact seems likely, though Wood himself insisted that his subjects did not constitute boosterism for any particular locale.[45] But when closely examined, Wood's landscapes bring to mind not just cartoon art but also advertising art, with which Wood's works have a number of features in common. The works are intended to promote the state of Iowa; thus like all advertisements, they are meant to "sell."

As Mumford discovered, comparisons between the works of Grant Wood and those of Arthur Dove are revealing. Consider, for example, two superficially similar landscapes: Wood's *Fall Plowing* of 1931 (figure 11) and Dove's *Morning Sun* of 1935 (figure 12). Wood's painting, like Dove's, is a horizontal landscape with a distinct foreground, background, and midground. Both works are marked by a modernist use of color and form, rather than perspective, to suggest distance. But in other respects, the painters employ color and form quite differently.

Grant Wood's *Fall Plowing* is vivid in color. The unmodulated green of the foreground, gold of the midground, and lighter green hue of the background are deliberately heightened; the hues are artificial and nonnaturalistic. Though not consistent and unitary, the artist's point of view is primarily a bird's-eye view borrowed from the early Netherlandish painters whose work informed Wood's European studies. This choice values distance, refuses intimate knowledge of the subject, and thus denies the particularity of the land depicted.

A solitary object in *Fall Plowing* rivets the viewer's attention at the center foreground: an abandoned plow suggests human inhabitants, as do, more subtly, the diminutive farm buildings and windmill portrayed among the background hills. Wood's landscape, like Dove's, is striated. And, as in Dove's work, this device indicates human cultivation of the land, the ageless human art of agriculture. But Wood's image caricatures the land's natural shapes. A sophistication, indeed slickness, of rendering that flatly denies the values of the autodidactic or folk artist pervades Wood's rendition. This is the view neither of the native nor of the naïf. Here the contours of the hills, trees, and shrubs—the land itself—are all subjected to the same simplification, which denies their natural irregularity and roughness. Instead we are presented with an image of nature thoroughly tamed by human control. The same concept of land management that regulates this midwestern landscape also impressed an unnatural gridded form on midwestern cities. The calculating "art" of the Great Plains farmer in accomplishing this domination is heralded by the painter's comparable domination of the canvas. In *Fall Plowing* all is order, stillness—the land is chillingly silent. No breath of life is suggested.

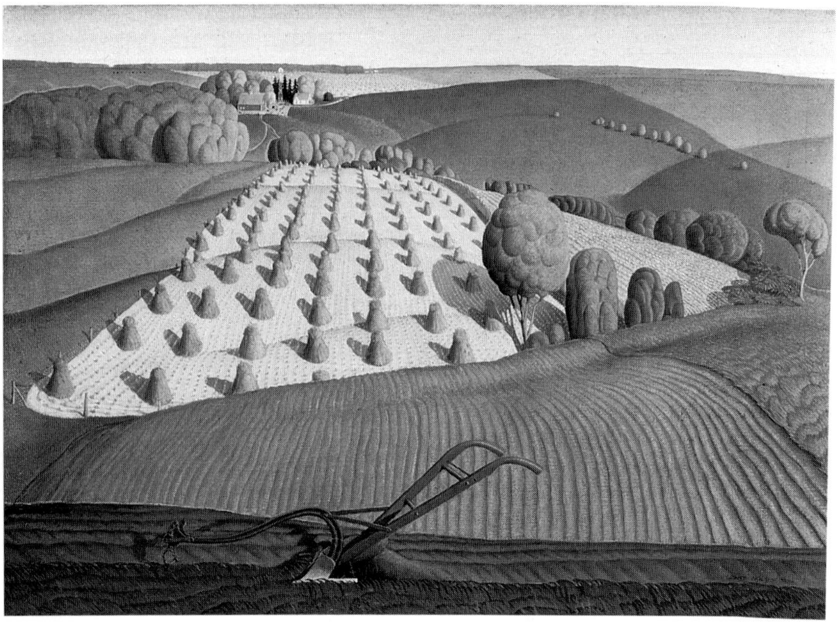

11. Grant Wood, *Fall Plowing,* 1931, oil on canvas, 29 ¼ × 39 ¼ in.
Deere and Company, East Moline, Illinois.

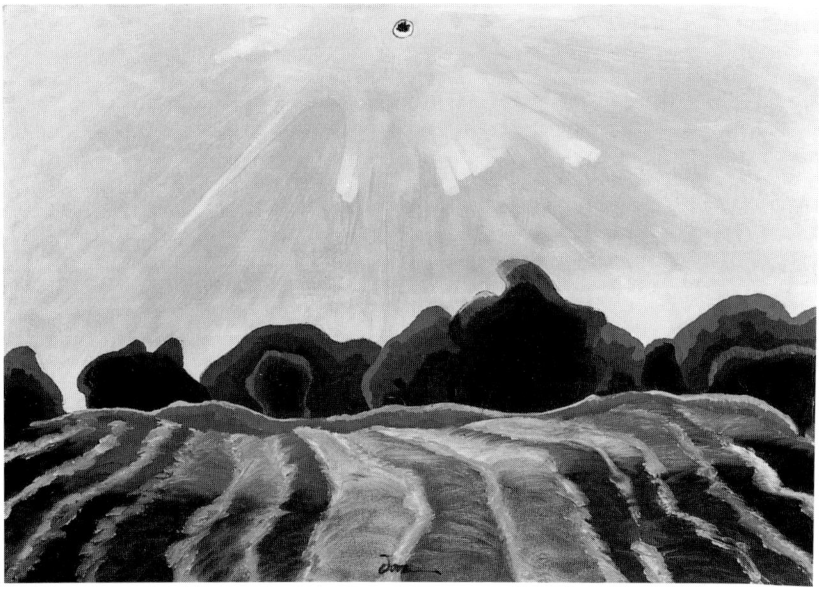

12. Arthur Dove, *Morning Sun,* 1935, oil on canvas, 20 × 28 in.
Acquired 1935, The Phillips Collection, Washington, D.C.

Wood's characteristic fashion of representing landscape depends on the simplification, clarity, and hard-edged exactness of advertising design. Here, too, viewers can take in the whole image immediately—slow, thoughtful reading and appreciation are not required. The work is deliberately not subtle, nor does Wood value subtlety and complexity. There is no element of surprise. Additionally, like a successful adman, Wood uses the power of suggestion rather than of expression. The painting not only attempts to promote Iowa, to "sell" the viewer on its importance and interest, but also simultaneously privileges white, middle-class, midwestern values: uniformity over irregularity, conformity over individualism, regimentation over spontaneity, seriousness over whimsy, sobriety over joy. Wood's decisions about representation and composition speak loud, both in what is absent and what is presented. What his work shuns, Dove's celebrates.

Arthur Dove's *Morning Sun* is subdued in color—unusually so, for the artist. The tones are all derived from hues found in nature, but muted. The overhanging image of the sun, centered in the uppermost register of the composition, is made to suggest a hollow navel of the world, poetically surrounded by a pale yellow aura of light. The trees of the landscape suggest pieces of children's puzzles; they are shapes as easy for the mind as for the small hand to grasp, elemental shapes that imply the literally elemental basis of the natural world.

The mood is lyrical, whimsical. The furrowed earth is beginning to heat up under the sun's rays, and a shadowy pattern of overhanging clouds adds further variety to the striped landscape. Dove's chin is (as Hartley prescribed) figuratively on the ground, in the rows of tilled soil. In this choice of point of view he, like other members of the Stieglitz circle, obeys the injunction to make art from the American earth. The humble perspective also contrasts starkly with Wood's dominating, overseeing viewpoint. Rather than promote the American land, *Morning Sun* joyfully celebrates it. It is a painted chant, like a Whitman poem, in praise of the American land and the American spirit. Dove's landscape is concerned not merely with describing a place (as in a promotional advertisement) but with expressing the pleasure of beholding. What is conveyed to viewers immediately, through Dove's use of abstract and simplified form, is the artist's joy in seeing nature. Indeed the human emotion of joy itself is the subject of the work. Dove represents his elation in contemplating the American landscape and all its myriad meanings for viewers to recognize and enjoy vicariously.

The point of view and message of the Regionalists sharply distinguished them from other contemporaries as well as from the Stieglitz group. Antagonisms between the Regionalists and various factions of the Left ran high, reaching a fever pitch by 1935; the Regionalists were attacked not only for their nationalism but also for their incipient fascism. As other critics have noted, the aesthetic ideas of Thomas Craven and Adolf Hitler are similar in a number of ways.[46] And because Hitler's attacks on and repression of Jewish artists were regularly reported in both art journals and the popular press, parallels between German and American nationalism of the thirties are easily documented. The connection appeared even stronger after Craven published his scandalous anti-Semitic slur in *Modern Art* (1934), calling Stieglitz "a Hoboken Jew without knowledge of, or interest in, the historical American background."[47]

Despite Craven's protestations to the contrary, none of the three most important Regionalists introduced new ideas or approaches into American art. They (especially Craven's favorite, Benton) recast—often in bigoted and malicious ways—ideals and attitudes that were already present in the culture, articulated in print and artwork since at least the mid-1910s by members of the Stieglitz collective and others. As the search for native expression in the 1920s gave way to nationalist impulses in the 1930s, a crucial idea was lost: that national identity was compatible with variety in individual expression. Artists and critics today might benefit from considering how that loss happened, as the conditions that enforce conformism continue to threaten art makers.

The cultural nationalism of the Depression decade supported neither experimental art nor radical social ideals. Cultural nationalism of a very different kind had galvanized the American avant-garde of the 1910s, as Craven and Benton were well aware. However, it served the self-interest of these proponents of "American art" not only to disavow knowledge of their immediate artistic predecessors but to discredit them. Craven's *Modern Art,* a biased history of the development of art in modern times that championed the influence of Mexican muralists and supported, above all, the work of the American mural painter Thomas Hart Benton, was immediately recognized by the Stieglitz circle as a direct attack. Craven's account challenged the group's version of modernism's history, the status of the arts, and art's function in society. In a letter to an artist outside the circle Stieglitz commented, "Craven has a new book out Modern Art in which he makes monkeys out of all 'Abstract' Art—wiping the floor with Matisse, Picasso, etc.—A very clever book Catering all that's ignorant. A best-seller.—Takes a lick out of '291' too. Still the book is written well.—Benton is his hero!—He leads the way. All others are doomed & damned."[48]

Powerful supporters of the Stieglitz circle's values were quick to counterattack. Prominent among them was Lewis Mumford, who wrote to Stieglitz: "The praise Craven's book has received from the reviewers makes me wish my own had been received only with abuse. I have tried to even up accounts a little in a review I just did for the New Yorker—but it would take more patience than I have to plumb all its badness—which was pervasive, like the smell of skunk."[49] One reason for the "smell" is the offensive and pervasive racism in Craven's treatment of the introduction of modern art to America. In a chapter sarcastically titled "The New Gospel," he mocks the modernists who, in his view, did nothing but distort the "pure" American heritage. With much derision he rhetorically segregates them from "painters of the true American lineage," whose work he approved: "What fine old American families were represented in this assault on the fortresses of academic culture! Benn, Bouche, Bluemner, Dasburg, Halpert, Kuhn, Kuniyoshi, Lachaise, Stella, Sterne, Weber, Walkowitz, Zorach—scions of our colonial aristocracy!"[50] Craven thereby links his concept of "the native" in art to a notion of racial purity. It was not only Stieglitz, the Jew of German extraction, whom Craven judged un-American, but any artist of immigrant stock—first, second, or even third generation.

Although quite democratic in dispensing his ethnic and racial slurs, Craven had much to gain by singling out the famous photographer as the antihero of his revised history of the development of modern art in America. His rhetorical strategy is transparent. If Craven could depose Stieglitz and his circle from their widely acknowledged place at the center of the American art scene, he and his supporters might have at least a chance to occupy that position. That he devotes nearly an entire chapter to an attempt to discredit the group itself attests to the members' authority and influence in the art world at the middle of the decade. Art historians have too often uncritically accepted historical accounts based on Craven's assessment and have consequently underestimated the importance of the post-291 galleries.

To fully appreciate Craven's personal attack on Stieglitz, we must examine it in its original context:

> Stieglitz, a Hoboken Jew without knowledge of, or interest in, the historical American background, was—quite apart from the doses of purified art he had swallowed—hardly equipped for the leadership of a genuine American expression; and it is a matter of record that none of the artists whose names and work he has exploited has been noticeably American in flavor. . . . In spirit, his present gallery, An American Place, is a dwindling continuation of the spirit of 291—alien to the current drive for an explicitly native art. The new trend of painting, following Benton's pioneering example, is toward strong representation and clearly defined meanings which may be shared and verified by large groups of people; and in this movement the elusive apparitions of the Stieglitz group have no function. (pp. 312–13)

In this and earlier passages Craven both identified Stieglitz and the artists in his group exclusively with 291 and the introduction of European modern experiments (i.e., with abstract, nonrepresentational art, presumed to be of foreign origin) and intimated that the trend toward abstraction continued unchanged after World War I. In so doing the critic glossed over developments in the circle's ideas and aesthetics after 1917.

Craven must have known that in 1918 Hartley had called for New Realism and that in 1916 O'Keeffe and Strand had reconfigured the approaches to realism in the Stieglitz group repertoire. But he left these facts out of his narrative. Referring specifically to the developments of the late 1910s and the 1920s would have forced Craven to reveal his own earlier efforts to win the attention of the critical press, which he saw as excessively focused on the Stieglitz coterie. A 1924 letter from Rosenfeld to Stieglitz documents this earlier phase in the competition for status. Rosenfeld reported the substance of his conversation with Lewis Mumford the previous evening: "The talk turned about Craven, Mumford says he can answer Craven perfectly on his own ground, and so I said do so and I'll publish it in the form of a MSS if you can get it published no wheres else."[51] It was not only Craven who was already on the attack in the twenties. A now largely forgotten article by Thomas Hart Benton, which appeared in the *Arts* in June 1924, touted the importance of subject and form in painting.[52] This conservative manifesto also attempted to challenge the cultural status of the Stieglitz group.

In the long run, Benton and Craven have had a great deal of success; their articles and books implanted the persistent but incorrect idea that the Stieglitz circle, except for its engagement with European modernism during the 291 years, made few contributions to the history of American art. And Craven's *Modern Art,* well received by influential reviewers, is largely responsible for our view of the Stieglitz circle as a group of elitist and socially disengaged artists.

After his lack of success in the 1920s, Craven changed tactics. In *Modern Art* he attempts rhetorically to strip his adversary of power by figuring him as aged and frail, benign and harmless. The book presents an extremely skewed portrait of Stieglitz: "A picturesque figure—now past seventy, in ill health but remarkably active, still talking, exhibiting, proselytizing. I have quarreled with him for many years, but he has never allowed differences of opinion to disrupt friendly relations; he has always welcomed me to his seances with disarming cordiality" (p. 314). He is a toppled monument, softened by time; "seances" is a barb meant both to question Stieglitz's more inclusive philanthropy, which extended to artists and styles Craven thought unworthy, and to present him as a crank (and a feminized one at that). Craven makes one final effort to erase the towering figure from the story of the search for American expression. He strategically supplies a complete list of 291 exhibitions, thus buttressing his one-dimensional portrayal of Stieglitz as promoter of alien European modernisms. Craven concludes his extensive but quite selective history by declaring that the photographer's introduction of foreign and novel ideas to America had "a debilitating effect on native talent" (pp. 314, 316). In a single chapter, Craven rhetorically effaced twenty years of historical development.

Predictably, *Modern Art* has an artist at hand who can take Stieglitz's place on the American art scene. Craven's mythicizing account of Thomas Hart Benton is a story of conversion—or, more accurately, reconversion. Benton is depicted as a prodigal son; the narrative cycle takes the reader from the painter's "thoroughly American boyhood . . . in southwest Missouri of a family famous in the West since the rule of Andrew Jackson" to his years as a naive and deluded prewar art student who had arrived in New York fresh from Paris, where he had undergone a (temporary) conversion to French visual and literary culture. In the climax, Benton is awakened to his true status as heroic American painter by his experiences in army basic training: "Having readjusted himself to the native background, and recovered his youthful ability to participate psychologically in the life of America with its emotional ties, prejudices and sentiments, he began, step by step, and scene by scene, to build an art of and for the American people" (p. 335). Ironically enough, Craven's argument echoes European art criticism from Vasari through Baudelaire, and it suffers from the narrowness of the traditional form. On this account, America must have a single artistic voice; pluralism is not allowed. Benton alone—whose art, for Craven, paradoxically "embodies the collective American spirit" (p. 335)—is the virtuoso intended to replace the varied styles and tones of voice of the American modernists who were his contemporaries.

Not satisfied with simply discrediting Stieglitz, Craven assaults the circle's view of the function of art. The American modernist, he asserts, "was so awed by the French trade-mark on his instruments" that he made the mistake of "us[ing] his tools, not to disclose and to sharpen the meanings inherent in native subjects, but as exhibits of themselves"; and in his conclusion to *Modern Art,* he adds: "The day is past when exhibition of tools entitled a painter to the name of artist" (pp. 317, 365). The modernist delight in calling attention to craft, valued by countless artists in the United States and abroad, means nothing to Craven. Nor is he sympathetic to other tenets held dear by William Morris and his followers. He instead supports the tradition that separated and maintained a hierarchy of the "fine" and applied arts, effectively denying the value and meaning of the act or process of human creation. But even while his theory disparaged the artists' tools, it promoted an art of "the worker." Consistency mattered little next to his main goal: to dismantle the theoretical underpinnings of the entire modernist social and aesthetic program, including the American variant that the Stieglitz cooperative had played a key role in establishing.

In 1934 Waldo Frank and others published *America and Alfred Stieglitz,* a collection of essays on the accomplishments of Stieglitz and the circle to date. In form and content the editors sought to make the book profoundly democratic. It includes a chorus of voices that tell the history of modern art in America from various points of view—the structural opposite of Craven's monolithic history, told from a single perspective. Indeed, the two books emblematize the contrasts between a monoperspectival system, following the tradition of the Italian Renaissance, and the modern pluralist approach of the twentieth century. *America and Alfred Stieglitz* resembles a quilt stitched by many hands, a democratic patchwork history incorporating the quality craftwork of a cooperative—a group of individuals committed to shared ideals.

Moreover, the equilibrium of *America and Alfred Stieglitz* makes apparent the nature of Stieglitz's accomplishment: the creative harnessing of the friction between the individual ego and the collective will. What Stieglitz enacted with the aid of his colleagues (and what we see again in the celebratory text) is a careful balancing of soloist and chorus in a complex musical counterpoint that displays a productive tension. Once the difficult balance is achieved, the individual artists can, theoretically, thrive within their communities. As a work of literary art *America and Alfred Stieglitz* demonstrates that successful and highly individual artists can act collectively. It portrays not just the photographer but the cooperative model he championed; the contributors displayed their continuing dedication to a set of social and aesthetic ideals intended to serve a broad public. The collection provides a useful reminder of the stakes in the art world's struggle: the diatribes of the Regionalist faction can be seen as the first questioning of modern art's ambition to change the social order, their proclamations of the "failure of modernism" as precursors of the accusation often heard from prominent art historians in the 1980s. For the full story behind these early complaints we must examine the motives of those struggling in our own time for cultural prestige and professional status.

By the early 1920s controversies in the American art world focused not on the borrowing of "foreign" forms and styles but on the issues of ethnicity and race that Marsden Hartley addressed in his groundbreaking articles. Thomas Craven, who publicly questioned whether members of the Stieglitz circle could legitimately participate in the creation of true American culture and taste, was only one among many whose nativism thinly veiled their racism and prejudice toward artists who did not satisfy their sense of American ethnic purity.

By the mid-thirties, when the pivotal events in the struggle over representation were commemorated by *America and Alfred Stieglitz,* the New York scene had already produced a distinctive American visual art, competing theories of art, and critical debates that were international in both ambition and importance. The first New York avant-garde labored to create, in print and in artworks, what Walt Whitman had predicted in his poems: a remade America that was "not merely a nation but a teeming Nation of nations."[53] The value that it placed on an inclusive sense of national community, history, and social relations makes the emphases on separation and difference in our contemporary cultural arena seem narrow and inadequate. Perhaps most worrying is the erasure by the postmodernist discourses fashionable in the 1990s of any notion of human subjectivity or agency capable of embarking on the kind of social and cultural transformations successfully undertaken by earlier artists' collectives.

5

THE COUNTRY

THE STIEGLITZ CIRCLE'S CONSCIOUS REMAKING of representations of the rural American landscape takes on added significance when we realize that early-twentieth-century American writers, fascinated with the growing cities, commonly attacked the small town. Members of the rural press responded heatedly to the dyspeptic assaults of H. L. Mencken and other detractors of the period. The fierce rhetoric helped make citizens of rural America themselves aware that, as a later historian put it, "in song and story the ethos of millions of Americans was changing in a novel and dangerous fashion."[1] However, they were not aware that they had allies in their fight to remain custodians of a true American ethos: a small band of visual artists and critical theorists who distributed their products in the art and literary marketplace of New York City but in most cases lived and worked in the countryside. In a sense, the Stieglitz group was deliberately expanding the traditional role of the American artist, for painters, poets, novelists, and essayists had long supported and celebrated the rural environment, its varied lifestyles, its communal values, and its economic self-sufficiency. Aiming at a truly democratic concept of audience, the circle aspired to be the voice of land-bound rural people as well as uprooted migrants to the city. In the interest of both these groups they contrived to refigure the American land as common ground, a shared homeland.

Even as modern authors such as Mencken and F. Scott Fitzgerald became mouthpieces of speculative interests that were taking over farmland and destroying the values of the countryside, the Stieglitz circle promoted traditional democratic values and an ethos of belonging. The artists identified with the struggles of the rural dweller as well as of those newly arrived in the cities; as visual artists, they too keenly felt their prestige slipping away. Like rural citizens, these artists saw themselves as custodians of American values and morals. Such traditional social positions were hard-won, strategic, and prestige-laden; neither artists nor farmers were willing to relinquish them.

Although the clash of metropolitan and rural values did not enter national political discourse until the 1920s, the roots of the conflict are as old as the first cities themselves. Throughout the nineteenth century, the interests of the countryside had dominated American politics. Even after the Civil War, as America quickly began shifting from an agrarian to an industrial society, its chief political figures came from rural areas. In fact, until the twenties, the politician's claim of having been born in a log cabin was his surest political appeal.[2] And despite dissent within their ranks, those in the American provinces remained in control of American public life until after World War I.[3] The antirural rhetoric of the period must be understood in this broader context. As social historians have aptly noted, "To encounter provincial America only in the writings of those who had declared war on it is finally to see merely a bizarre, pathetic, and infinitely comic phenomenon. . . . H. L. Mencken could conjure up the simple yokel whose five thumbs made him a lower order of creature, but that view is disabling in respect to the yokel's political strength."[4]

Rural attacks on the metropolis were also changing. Previously, specific grievances had been laid against the Wall Street financier and the railroad magnate. Now, however, rural critics lambasted not so much the capitalist's economic power but the way he made his living and lived his life.[5] What raised the hackles of the modern rural citizen, according to one scholar of the 1920s, was "less the sheer existence of wealth than the way in which it was acquired. The village dweller was outraged at a world in which chicanery was rewarded so generously." As country dwellers and their representatives saw it, "the capitalist was unable to create a meaningful existence in the city; and so he and his family dulled their senses in a kind of Roman voluptuousness that was utterly depraved."[6] Although a cosmopolite, Lewis Mumford had much the same impression. In a letter to Stieglitz outlining the plans for his latest book, Mumford compared modern America under the spell of rising urbanization and industrialism to Rome before its fall.[7] Mumford was hardly alone; such ideas were disseminated on a broader scale by popular filmmakers of the period such as D. W. Griffith. The vision of America in which country life stood for personal warmth, independence, and simplicity (while urban life represented nearness without feeling, action without independence, and existence without sanity) was promulgated in regional dialects as well as the suave media of the Stieglitz group.

What members of the circle did share with the broader community of authors and intellectuals in the 1920s was a deliberate turning away from the world political scene to concentrate on their own backyard. On its face, such narrowing of vision would seem to have much in common with Fitzgerald's familiar maxim that life is a personal matter. But given the circle's allegiance to American small-town values, their position should not be interpreted as political retreat, as the isolation of most intellectuals of the twenties is generally viewed. Rather, this turn inward, which accompanied their interest in the welfare of a small community of craftworkers, was the manifestation of a regionalism that was only later stripped of left-leaning political content. Powerful American myths (buttressed by both biblical and republican traditions) represented the self-reliant and moral citizen as the small farmer or independent craftworker, giving rise to an equally potent form of individual political rhetoric. It is this rhetoric that the Stieglitz circle appropriated and adapted in their cultural production.

In complex ways the image of the country, specifically its pastoral landscape, had come to represent America as a whole. An early-twentieth-century artist who used rural land as a theme could be certain that the audience would comprehend the image as symbolizing values associated with the American village—simplicity, peace, security—values continually praised in the rural press when burgeoning urban economies based on industrial capitalism eroded hard-won farm prosperity.[8] These values were promoted not simply for their own sake but for their result: a kind of independence. The rustic environment, it was argued, made an essential contribution to the contentment of the countryside—the natural beauty of its setting; the sights, sounds, and smells of the pastoral world (which contrasted so dramatically with the new urban scene). It is this same pastoral setting and its direct, refreshing appeal to the senses that Paul Rosenfeld praised at length in his art criticism. We would hardly be surprised if we were to learn that he was the anonymous tabloidist in the *Goshen Democrat* (of rural New York) who penned a panegyric on the "little country town where the only lights come from the windows that glitter down the lane," and the silence is punctuated only by "the lowing of the cattle in the fields and the sighing of the winds through the trees."[9]

The urban New York essayist Rosenfeld shared this style of provincial propaganda with his rural colleague. Identifying the roots of Rosenfeld's evocative prose enables one to fully appreciate passages such as his rapturous appreciation in *Port of New York* of Arthur Dove's depictions of cows: "The brownish, cream-white, pastels made from the herds of cows bring the knowledge of someone who has almost gotten into the kine themselves; and felt from within the rich animality of their beings, felt the thrust of the thin legs, and toss of the horned front, the unashamed, udderful, fecundity; and then given it out again in characteristic abstraction and soft, sensitive, fuzzy, spotting" (see figure 5).[10] The sentence contains high poetic praise of the artist's anti-Puritan, antirational primitivism and sensuousness; his identification with the humble beasts; and his immediate and direct participation in the natural world.

Investors took a somewhat different view of the natural world. Americans, whose savings mounted rapidly from the early 1910s through well into the 1920s, also continued to invest in traditionally valued commodities. During this period land and mortgage speculation became rife, and land prices soared as inactive savings were pumped into fabulous real estate projects. What captivated the speculator's attention was rural land, often farmland: the traditional symbol of American "rootedness" and of Jeffersonian democracy itself. Prices for rural land peaked in 1920, and by 1922 the market for farm mortgages was saturated. Following on the heels of this boom was a second, related phenomenon: the rapid and wide-scale development of urban properties caused by large migration to metropolitan areas. Indeed, by the mid-twenties, for the first time in American history less than half the population occupied rural villages.[11] The urban migration provoked critical inspection of rural mores and values in many quarters and with unprecedented vigor. The dramatic changes in both the use of the American land and its ownership deeply affected all citizens, urban and rural. For the Stieglitz group (who between 1924 and 1934 produced mostly landscapes), as for all Americans, the old meanings attached to land had been forever altered. The visual artists and critical theorists rendered their commentaries on these social changes, which they often felt in profound and personal ways.

In the 1920s, rural land—pastureland and fertile fields, the traditional embodiment of American ideals and of American freedom itself—was fast being turned into one more commodity. Land, once intimately known and valued as home, was now, with alarming frequency, treated as a devalued and impersonal object. To artists witnessing its exploitation, rural American land became an ideal metaphor for the contemporary American art product. American art, like American land, had by custom been highly valued by the public for the ideological weight it carried; but now it was increasingly possessed by only a few and assigned only monetary value. When the newcomers to the cities left the rural homeland, they were fleeing not just a place but a time. They were trying to escape the past that the visual artists of the Stieglitz group evoked and attempted to use. In that past, artists' products (like those of the farmer now also threatened by mass production) were highly esteemed by the American public. In the view of the Stieglitz group, it could be restored, along with its attendant values, only if artists maintained the high standards of craft of those earlier times—standards that had won prestige for the artworks and their makers.

Beginning with the publication of Edgar Lee Masters's *Spoon River Anthology* of 1915 (a work that deeply influenced Paul Strand) and continuing into the 1930s, literary dissections of American rural ways were conducted like inquisitions.[12] The diatribes of Mencken stood out as a frontal attack on a form of American life and an ethos already weakened. As the historians George Mowry and Blaine Brownell have pointed out:

PLATES

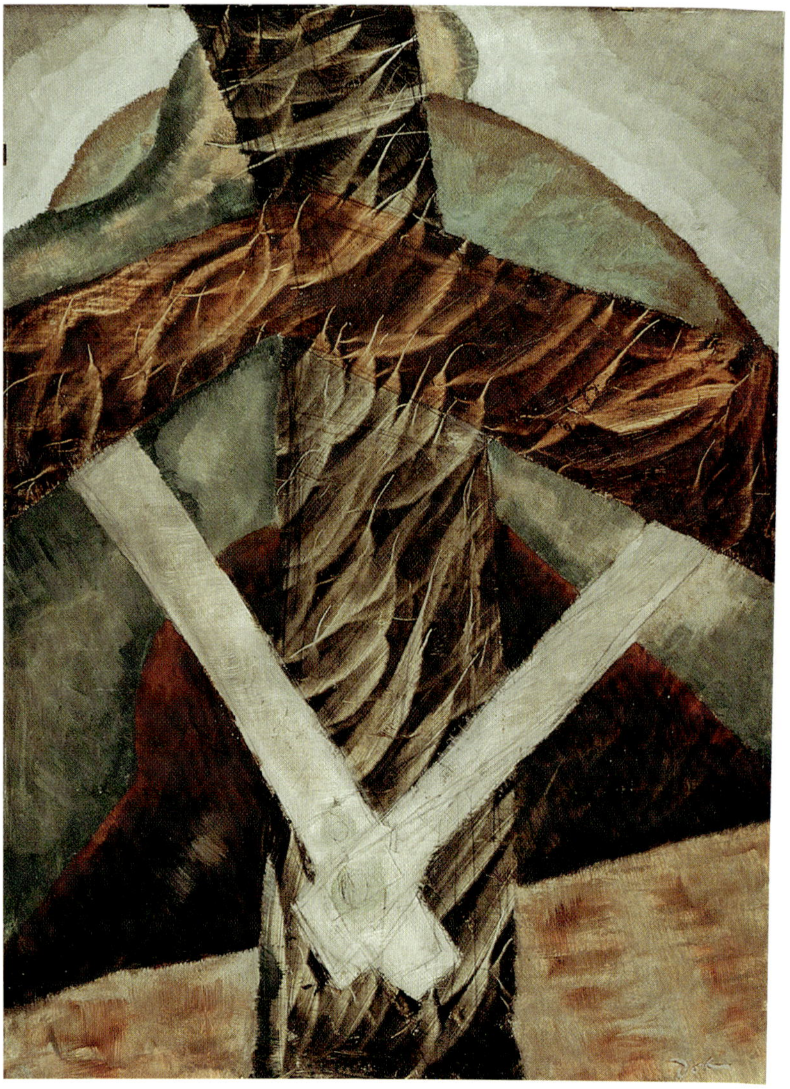

1. Arthur Dove, *Telegraph Pole,* 1929, oil and metallic paint on metal, 28 × 19 3/4 in. The Art Institute of Chicago, Alfred Stieglitz Collection.

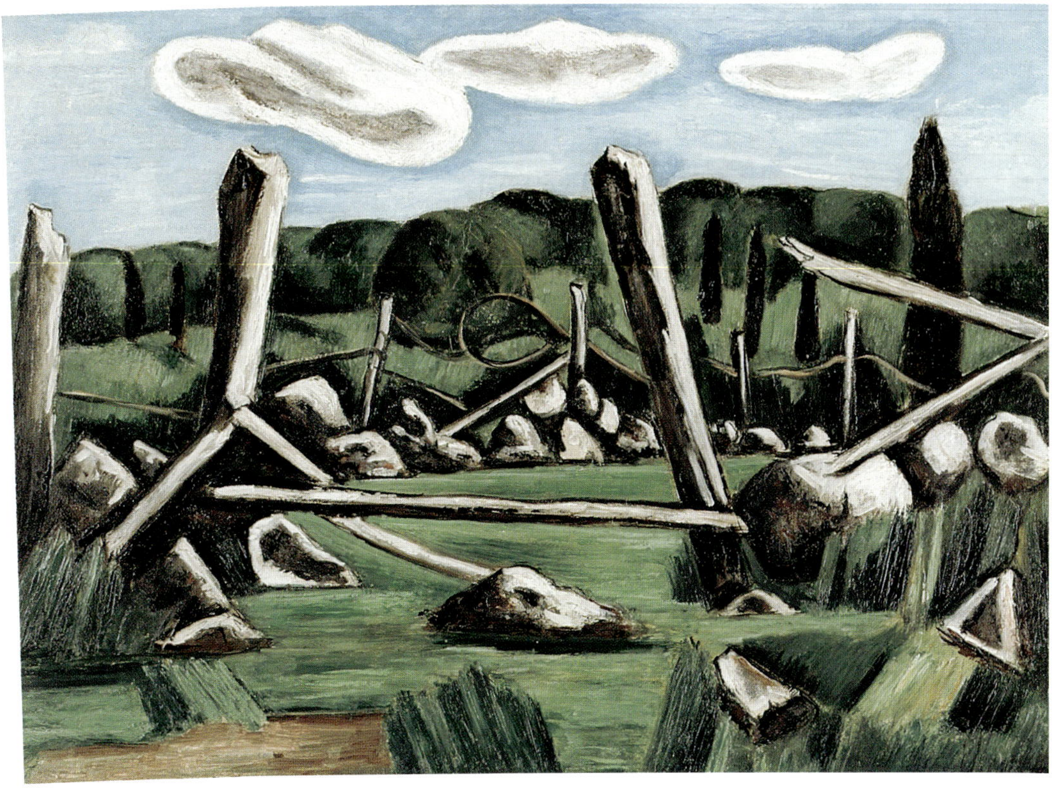

2. Marsden Hartley, *The Old Bars, Dogtown,* 1936, oil on composition board, 18 × 24 in. Purchase, Collection of Whitney Museum of American Art, New York; photography by Sheldan C. Collins.

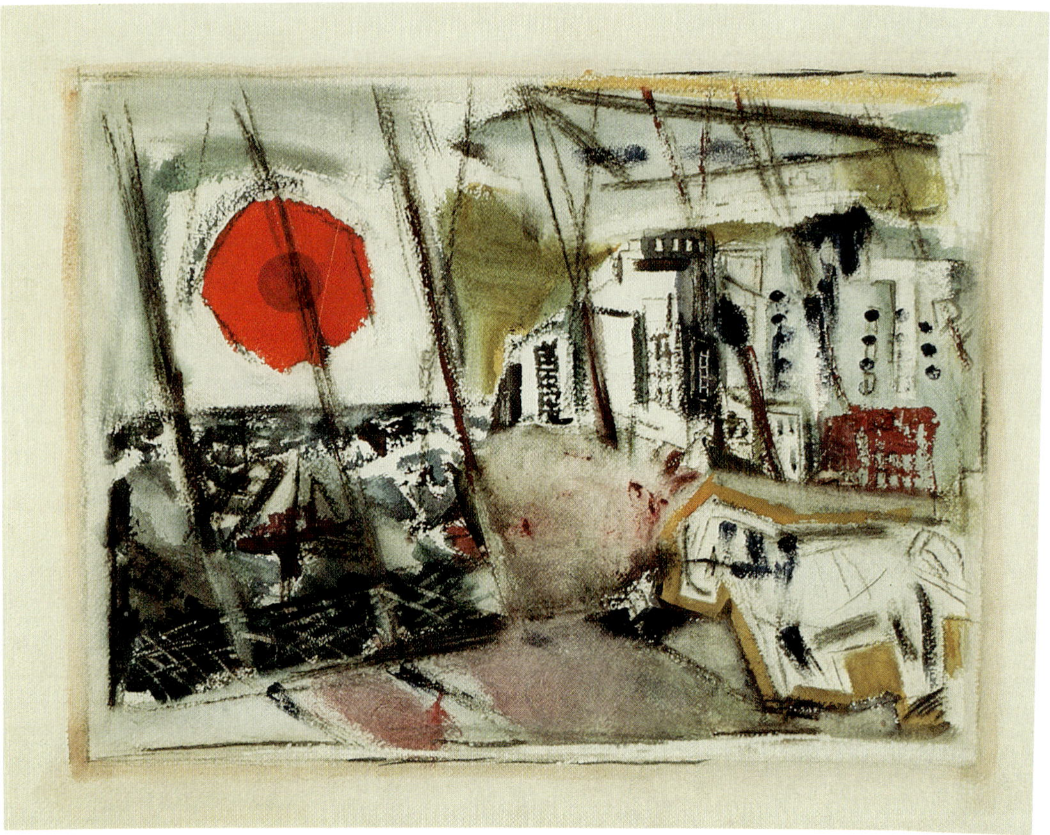

3. John Marin, *Red Sun, Brooklyn Bridge,* ca. 1922, watercolor with charcoal on white wove paper, 21 3/8 × 26 1/8 in. The Art Institute of Chicago, Alfred Stieglitz Collection.

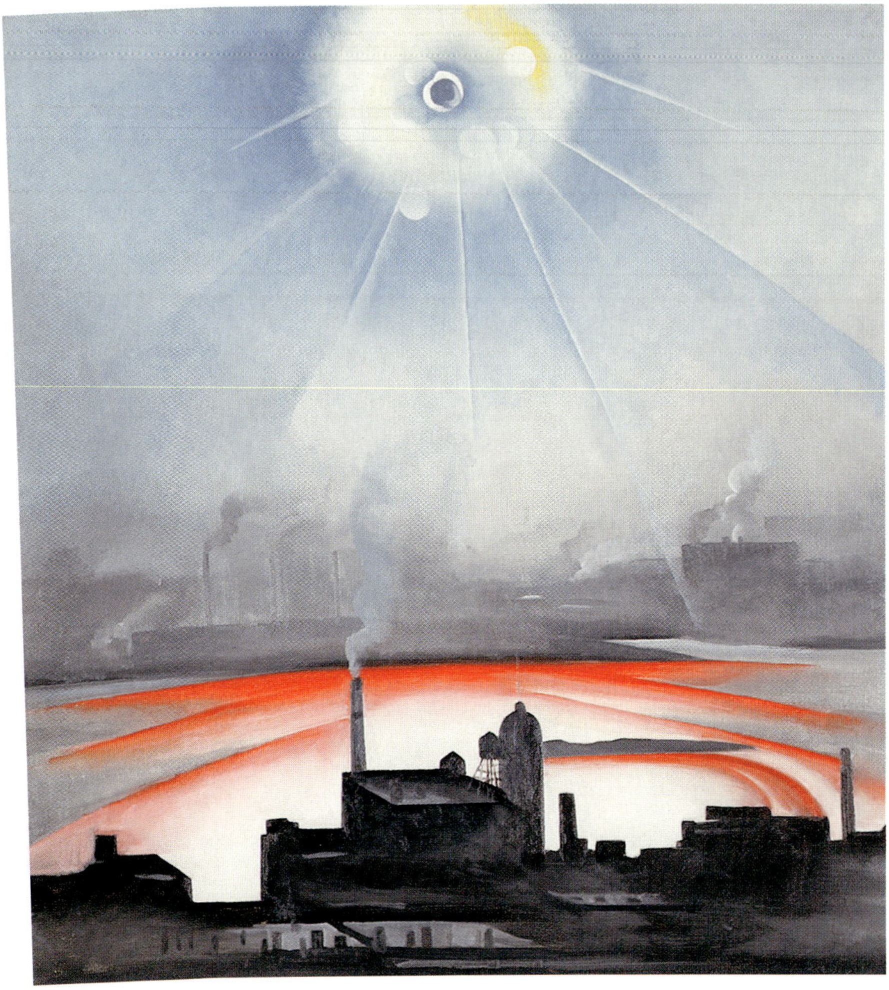

4. Georgia O'Kee e, *East River from the Shelton,* 1927–28, oil on canvas, $27\ ^{1}/_{16} \times 21\ ^{15}/_{16}$ in. Purchased by the Friends of the New Jersey State Museum with a Gift from Mary Lea Johnson, New Jersey State Museum Collection, Trenton.

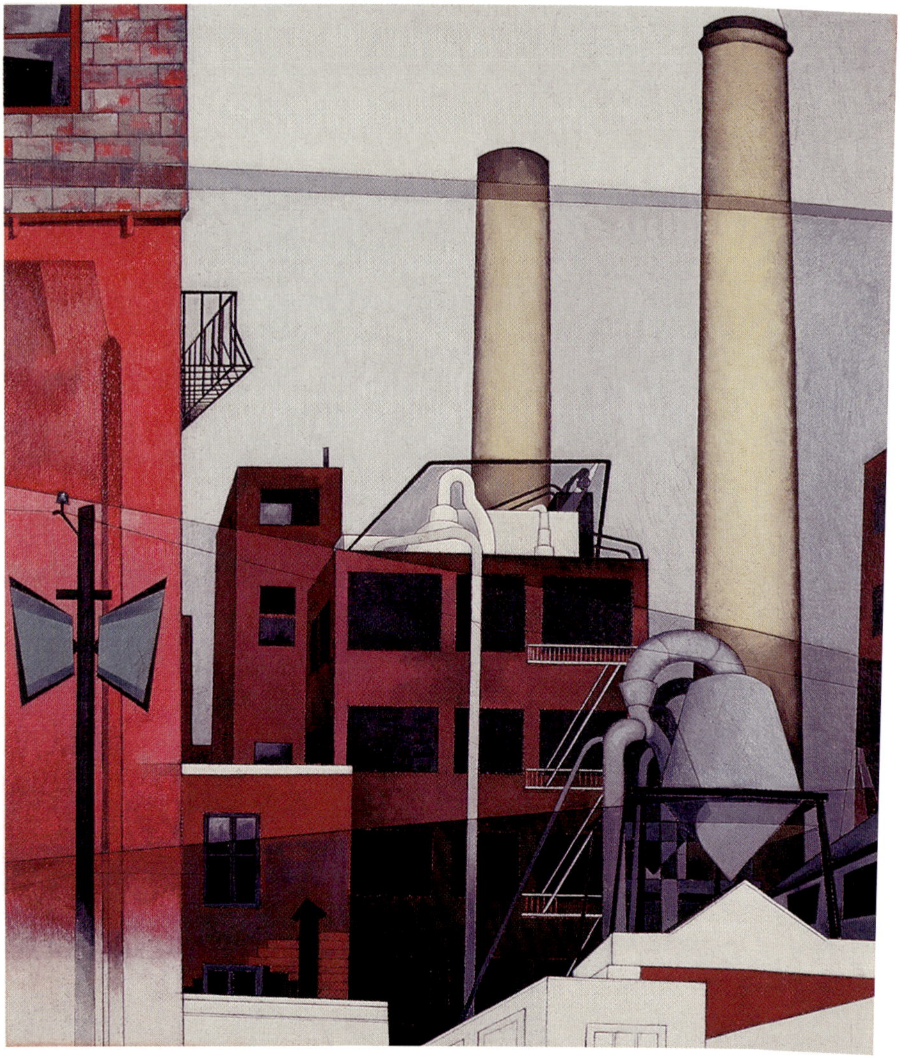

5. Charles Demuth, *After All*, 1935, oil on composition board, 36 × 30 in. Collection of the Norton Museum of Art, West Palm Beach, Florida.

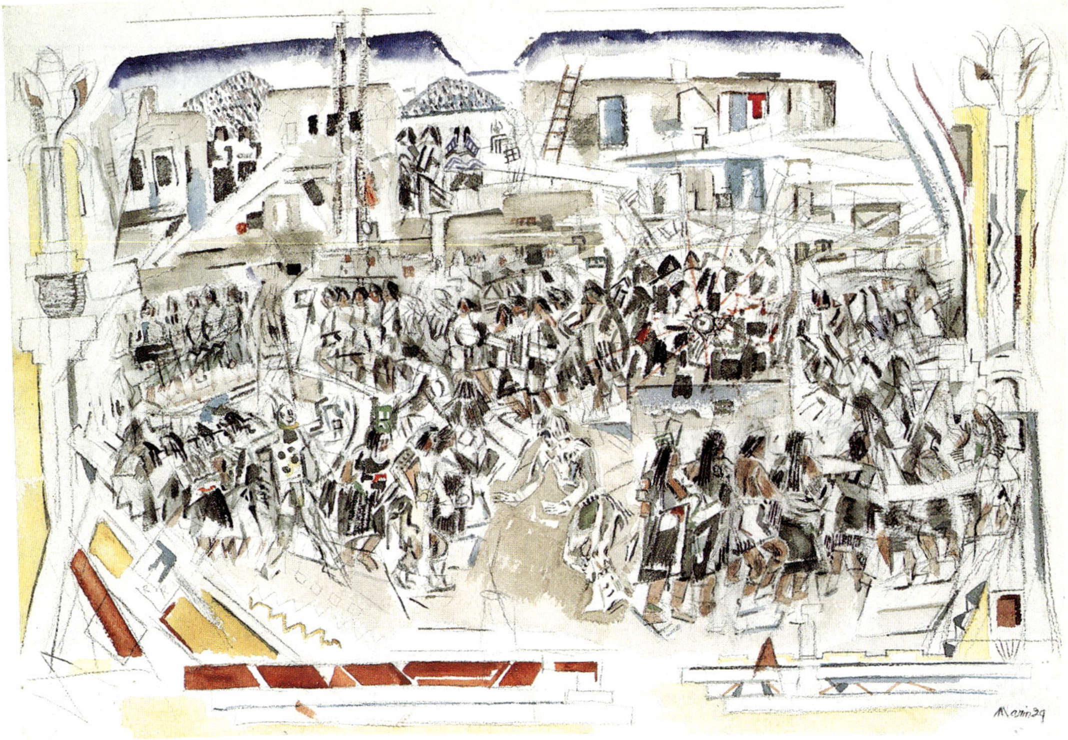

6. John Marin, *The Dance of the Santo Domingo Indians (The Corn Dance)*, 1929, watercolor and charcoal on paper, 22 × 30 ¾ in. Acquired 1949, The Metropolitan Museum of Art, Alfred Stieglitz Collection.

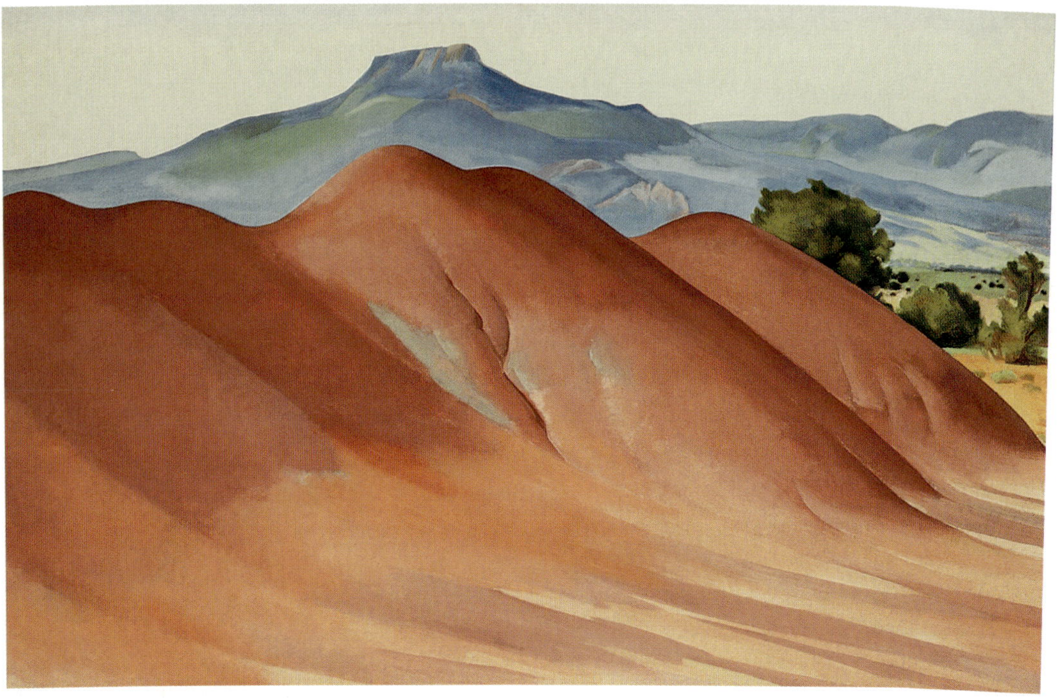

7. Georgia O'Kee e, *Red Hills with the Pedernal,* 1936, oil on linen, $19\,\frac{3}{4} \times 29\,\frac{3}{4}$ in. Bequest of Helen Miller Jones, Collection of the Museum of Fine Arts, Museum of New Mexico, Sante Fe.

Whether the new moral and ethical climate of the twenties was brought about more by the ideas disseminated by towering thinkers like Freud, Bergson, and Einstein, and by those of the lesser essayists and the creative writers, scholars, and artists, or more by such mundane and objective factors as urbanization, the rapid change in technology, and the complex forces let loose by the creation of the mass-production-consumption society is a historical argument without apparent end.[13]

In the twenties, "objective" social factors unquestionably exerted influence equal to that of individual thinkers. The new system of values was also spread through the movies, daily papers, and confession magazines, which were influenced more by popular tastes than the highbrow novelists and essayists who were conveying similar notions.

Cultures labeled "high" and "popular" were already intermingling by the twenties much more significantly than Van Wyck Brooks had anticipated or later historians ever acknowledged. Better distribution of all forms of printed material was in part responsible for the change. The vast migrations to cities from the American hinterland and from foreign shores caused an unprecedented mixing of classes, ethnicities, and cultures. Advertising, the infant prodigy, expedited (as it still does) the rapid promotion of the new values and new identities born of new American experiences and experiments that it both commemorated and attractively reified. Members of the Stieglitz group determined to create artworks that would be as effective as advertising's commercial media in promoting the traditional values they favored.

The Stieglitz circle's own identity was derived, above all, from the American landscape. As we saw in chapter 1, Van Wyck Brooks's writings reactivated Whitman's compelling notion of "rootedness," positing a relation between the renown an artist can attain and that artist's rootedness in a society. Brooks believed that historically the key to fame was a specific geographical identity. Following this lead, circle members displaced "alienation," the stance toward society that Baudelaire had popularized for artists and that contemporary French modernists still held, with the socially engaged idea of rootedness.

The issue of the artist's alienation itself was variously addressed by the group. Though the best-known example is Stieglitz's *The Terminal* (1893), there are many others. John Marin's watercolor titled *The Pine Tree, Small Point, Maine* (1926; figure 13), in the selection of location and of object, elegant color, exuberant tone, and dynamic structure, suggests that the artist cared deeply about this particular site at Small Point, and indeed this particular tree. This impression is conveyed even more emphatically by Marin's chosen point of view. He observes the pine (a common American subject) almost as closely as O'Keeffe inspects her mammoth flowers, thus intimating that he, a citizen of this rural environment, frequents this place. As in some of Stieglitz's photographs and some of Dove's works, the chosen view also suggests an empathy between the beholder and the thing beheld: Marin identifies directly with an object of the natural world. By equating the creative energy of the act of representation to the creative energy of the plant form depicted, the artist implies that artistic talent is part of the natural scheme of things.

In other works, Marin proves that it is not necessary to use the device of close observation to suggest intimate relation with or rootedness in the American land. *Maine Islands* (figure 14) of 1922 is an especially good case in point. A characteristically "vignetted" ocean view, the watercolor is a strong, proud statement about the uniqueness of the place, the island group where the painter lived. His vantage point is that of one who frequents a specific locale: one who knows just where to stand to take in all the important information about the islands, like the fisherman who has learned where to find the best catch. Marin invites his audience to share the privileged standpoint of an inhabitant, not the superficial view of a tourist or outsider.

Two other exemplary Marin landscapes should be considered in this context: *Hudson River near Bear Mountain* (1925; figure 15) and *Mount Chocorua—White Mountains* (1926; figure 16), of the "White Mountains" series. *Hudson River* is striking for its intimate scale and its delicate, poetic drawing. Both features signal lyricism and a praise-of-place theme. The quiet tone and hushed color of the work suggest Marin's reverence for the place, as well as a certain reluctance to "advertise" it, to encourage too many others to visit. Marin's delicate handling of the passage from mid- to background (the distant hills) in fact provides a direct contrast to advertising art. The small touches of turquoise, to the left, are like polished gems; their glow calls attention to the land's rich mineral deposits. The softly washed and lyrical passage of paint to the right, which swirls turquoise with a rich brown shot through with olive and gold, describes not just the land but also Marin's pleasure in it. It celebrates the painter's ability to express through this volatile medium both the look of the land and his emotional reaction to it. More subdued is the foreground drawing, a whisper of pencil barely hidden by washes of gray and light turquoise. Here and in the point of view adopted in the work, one clearly senses the artist hushing his style to blend into his environment. The democratic New Realism encouraged artist and audience to identify with the land and to imagine being an integral part of it, rather than take the detached stance conventional in Renaissance art.

The new democratic mode depended as much on intimate scale and on replacing an impersonal and detached rhetoric with a more personal, engaged voice as on obvious point of view. Dramatic works such as *Mount Chocorua*, a highly charged landscape with a theatrical sky, could also convey a sense of personal knowledge, increasing the powerful effects of the surface of the work itself, which is democratized by its even texture. The objects in the landscape are not hierarchically ordered, and the space is legible but collapsed: that is, there is a clearly discernible foreground, midground, and background, but they are distinguished only by tone. This representation, unlike Frederic Church's extravagant South American landscapes of the mid–nineteenth century, is not intended to elicit awe. Instead, it praises the natural

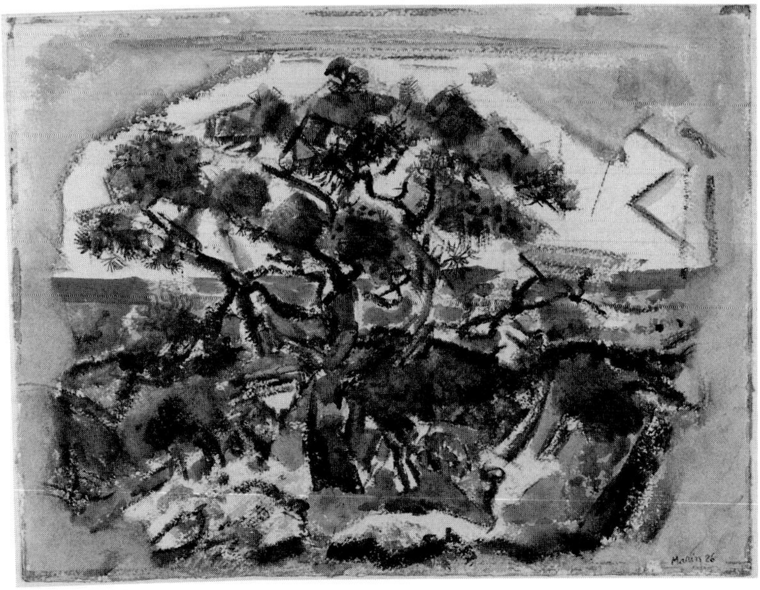

13. John Marin, *The Pine Tree, Small Point, Maine,* 1926, watercolor with charcoal on ivory wove paper, 17 ¼ × 22 in. Acquired 1949, The Art Institute of Chicago, Alfred Stieglitz Collection.

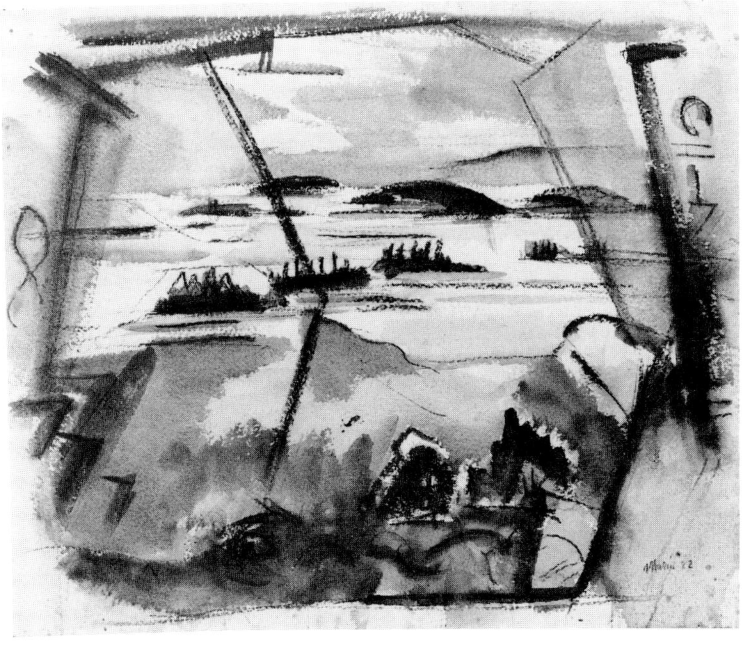

14. John Marin, *Maine Islands,* 1922, watercolor and charcoal on paper, 16 ¾ × 19 ¾ in. Acquired 1926, The Phillips Collection, Washington, D.C.

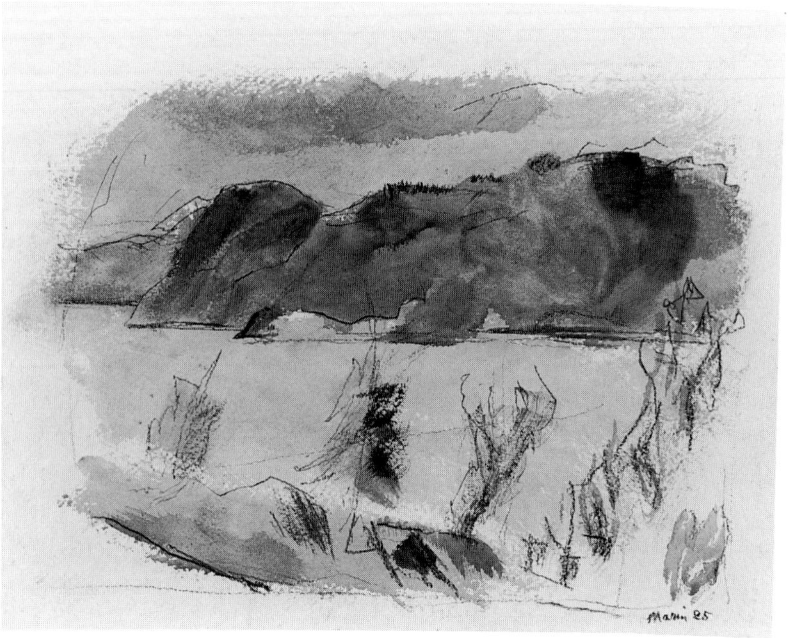

15. John Marin, *Hudson River near Bear Mountain,* 1925, watercolor, 13 × 16 in. Acquired 1927, The Phillips Collection, Washington, D.C.

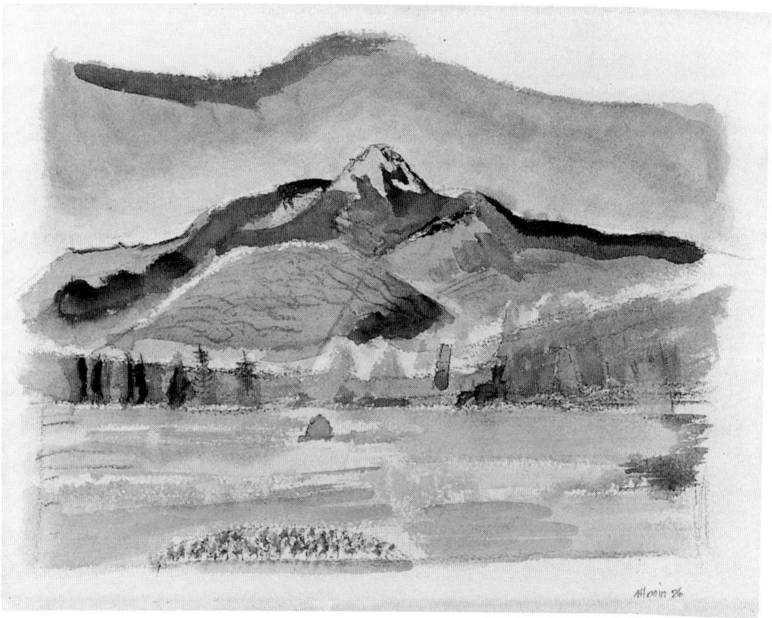

16. John Marin, *Mount Chocorua—White Mountains,* 1926, watercolor, 16 ¾ × 21 ½ in. Acquired 1926, The Phillips Collection, Washington, D.C.

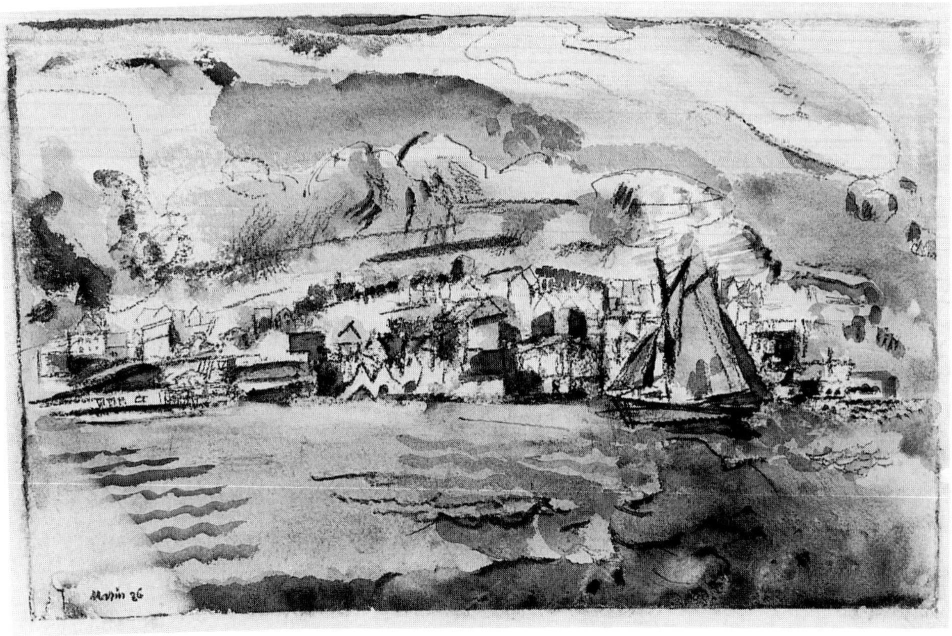

17. John Marin, *Movement, Stonington Harbor, Deer Island, Maine,* 1926, watercolor, 11 1/4 × 17 1/4 in. Acquired 1949, The Metropolitan Museum of Art, Alfred Stieglitz Collection.

beauty of a place that many previous artists thought unworthy of attention, in a scale and medium also thought of lesser status. Marin's extraordinary skill argues—successfully, I think—for a reevaluation of the American land as subject and of watercolor as an artistic medium for modernist styles. Stieglitz's photographs of city and country similarly elevate their devalued subject matter and medium.

Members of the circle sought to achieve yet another quality in their productions. A viewer examining a work such as Marin's *Movement, Stonington Harbor, Deer Island, Maine* (1926; figure 17), may at first be disappointed by the lack of incident. Although the work's mood is very subdued for this artist, it is not poignant (like a Whistler), nor does it impart a feeling of nostalgia (as often happens when an artist reflects on the past). Rather, the watercolor is a present-centered appreciation of a particular foggy day and a particular sleepy town. The touch, for Marin, is unusually slow and methodical. One need only recall his contrasting renditions of the city to realize that this painting constitutes an homage to the pedestrian life of the American small town. The image further suggests that the modern artist has found a haven in the rural community. The subject is the type of modest regional landscape that (in the view of the circle) can be effectively depicted only if the modern American painter invents new conventions of representation. *Movement, Stonington Harbor* is a pointed testament to Marin's own brand of American ingenuity.

Although Stieglitz circle members were all city dwellers (at least briefly), their permanent residences were in smaller communities. Charles Demuth, for example, was rooted in Lancaster, Pennsylvania, sharing the family home with his aging mother. Until the early thirties, when he inherited his father's estate on Long Island, Arthur Dove farmed in Connecticut to make money. Marin purchased an island off the Maine coast, where he lived in summer; in winter he returned to the (then small) city of Newark, New Jersey, the community of his childhood. All three men visited New York principally to deliver artworks to the circle's galleries and to study recent work by others. Marsden Hartley, early attracted to the art capitals of Europe, immersed himself in the late 1910s in America's natural habitats far from cities, beginning with his explorations of New Mexico. His eventual return to his birthplace in rural Maine was celebrated (and virtually mandated) by several contemporary critics.

Paul Rosenfeld, with an independent income, purchased and maintained a retreat in Westport, Connecticut, probably influenced by his visit to Sherwood Anderson in the wilds of Virginia.[14] He wrote enthusiastically to Stieglitz of Anderson's new home:

> I had a perfect eight days in Troutdale. Sherwood and Elizabeth are very much away from the world of small irritations, and indeed it would be difficult not to be, located as they are. They have land in a little hilltop valley three thousand feet high, and even the nearby hills in that part of Virginia are the warm tender blue one associates with Claude Lorraine. Blue is everywhere, somehow under the leaves of the trees, while the soil of the part bare, partly richly wooded country is red, and chocolate at a distance. They are building themselves a stone house in their little valley. A brook rushes closeby, and is the loudest thing one hears at night; old apple trees surround the site, and the stone comes out of their own territory and is the sort of fieldstone both yellowish and purplish. The labour is extremely cheap. Sherwood gets fun out of the building and out of the work-men, who take one back to the Civil War and before. The people have a desperate time organizing a living, and have poor houses; but they are independent, loving their soil and also unlike the city people striving to speak as well and fully as they can.[15]

In addition to displaying his tendency to view nature through the medium of art, Rosenfeld, in his sensitive and observant evocation of the Virginia hill country, captures more than just the land itself. He shares Anderson's interest in the workers in telling terms, attuned to those aspects of a rural economy that keep its folk poor but (he believes) independent. They have a voice that their urban counterparts lack. Rosenfeld's account underscores Anderson's own interest in the unsung histories of the American folk. Opinions voiced by rural citizens, containing wisdom derived from personal experiences played out on a provincial communal stage, were valued by both the sociocultural critic and the literary artist.

Questions of relatedness and belonging, of rootedness in a past and a community, were inescapable in 1920s America. Members of the artistic community (especially those freshly returned from war-ravaged Europe) were particularly susceptible to musings on and interpretations of these issues. In *Exile's Return,* his account of American writers of the twenties and early thirties, Malcolm Cowley spoke for his generation, naming the phenomenon he was himself caught up in and giving it an intelligible shape. He saw that his contemporaries "had been uprooted from something more than a birthplace, a country or a town. Their real exile was from society itself, from any society with purposes they could share, toward which they could honestly contribute and from which they could draw new strength."[16] Both this alienation and the desire to reestablish functional relations within American society were felt generally by artists and authors of the time.

Settling in a rural community enabled the early modernist artist to assume a different and much-desired voice. From this privileged vantage in a network of established relations, artworks could be produced that represented not only the observer's perceptions of the rural surroundings but also his or her position in and stance toward it. Here, point of view is negotiated by engagement with a community.

But the new arrivals could not replicate the bonds with the land enjoyed by long-established residents. Instead, they consciously added their own ideology to the old communal patterns of interrelatedness. To combat alienation and prevent the disintegration of identity, the Stieglitz circle invented a psychosocial "community," located primarily in the collective imagination: the locus of human myth, ancient and modern, and of the mythmaking and art-making faculties themselves. Out of their pressing need to adapt, they theorized this modern "superreal" community and imposed it on the rural landscape. In this new schema, the circle's attitudes toward nature and the American soil itself (derived from the writings of Walt Whitman and of Hippolyte Taine) by and large remained constant. Rather than provide an occasion to criticize human folly or remark on the ephemerality of human existence and of human marks made on the earth's surface, rural subjects gave group members the opportunity to celebrate the sublimity and permanence of nature.

Perhaps the circle's most fascinating ongoing relationship with nature and with belonging was that of Stieglitz himself. The biography by Stieglitz's niece Sue Davidson Lowe recounts in detail his experiences from childhood to adulthood at his parents' home in Lake George, in upstate New York.[17] Lowe's narrative includes the annual summer retreats that Stieglitz (accompanied after 1923 by Georgia O'Keeffe) made to the small lakeside village. It was there that he could most comfortably play the host and patron to Waldo Frank, Sherwood Anderson, Paul Rosenfeld, Paul Strand, and the other artists who were his guests, sometimes for months at a time, while they worked on their own projects. In a series of photographs of the environs of Lake George, Stieglitz composed an image of "the country"—specifically of the family

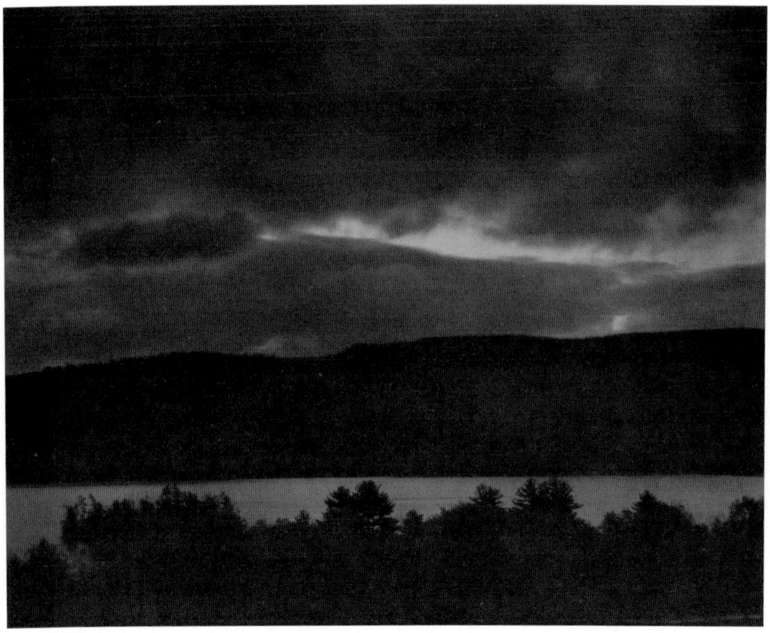

18. Alfred Stieglitz, *Lake George,* probably 1921, platinum photograph. National Gallery of Art, Washington, D.C., Alfred Stieglitz Collection.

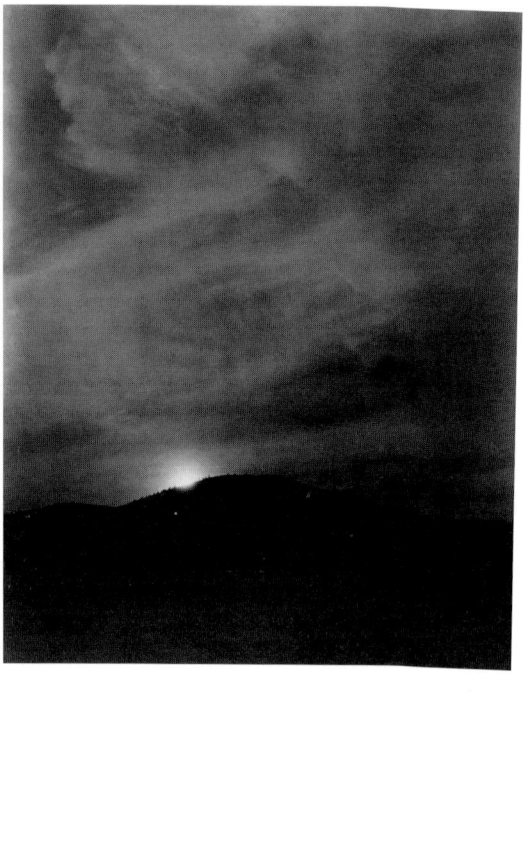

19. Alfred Stieglitz, *Later Lake George,* ca. 1922–23, gelatin silver photograph, 9 ¾ × 7 ½ in. Acquired 1949, The Art Institute of Chicago, Alfred Stieglitz Collection.

homestead, where the extended Stieglitz clan spent their summers. For him, the land surrounding the lake held memories of years past, of close familial relations and sustained social contacts. And it was at Lake George, away from urban stresses, that Stieglitz was most productive, capturing nature and developing its image on his plates as if he were acting out Van Wyck Brooks's assertion that "If something vibrates in the air it is without doubt the expectation of a social ideal that shall act upon us as the sun acts upon a photographic plate."[18]

Of the large and (in 1924) crystal-clear lake itself, Stieglitz wrote to Sherwood Anderson: "The lake is perhaps my oldest friend.—Gosh! What days and nights we've had together. On and in and every which way. Calm beautiful hours. Mad ecstatic ones.—Dream hours.—Hours and days of quiet wonder. Ever the same lake and hills, never a moment of deadness."[19] Stieglitz translated his love of Lake George and its natural surroundings, and all the contrasting resonances of its meaning for him, into his photographs. A platinum print titled simply *Lake George* (figure 18) presents a sublime vision of the silvery-gray, calm surface of the lake, whose low-lying placement imparts a feeling of stasis and perfect balance. Its opalescent veneer stretches across the entire low midground. The time is sunset. The clouds, which constitute the top half of the image, provide a great sense of movement and drama, achieved through the fascinating irregularity of their forms and the fiery, alchemical patterns of the light they absorb and reflect. The sky itself is dark and somewhat threatening, as if a sudden shower is imminent. The great contrasts—light to dark, tranquillity to movement, smoothness to irregularity—lend a theatrical air to the photographic print, which offers high praise to nature's sublimity.

In creating the image Stieglitz aimed the camera to capture a layered landscape. The uppermost register, the sky, is very dark, as is the immediate foreground that depicts the silhouettes of trees on the near side of the lake. Below that topmost black layer stretches the bright silver of fast-moving clouds. Their sleek forms and shimmering tones give the print movement and life. Beneath the clouds a third layer, slightly less dark, depicts the tree-covered hills on the far side of the lake. These multiple levels, along with that of the pearly lake surface itself, create a striated effect that suggests the calm balance Stieglitz attributes to the anthropomorphized lake in his letter to Anderson. It also presents viewers with an unusual abstract surface pattern, as interesting as the larger subject of the work. And while the "chemistry" of the electrical storm brewing in the sky celebrates Stieglitz's more impassioned hours at the lake, it also refers slyly to the chemical processes through which such natural splendor is caught and preserved on film.

A vertical view of the lake's environs, made about 1922 or 1923 and titled *Later Lake George* (figure 19), records Stieglitz's continuing interest in and devotion to the particular landscape near his family's summer home. So does a series of letters written by Stieglitz to Paul Rosenfeld from the summer of 1923 into late fall. Stieglitz's correspondence details the events that can be considered the subtext of the visual works he was then producing. In one undated letter, probably written in October, Stieglitz himself endorses such an interpretation, noting of the four photographs he was sending: "They will serve as a 'souvenir' of the Hill, Summer, 1923—I should say, Autumn's Beginning, 1923." The prints bear a direct relation to the particular history, largely autobiographical, of a specific place, "The Hill" (his affectionate name for the summer home), and a specific time. Although they may seem at first to present neutral views, the landscape works were intended and, on close inspection, appear in fact to be highly individualized moments in a private history. According to Lowe, hundreds of photographs by her uncle exist that form a lengthy historical narrative of the extended clan. The still largely unknown body of Lake George works to which she refers should be reintroduced into Stieglitz's history.[20]

In the same autumn letter to Rosenfeld, Stieglitz declared:

> A few days ago the whole landscape was a yellow mass—I never saw such a living yellow. . . . A few hours of rain and a little wind and the yellow was gone. Many trees are denuded. Bleakness is setting in—although when the sun is brilliant & the sky real clear the hills on the opposite side of the Lake seem a source of constant wonderment to me because of their everchanging color—form—mood—line—I always discover something new at the *roots* as it were of the "simple" thing before you. It's so maddeningly "simple."

Later Lake George may be from the series of photographs from which Rosenfeld was given a few prints. The foreground is pitch black. The lake lies blanketed in darkness while the figure of The Hill presides. The saturated black of the foreground is set off by the exceedingly bright setting sun, which casts an aura over the dark, complex forms of the background hills on the far side of the lake. A highly enigmatic sky (a subject that here shares center stage with the landforms but will take on the leading role in two later series of Stieglitz's prints) is allotted a full half of the composition. The forms of clouds—swirled, veined, and entrancing in their irregularity—appear to be softly etched on the print's surface.

The print is a sober celebration, a more reverent hymn of praise for the beloved homescape than Stieglitz's earlier, more histrionic, display of affection. It seems to pose the important questions asked by many in the postwar years, in America and Europe: What is left for moderns to praise? to value? Stieglitz's answer, shared by his coterie and put forth in this work and others, is that nature's sublimity and continuity in constant change, its resilient power to affect human emotions, perpetually inspire and solace humankind. All these values, which the circle found presented in wild nature, they sought to represent in artworks intended to celebrate and preserve those same attributes.

No one familiar with the full production of the Stieglitz circle can view *Later Lake George* without recalling treatments of the subject by other members. Perhaps the first to come to mind would be Georgia O'Keeffe's well-known *Lake George with Crows* (1921, private collection), a landscape doubtless adopted from Stieglitz's photographic

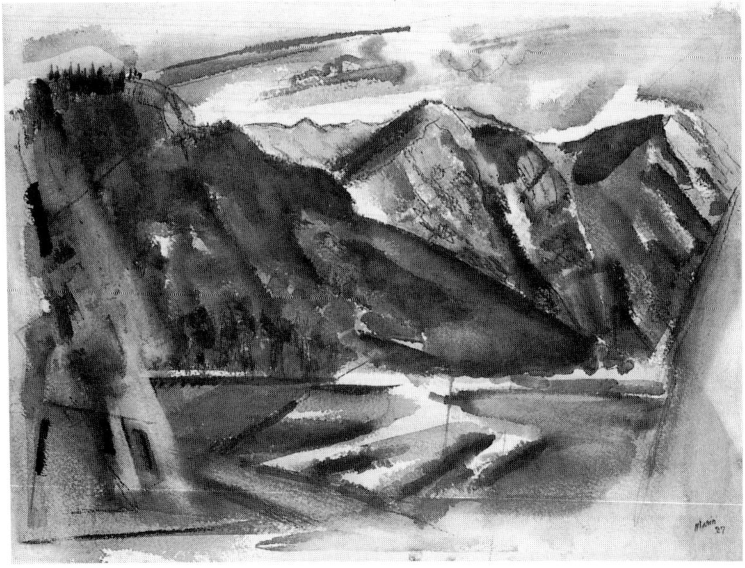

20. John Marin, *Echo Lake, Franconia Range, White Mountain Country*, 1927, watercolor and charcoal over graphite, 17 3/8 × 22 1/4 in. National Gallery of Art, Washington, D.C., Alfred Stieglitz Collection.

treatment. Like Stieglitz's print, O'Keeffe's painting is distinguished by a firm (and ultimately successful) determination to represent a remarkably wide yet subtle range of tone. In O'Keeffe's rendition this variation is handled in colors—blues, blue-violets, reds, and red-oranges. Playfully and pleasurably, the figure of the lake reads "up" the canvas. Traditional perspective is denied and distance is collapsed, as in most of Stieglitz's prints. The colored shapes on the canvas surface deliberately suggest a child's jigsaw puzzle; they recall Dove's use of similar devices that reiterate the flatness of the canvas surface and also evoke the child's fresh view of the world. Here that view arises from O'Keeffe's attempt to subvert the conventions of Renaissance perspective that she knows well but professes not to need. The reference to and celebration of folk art's flatness and "naïveté" are unmistakable.

Even unschooled viewers of *Lake George with Crows* and the many other lake pictures produced by Stieglitz circle members would almost certainly be aware of yet another level of meaning. For in addition to commenting on art and art-making practices and referring to the artists' private histories (individual or familial), their depictions of lakes resonate with references to Thoreau's *Walden*. In this connection one thinks particularly of the much-reproduced early lake pictures of Marsden Hartley. His *Mountain Lake—Autumn* (ca. 1910, Phillips Collection), for example, is childlike in the freshness of its nonperspectival view, its landscape masses represented by simplified shapes in bright primary colors.

John Marin, too, made the beautiful forms of natural lakes an occasion for artistic commemoration and praise. *Echo Lake, Franconia Range, White Mountain Country* (1927; figure 20) is a good example of the painter's response to that environment.

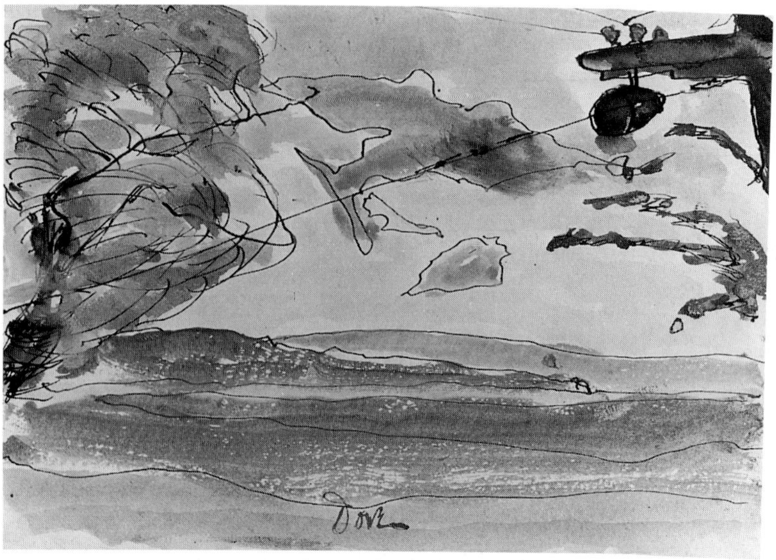

21. Arthur Dove, *Seneca Lake,* 1935, watercolor and ink, 5 × 7 in. Acquired 1949, The Metropolitan Museum of Art, Alfred Stieglitz Collection.

A horizontal landscape bisected by the image of a lake placed a touch to the right of the middle ground, the work is similar in composition to Stieglitz's early photographs of Lake George; it too attempts to suggest a stability and balance inherent in nature. And, as in Stieglitz's works, the sky appears to move very fast, its movement contrasting with and thereby emphasizing the calmness of the lake surface. Unlike the artist whose medium is photography, however, the watercolorist implies rapid change and transition through touch. Like most works of these early-twentieth-century modernists, *Echo Lake* demands a close reading. At first glance the color appears dark, but on a more leisurely viewing it is revealed as a subtle and sophisticated blending of blues, greens, browns, and violets. In his complex choice of palette Marin seeks to reproduce not "local color" but knowledge of the complexities of natural coloration that he claims, by his manner of rendering them, are more intricate than the casual eye perceives. As usual, Marin structures the forms of the natural landscape in complementary, irregular bands that accentuate his color choices just as dark bands of metal gird and accentuate a cathedral's stained glass. Through a careful study of his painted commentary one gradually comes to realize and appreciate nature's manifold properties and complexity, as well as its remarkable ability to bear human meaning.

Arthur Dove's *Seneca Lake,* a small, thoughtful watercolor (1935; figure 21), fits nicely into this discussion. The work is characteristic of the artist in form, yet the color—muted grays, greens in softened shades—suggests an unusual mood: not celebratory but serious, elegiac. The lake itself plays a minor role in the work, for at the upper right of the composition an electrical power pole with its crossbar and dangling insulator, dark and ugly, intrudes on the natural scene. Against this modern antagonist

22. Alfred Stieglitz, *Lake George in Winter,* 1923, gelatin silver photograph. National Gallery of Art, Washington, D.C., Alfred Stieglitz Collection.

stands the protagonist, a tree at the top left of the composition. The lines that give the tree its form are electric, full of life; those of the power pole clumsy and awkward. This small, unsung watercolor both addresses the intrusion of modern technology on the landscape and, unambiguously, expresses the artist's concern about its effect on the American wilderness.

Modern technology and its products are also introduced as characters in Stieglitz's photographic commentary. Here such objects cannot be taken as figures of "modernity," as in the works of many contemporaries not connected with the Stieglitz circle. Circle members use them either literally or as emblems of artistry. For example, in *Lake George in Winter* (1923; figure 22), a horizontal night landscape, Stieglitz admits a telephone line and poles into the composition in the lower midground for specific reasons. The winter scene conveyed in the photograph is highly poetic. The composition deliberately recalls both Hartley and Marin in its "registering" of objects—sky, hills, trees, and foreground—in discrete, flat planes. The contrasts of tone in the print are not played for drama, as in some of Stieglitz's photographs of the lake; instead, they create a more subtle lyricism, which recalls the tone of certain poems of Whitman. Even more important is the intimacy suggested by this softened tone. Stieglitz's perspective, like Marin's in the painted views of his Maine island, is that of inhabitant and settler, not of outsider or tourist. Prints like *Lake George in Winter* ensure Stieglitz's place as an early regionalist because they show how he intentionally captured and celebrated a distinct, familiar region of American land.

The bright moon hangs prominently in the nighttime sky of *Lake George in Winter.* Stieglitz explored mysterious night in his earliest New York prints, which were produced, exhibited, and critically acclaimed just before the turn of the century. Now, in the twenties, French surrealists regularly used the night to evoke a sense of reflection, memory, and dream. In this 1923 print the telephone apparatus portrayed in the center of the composition adds just the right touch of irony as it announces that this is not a nostalgic work. The photograph's mode of representation, while lyrical, is not romantic in the nineteenth-century sense. While his French contemporaries used disjunctive images in their visual art and poetry to overturn accepted artistic conventions, Stieglitz juxtaposed the objects of modern technology with nature to surpass the subject matter of his American artist predecessors. Beauty and charm are in the method of portrayal, not just in the object portrayed, Stieglitz's photograph asserts. These valued properties can no longer simply be uncovered in nature: they must also be created through the artist's transformative power. Through art, the forms of technology could be appropriated and converted into something with visual appeal.

Other works by artists of the Stieglitz circle also make use of apparatus of the modern age to comment on the nature and function of representation. Dove's *Fall Brook Railroad,* a small pencil and watercolor (1934; figure 23), is in one sense a typical landscape. Though it is more conventional than Dove's best-known works—clearly legible buildings, grass, and trees are depicted more literally than abstractly—the title of the work remains highly allusive. Without the picture in hand, one might imagine its subject to be the fuming iron engines of Stieglitz's famous *Hand of Man* (1902). Dove presents us not with a railroad train, however, but only with reminders of one: the train tracks that pattern the foreground of the work. Instead of an image of a train, a towering telephone pole, its wooden arms outstretched like a cross, is centrally placed in the composition. Wires extending from the pole literally parallel and reiterate the meaning of the tracks depicted below; both indicate communication over distance. Yet the work is not an attack; Dove accepts technological progress as the nineteenth-century advocates of Arts and Crafts aesthetics never did. Forms of modern communication can by analogy provide what Dove (and the other members of the group) saw as the ideal social function of works of art: widespread communication, binding together the many diverse regions of the nation in common discourse.

But more often, the nation's pressing issues were figured in the familiar regional landscape. Stieglitz loads a letter to Frank of August 1927 with political and socio-

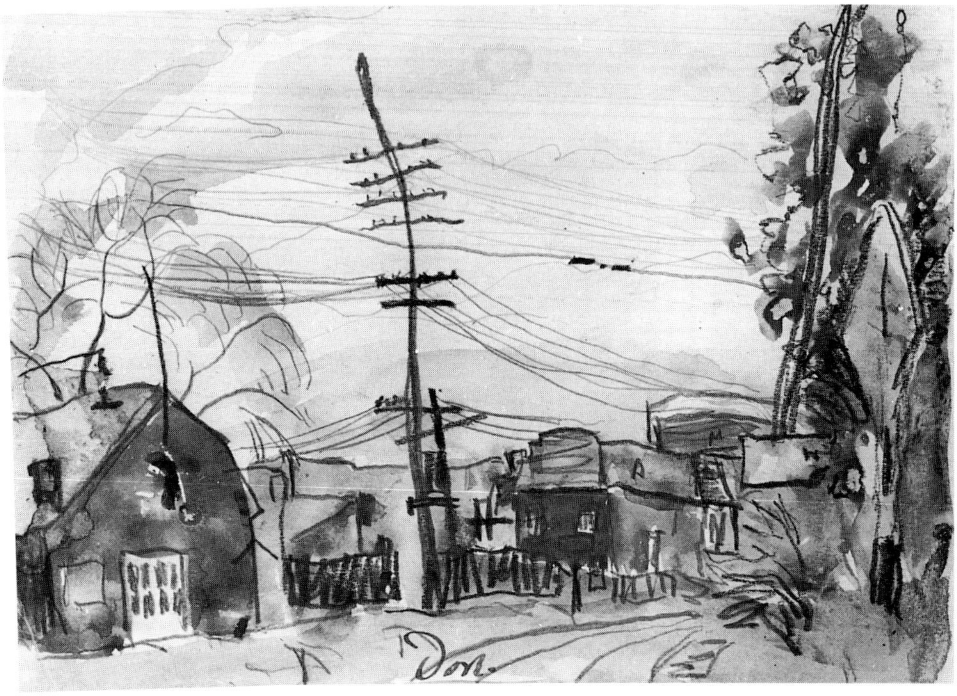

23. Arthur Dove, *Fall Brook Railroad,* 1934, pencil and watercolor, 5 × 6 15/16 in. Acquired 1949, The Metropolitan Museum of Art, Alfred Stieglitz Collection.

economic implications: "Everything seems real enough & still it is as if an immovable haze hung over it all—much like the summer so far—the hills rarely sharply outlined—rarely edges—listless mists—much indecision every where. Coolidge—Gov. Fuller—Geneva—many 'thinking' people stunned—'panic' in Wall Street."[21] Stieglitz is asserting the validity of the pathetic fallacy, the notion (particularly dear to the romantics) that nature is sympathetic to human moods; the appearance of things changes, John Ruskin observed in naming this phenomenon, "when we are under the influence of emotion, or contemplative fancy."[22] In his verbal sketch the usual appearance of Lake George, in the heat of summer, represents the indecisiveness of contemporary American leaders and the uncertainty of the future.

In other cases Stieglitz did depend on prior literary conventions to convey his more private or autobiographical meanings. Trees, specifically the trees that enlivened the landscape in the family yard at Lake George, were frequently the subjects of his photographs. About to leave New York City for the lake, he wrote to Sherwood Anderson: "I'm curious to see my old friend the Dying Chestnut on the Hill—What a wonder that lone tree is.—Maybe this year I'll manage to get a real picture of that heroic figure."[23] Through personification, the chestnut tree becomes a human actor. The particular significance of that tree becomes clear when we read another letter, written in the summer of 1922 and published as an article in the *Amateur Photographer* the following September. Throughout the summer, Stieglitz wrote, he had watched his mother dying and "[o]ur place going to pieces. The old horse . . . being kept alive by the 70-year-old coachman. I, full of the feeling of today; all about me disintegration—slow but sure: dying chestnut trees. . . . [T]he pines doomed too—diseased; I, poor but at work; the world in a great mess; the human being a queer animal—not as dignified as our giant chestnut on the hill."[24] The remarks of Stieglitz's niece, Sue Davidson Lowe, reveal more about the loaded and complex meanings of the trees that "peopled" the family estate: "Any change in his immediate landscape was excruciating [to him]. The velvet-weathered barn siding could be on the verge of rotting before new stain was allowed; there was a two-year battle over placement of telephone poles that Alfred insisted would ruin his vista. . . . Alfred refused to permit the felling of the three dead chestnut trees he considered a special legacy from [his father] Edward."[25]

Stieglitz's many images of trees celebrate natural forms; but they also commemorate the passage of time in an individual's life, the familial human drama of life and death taking place as he watches. In many of the photographs, the trees at Lake George—with their imposing presences, dominant placement in the compositions, and especially their eerie tonality—are presented as numinous surrogates of the beloved dead. This fictive remaking of the trees into powerful personal icons may pay homage to nonliterate or folk cultures, which had held the attention of the circle since the days of the 291 gallery. It also marks Stieglitz's own quite human need to memorialize the respected ancestors in palpable form. The photographs themselves serve this latter purpose quite well, representing the life cycle and endowing it with a significance it rarely received in twentieth-century America outside of traditional religious observances.

To be sure, many of Stieglitz's tree pictures have meaning beyond the autobiographical, and not all are used to address the difficult subjects of change and death. The vertical landscape photograph *Two Poplars on the Hillside, Lake George* (1933; figure 24) is a good example of the subject portrayed in a different tone. The poplars are certainly the protagonists of the image, dominating the photograph as decisively as do the vertical building forms of Stieglitz's cityscapes. The vantage point is a close one, underscoring that this is a "heroized" rendition. The tone, by contrast, is very subtle, delicate, and nondramatic. The careful depiction of small details of each slender branch requires an intimate viewing. Myriad natural reflected lights are captured, as are the slender blades of grass beneath the poplars at the soil line. Numerous clouds crowd the sky, dark and rain-bearing; a storm is coming soon. Yet the mood conveyed is one of quiet contemplation. The photograph meditates on the inevitable transformations in nature.

In several letters describing the same poplars to friends, the trees figure even

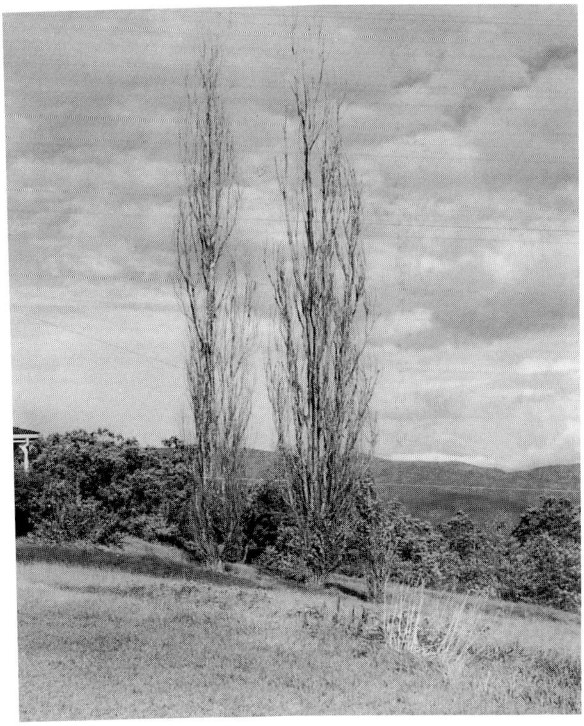

24. Alfred Stieglitz, *Two Poplars on the Hillside, Lake George,* 1933, gelatin silver photograph, 4 ⅝ × 3 ⅝ in. Philadelphia Museum of Art, The Alfred Stieglitz Collection.

more deeply in Stieglitz's rumination on human fate. One such letter of 1929, written to Waldo Frank from the lake, is especially telling: "Of course the crash in Wall Street altho' 'expected,' stuns one—It is as if war were imminent or death peering from around the corner. One feels such a damned fool—and so helpless. There are no regrets—one is just dazed & even wonders what *its* all about. Life having a grand time. . . . The poplars are bare—excepting here & there still a yellow leaf glowing yellow against a dark sullen sky. To think of New York when there is this is none too pleasant."[26] As in the landscape works of his regionalist predecessors—the Hudson River School painters of the nineteenth century, for whom Lake George frequently provided a subject—Stieglitz used the forms of nature to represent a sign of hope, a promise of renewal to humankind in the face of human folly and social disruption. But he differs from his predecessors not only in his medium, the photograph, but in his use of the trees in his own yard as symbols, a choice that adds another level of significance to the generic message: a private, self-reflective, and autobiographical layer of meaning. (We might note that Monet's poplars had similar connotations.)

In the case of *Two Poplars on the Hillside,* a small portion of the porch of the Lake George homestead is captured at the left edge of the print, grounding the image of the trees in a specific place at a specific moment. But the house itself is the subject

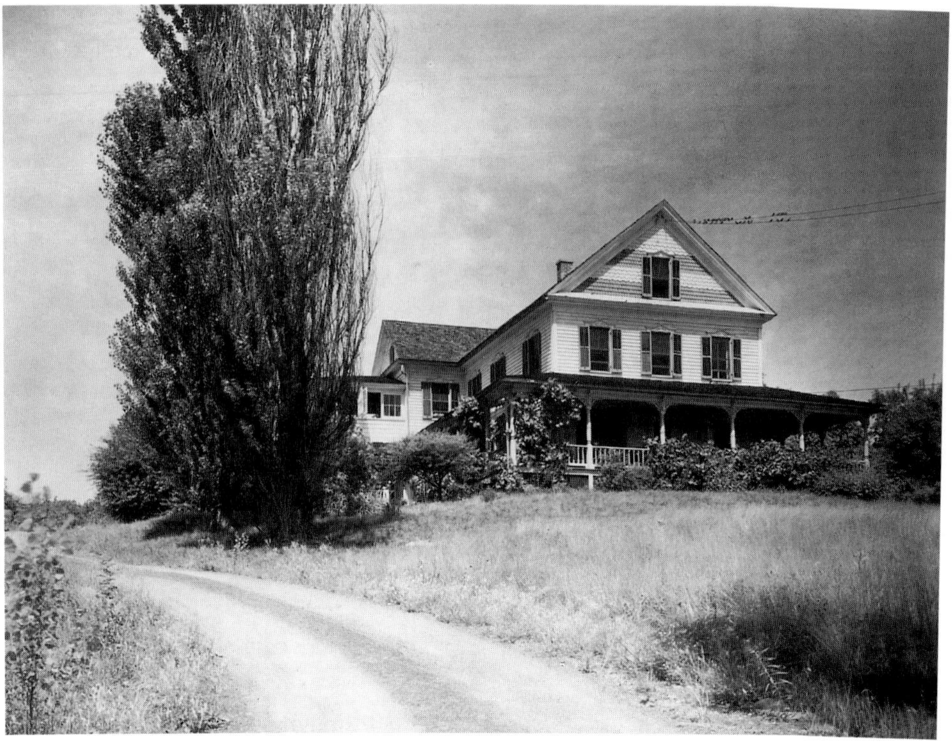

25. Alfred Stieglitz, *House on the Hill, Lake George,* 1932, gelatin silver photograph. National Gallery of Art, Washington, D.C., Alfred Stieglitz Collection.

of several photographs. One example that captures the Stieglitz family summer home in all its spaciousness and personal resonance is *House on the Hill, Lake George* (1932; figure 25). Stieglitz's favorite poplars to the left of the house play supporting roles. The foreground of the print is noticeably faint in tone. The various grasses in the foreground, right, are well described, and the architectural details of the house are clearly and crisply delineated. Stieglitz managed to capture the effect of a wide-angle architectural lens, creating the illusion of a broader foundation for the central character, the house, and rendering the porch exaggeratedly long and deep—suggesting the welcome and hospitality customarily associated with plantation mansions in the American South. Stieglitz depicts the dreaded telephone poles and wires in this winter landscape not to undercut the tone of seriousness but to gain expressive advantage. He waited patiently for birds to bejewel the strands of wire that, from his chosen angle, sweep gracefully into the distance off the charming gabled roof.

Stieglitz seems to have become accustomed to the intrusion of the telephone equipment, but he carefully denies one element of the landscape much say: to assert the primacy of the homestead and, by association, the extended family living there he described the road only faintly in the print. It seems that Stieglitz did not wish to lend power to the road, the modern embodiment of alienation and estrangement, which connotes the "progress" the artist questioned. It represented, for him, the intrusion of urban transportation (and increased commerce) into a rural community. Perhaps worst of all, it signified O'Keeffe's increasing absence; freed by the automobile, she had decided to spend summers alone in New Mexico. Stieglitz could not ignore the road or its many meanings, but with the powers of an art maker, he could diminish its importance by controlling tone and placement. What a telling contrast to the celebratory treatment of the road as a central figure of freedom in the later works of O'Keeffe!

Fall Brook Railroad is not the only example of Arthur Dove's use of the intelligible symbols of modern communication to comment on the power and inventiveness of art and art makers. *Telegraph Pole* (1929; plate 1), an exceptional work in a thoroughly modern medium—oil and metallic paints on a metal backing—exemplifies Dove's early use of such figures.[27] This visually stunning work, which flickers teasingly between abstraction and representation, is a vertical landscape. The background hills and the middle ground are rendered in a vibrant, electric green. The distinctive forms of the telegraph pole itself bear the artist's most inventive marks and solutions. The "bow" that crosses at the top of the pole is brown, flecked with shiny golden leaflike forms; the "bow" at the bottom is simply the unpainted metallic surface of the backing material, which Dove has allowed to shine through. The metallic surface is burnished with calligraphic patterns that anticipate similar designs in the work of such modern sculptors as David Smith. Some of the marks coyly mimic drawing on paper. The foreground of the painting is a distinctive blend of red on silver metal. The shapes that adorn the Vuillardesque central figure of the pole recall leaves blowing and curling in the wind. Through consummate artistry, Dove wittily makes of the modern form of the pole a thoroughly modern tree.

Dove's powerful artistic inventiveness in *Telegraph Pole* rivals that required to create the communication device his painting celebrates. Indeed, the painting indirectly addresses the function of the artist in American society. *Telegraph Pole* praises the inventiveness of the artist-creator of the apparatus, Samuel F. B. Morse, whom Dove posits as a worthy model for American artists. And the painting itself provides a good example of how the inspiration of a predecessor, here Morse, spurs on the twentieth-century artist to daring new heights of formal innovation. Dove goes beyond singing Morse's praises to make a very beautiful form from an ungainly one; even more, he fashioned a delectable object of art out of the detritus of modern civilization. On several complex levels *Telegraph Pole* reasserts the communicative function of art and the great transformative and inventive power of the American art maker; it does so primarily by merging the histories of artistic and scientific discovery and invention. This merger recalls not just Morse's accomplishments but a longer tradition of American intertwining of art and science (emblematized by Charles Willson

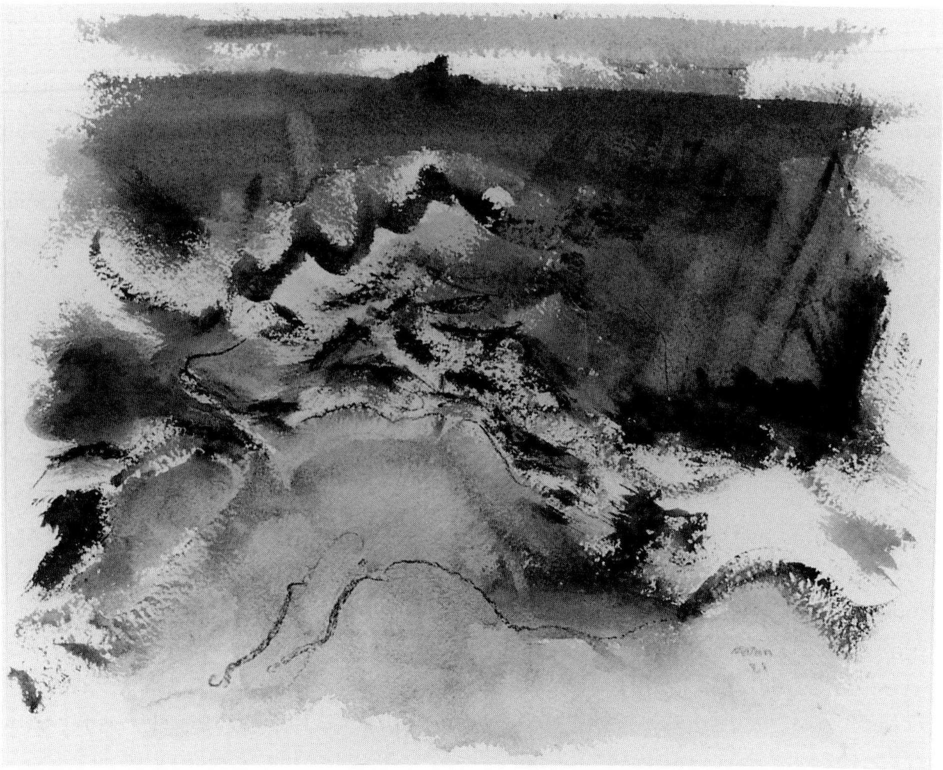

26. John Marin, *The Sea, Maine,* 1921, watercolor and charcoal on paper, 16 ½ × 19 ⅝ in. National Museum of American Art, Smithsonian Institution, Washington, D.C.

Peale's eighteenth-century museum, which contained objects of natural history and technology as well as portraits).

Other Stieglitz circle works address the issue of art's communicative role differently. What is finally to be communicated by art is a question raised in works like John Marin's watercolor *The Sea, Maine* (1921; figure 26). The central figure, as the title announces, is the Atlantic Ocean off the Maine coast. The Atlantic is depicted in deep cobalt and bright aqua blues, with a striking deep green striation at the horizon, placed high. A tall wave is suggested by a white hieroglyph in the middle ground. There are touches, subtly blended, of blue on the beach in the foreground, suggesting the reflections of light off the sandy ground. The artist's exuberance of expression, demonstrated by the great variety of touches and marks as well as by his wide range of high-intensity color choices, is compared here with the power of the ocean itself. Marin takes as his subject not simply a portion of the Atlantic that he was to observe for decades but also the way that nature's strong forces, represented by the ocean, both elicit and bear comparison to the strongest human moods—joy, ecstasy. In essence *The Sea, Maine* is about expression: about art's great capacity to capture and match the sublimity of nature in expansive, expressive, and enduring human response.

For the circle, nature could be celebrated as successfully by singling out small objects for contemplation as by reproducing entire landscapes. This idea is demonstrated with special power in the close-up views of unique natural forms found in the oeuvres of Alfred Stieglitz, Paul Strand, and (profoundly influenced by the photographic experiments of her two colleagues) Georgia O'Keeffe. In works such as Strand's 1928 photograph *Driftwood No. 1, Maine,* for example, the entire print surface is swallowed up by the image of a time-weathered, intricately shaped natural form that extends beyond the surface of the page. The contrasts of tone are understated and nondramatic, alluding to properties of the found object itself and conveying a feeling of quiet and reverence. The extreme close-up deliberately exaggerates the common human viewpoint. One rarely visually penetrates and examines forms at such close range. This device both demands viewers' visual participation in a new type of scrutiny and calls attention to the artist's practice of it. It encourages the discovery of details of form, texture, and striated pattern in the wood grain depicted. An erratic grass blade, much like a scratch on an etching plate, zigzags across the print's surface in the left midground. The bit of driftwood, for which we have no true scale, is captured and metamorphosed into an abstract shape recalling the fascinating irregular forms depicted in some of Arthur Dove's works. Among other things, Strand claims for photographers the transformative power customarily allotted to painters. *Driftwood No. 1, Maine* also remarks on the properties valued by early-twentieth-century modernists. A central proposition of the work is that the human mind cannot grasp the "whole" picture, just significant fragments. What is meaningful to represent, then, is beauty, irregularity, uniqueness, nonconformity, and naturalness, properties quite literally presented in the print.

Other works of the Stieglitz group evoke an especially powerful symbol of America's past, the farm. In a series of photographs begun in the early twenties and continued until illness forced him to put aside his camera, Stieglitz created images that reported the dramatic social changes that transformed the independent American farm. For this project he used the familiar sights of his family's Lake George homestead as symbols of a general condition.

In one work of the series, dated 1922 and titled *Barn, Lake George* (figure 27), there is a full-faced portrait of the old, weathered barn that Stieglitz (according to his niece) was so reluctant to refurbish. The structure discloses its history in the photographic print through the "character lines" that time has made across its aging facade. Through the point of view Stieglitz proclaims his intimacy with this subject and demands that his viewers closely scrutinize its every detail. Except for the mere shadow of a tree (outside the frame) that casts an intriguing pattern on the barn face and allows a bit of nature to enhance the human-built form, only the barn itself is portrayed.

Especially remarkable is the print's uncommonly light tonality, which gives the

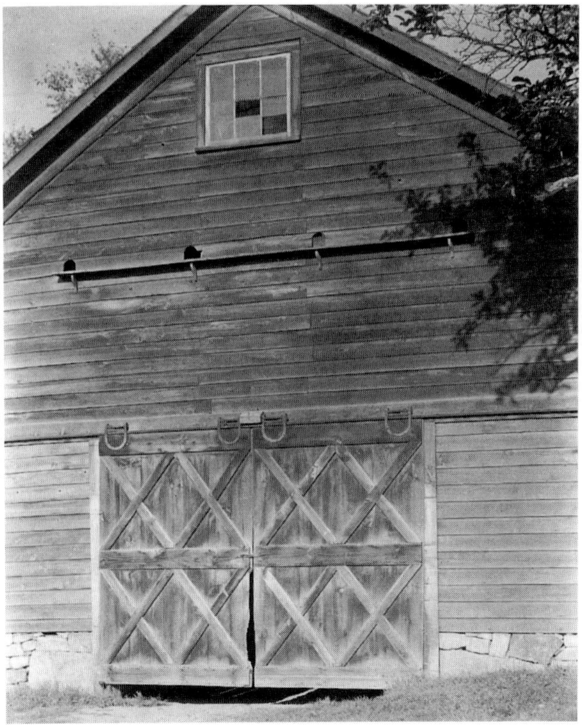

27. Alfred Stieglitz, *Barn, Lake George*, 1922, gelatin silver photograph. National Gallery of Art, Washington, D.C., Alfred Stieglitz Collection.

impression that the image has been effaced, washed out by time. The shadow in the empty interior of the barn is the darkest element of the composition, seen through the gaps between and under the rugged doors. The suggestion of empty interior space, the description of the broken panes of the single window that crowns the facade near the barn's peaked roof, and the detailed account of the breakage in the ledge above the doorway sum up the content of the image. All these features, combined with the deliberate bleaching of the tones throughout, inform us that America's agricultural heritage, emblematized by the barn, is defunct. The "soul" of the traditional architectural form, once the heart of farm activity, is empty; no productive life remains within. Four rusting horseshoes affixed to the barn facade as talismans ironically comment on the bad fortune of the American farmer. With undisguised poignancy Stieglitz's photograph meditates on the passing of a long-valued tradition of American economic independence. Though the Stieglitz homestead was not, during the family's ownership, an independent farm, it is used as an emblem of the type.

In a later version of a related subject, *Haywagon and Barn, Lake George* (probably 1923; figure 28), Stieglitz comments further on traditional American relations to the land. Here, by choosing a vantage point at a greater distance, he adopts the disengaged stance of anthropological observer of his own homestead. Although smaller

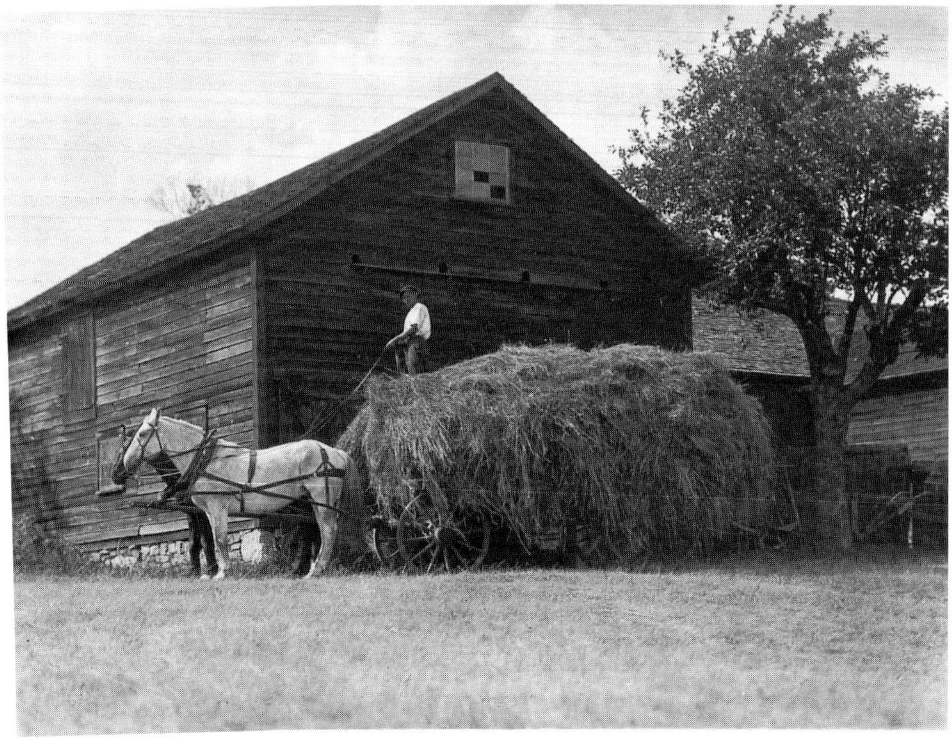

28. Alfred Stieglitz, *Haywagon and Barn, Lake George,* probably 1923, gelatin silver photograph. National Gallery of Art, Washington, D.C., Alfred Stieglitz Collection.

in scale than in the 1922 image, the barn is literally central to the work; also, its form is described more completely than in the earlier, cropped version of the subject. More important, the barn in this print shares the stage with other equally important figures: a farmhand and his horse-drawn wagon loaded with hay. The print evokes the past, implying that man, horse, wagon, and barn form an integral working unit. Their figures add up like words in a sentence, with meanings both individual and collective: worker and beast are interdependent. The print refers more generally to human culture—the acts of humans who devised the utilitarian wagon and by their ingenuity ensured the hay harvest.

By literally stepping back to gain distance, Stieglitz could note the interrelated components of agrarian self-support. The photograph does not depict the present but rather provides a memorial glimpse of the past. There is no attempt to suggest that the hay piled high in the wagon came from the Stieglitz barn (which the earlier print had presented as empty). Nor does Stieglitz direct the farmhand to play the role of happy farmer or proud possessor of the land and the tools for its cultivation. The

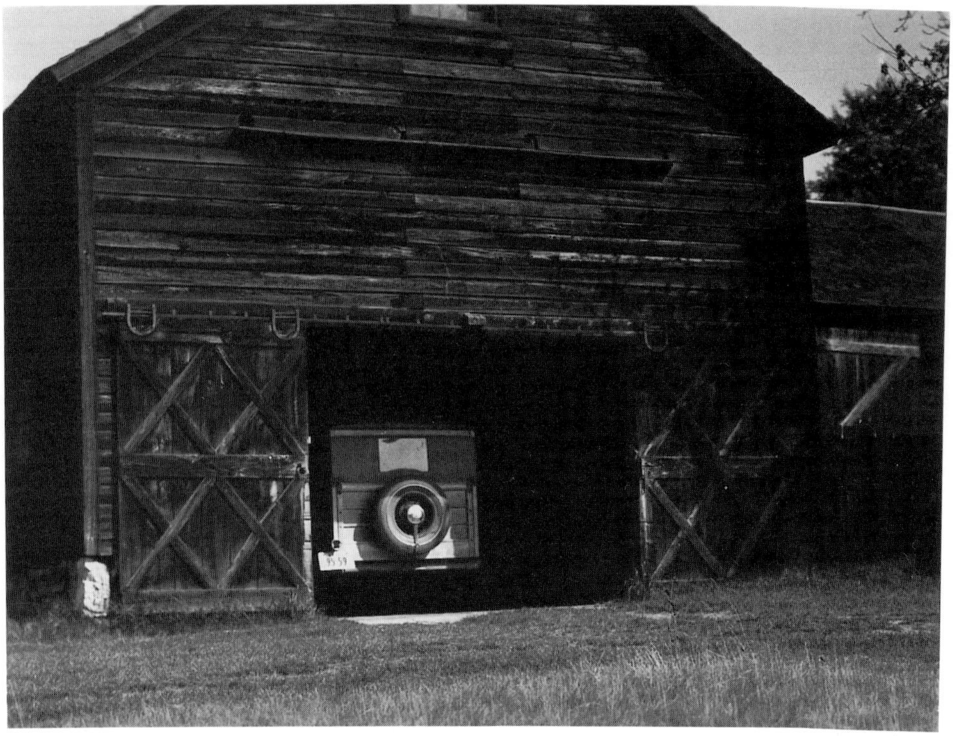

29. Alfred Stieglitz, *Barn and Car, Lake George,* 1934, gelatin silver photograph. National Gallery of Art, Washington, D.C., Alfred Stieglitz Collection.

photograph tells no story. The deliberately staged view is instead commemorative—an elegy for a set of relations to rural American land that are now being replaced. And Stieglitz's comments are unsentimental. The image is objective, crisp. The composition is not "beautified" or made picturesque but suggests, through its remarkable balance, the stability of the old economic system. All objects are formally bound in necessary and harmoniously functional relation. The America eulogized here is one of decentralized, unindustrialized, regional economic units celebrated in the theories of Lewis Mumford.

Not all the photographs in the barn landscape series are eulogistic; *Barn and Car, Lake George* (1934; figure 29) is ironic. It gives us an intimate view of the facade of the dilapidated Lake George barn. The vantage is close-up and the gable is cropped more severely than in most views, transforming the structure into something new and unfamiliar. In fact, this photo wittily comments on the barn's new function as garage, a shelter for modern mechanical beasts. The barn doors have been flung fully open to reveal the rear of an automobile; its license plate is the most prominent object in the image. The white rectangle of the plate reflects the natural light of the sun overhead. The photographer comments not only on the barn's new and somewhat amusing function but also, by inference, on the new human role of motorist. Humans now operate not horse-drawn carts but sleek vehicles; in them, they are identified not by their relation to the land traversed but by double sequences of numbers like those displayed so prominently on the car's back plate. Stieglitz notes these changes in the true spirit of a dada punster, with detached irony.

Stieglitz was not the only one of the circle alarmed at the plight of the American independent farm and the wholesale transformation of the American landscape. In "New England on the Trapeze" (1931), Marsden Hartley reported the changes he noted in the New England countryside after a twenty-year absence:

> It is to be expected of course that all this modernism would revolutionize the life of the farmers also, but the transition has turned them into something like cheap slaves masquerading in imitation of their masters and dictators, the rich summer sojourners, and if all those modern appliances, electrical devices and the like, lessen the strain of their labors, it certainly destroys the lyric charm of what one used to know as "the Farm," for all of its natural qualities have been effaced, and the buzz and click of machinery at every hand resembles nothing that you have known, nothing that is recognizable in the old satisfying form.[28]

While he decries the machine, Hartley makes the "effacement of nature" his principal subject. The American forests (which Hartley had earlier judged far superior to those of France)[29] had been transformed, much for the worse, by the state. Hartley rails: "Nature is no longer herself, everything is ticketed, labelled, and duly classified by the social and commercial enterprise of state organization which, in this case, being New Hampshire, is obviously bent upon developing its Yosemite of the east." The desire of state government to generate revenue by artificially barricading and displaying the American wilderness enrages the artist, who attacks the result: "New England has joined the circus; she has, I suppose for reasons of pecuniary embarrassment, which were always typical of her, joined the 'Greatest show on earth' projects; she has been disciplined to her modern trade; she is swinging on the trapeze of modern commerce, showing herself off at so much a turn."[30]

This legalized prostitution of nature is damaging the previously untouched landscape that artists of the Stieglitz circle wanted to preserve. Not only have the New England wilds been turned into "anybody's public lady," but

> As far as I could make out, everyone is sold out—everyone—and the whole dignified works has succumbed to modern traffic, the hills are covered with golfers from upper Broadway, and the valleys are strewn with inveigling signs to entice touring travelers to "stay with us"—"here is good rest—Simmons beds," etc.
>
> And there are traffic squads, police in their boxes, motor cops, parking plazas, room for several hundred cars in one case, with underground passage to dispose of foot traffic

on its way to give a look at Profile Rock, more commonly known as "The old man of the mountains."

You do not expect to find such intrusions in the midst of these very noble scenes of nature and, if you are a home-loving native, you will never get used to them.[31]

By promoting wilderness areas as places for rest and recreation, the state was encouraging crowds of tourists, who brought with them their noisy, smoke-spewing automobiles and, with their numbers, encouraged the proliferation of gaudy roadside billboards. For Hartley, as for others of the circle, woman personified the American landscape; in this case, she has been defiled. His reaction makes it easy to understand why his paintings, unlike Marin's jazzy city landscapes, never included images of advertising signs.

Elizabeth McCausland noted in her biography of Hartley that he "spent the summer of 1930 at Franconia Notch [in New Hampshire], a terrain which proved to be morally painful and enervating."[32] In a letter to Stieglitz from Franconia in July 1930 Hartley throws light on the reasons for his lowered morale:

> Here I am in the old country and I must say it is very handsome—but I must say that all I can see is that the country is sold out years in advance—it is all so like a three ring circus now—But the country is as beautiful as ever even if one must look over a parade of autocars to see it. . . . [It] is completely sold out and nature is robotized perfectly. The chipmunk eats his lunch out of refuse baskets in the state reservations when they don't get their backs broken trying to cross the state highways. Nature is being heavily preserved here—and when you want to see special beauties you pay a quarter and pass through a clicking gate—so much for progress.[33]

Like so much of the group's published cultural criticism, the first draft of Hartley's "New England on the Trapeze" was a personal letter to another circle member describing his firsthand experience of a well-loved landscape now dramatically transformed.

This belief that the American wilderness was being betrayed for profit by the U.S. government was not an eccentric point of view. A contemporary member of the Interior Department's Advisory Board on National Park Policy reported that when he looked down on Yosemite, which Hartley claimed New Hampshire was trying to rival, he saw little more than "long stretches of wide road, innumerable buildings, hotels, automobiles, and parking places."[34] In truth Yosemite itself was no longer the primitive, untouched wonder of Albert Bierstadt's paintings of the previous century but a heavily promoted resort, run by business. An impressive range of Americans joined in indicting the misuse of wilderness.[35] Like a poet who speaks the collective mind from his wilderness retreat, Hartley voiced social criticisms that rang true to the public of all classes, for whom reverence for the image of American land as Arcadia bound the culture in a tacit social contract.

One work by Hartley specifically addresses the issue of forest preservation. Al-

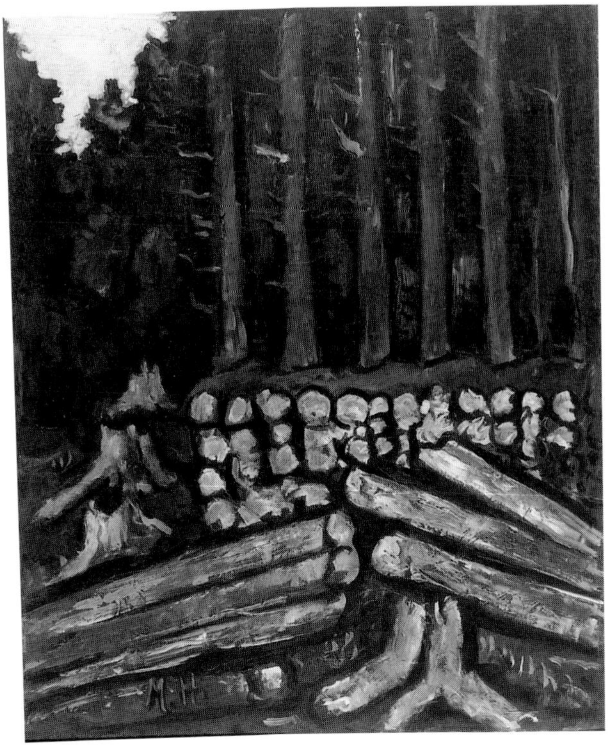

30. Marsden Hartley, *Wood Lot, Maine,* 1938, oil on canvas, 28 1/8 × 22 in. Acquired 1942, The Phillips Collection, Washington, D.C.

though its content is somewhat ambiguous, the subject of Hartley's *Wood Lot, Maine* (1938; figure 30) is clear enough. The title informs us that the artist chose to consider not the untouched New England forest but rather a cultivated lot of pine, in an unnatural grid formation planted strictly for commercial uses. *Wood Lot, Maine* is a vertical landscape in dark forest greens, browns, "flesh" tones, and white. The forms of the image are dramatized by a thick black outlining, characteristic of Hartley's late style. The artist's use of the tones one might see on the flesh of local Anglo residents suggests that he is personifying the painted trees, as he had New England itself in his 1931 article. The landscape is darkly somber, and it reads down the canvas "page," like a piece of critical writing. At the top is a dense and lush passage of living trees; at bottom, a pile of logs, their flesh-colored, exposed interiors jutting out at the spectator like accusing fingers. Perhaps more poignant are the two stumps of trees felled for their wood in the left foreground.

Hartley's scathing written attack on the government policy of "producing forests" is repeated in *Wood Lot, Maine* in the more eloquent and poetic language of paint. While being shown the exploitation of American forestland for profit, viewers are encouraged to attend to the grace of the painterly language. The lushness of even the felled trees underscores their essential value in the world of nature and natural beauty.

Through careful, indeed loving, brushstrokes and emphatic highlighting, the artist eloquently presents elements of the natural resources he most values. But Hartley intends to educate as much as to delight—to persuade viewers to value their properties as he does.

The very same Arcadian and communitarian mythos that supported the Stieglitz circle's interest in the preservation of the rural countryside and farmland and in the conservation of forests supported the parallel interests of urban planners. In 1925 Lewis Mumford argued that "regional planning is the New Conservation—the conservation of human values hand in hand with natural resources."[36] Urban "conservation," unlike rural, was aimed at utilizing natural resources exclusively to benefit city dwellers. Throughout the twenties, America's social planners employed the myth of Arcadia to remake both city and country. Much like Emerson and Thoreau, American visual artists, writers, and urban designers who regularly dealt in myths and symbols saw the undeveloped native landscape as a major determinant of the American character. The Stieglitz circle did not invoke Arcadia simply to revive nineteenth-century transcendentalism, however, for with Whitman, they valued nature as much for its aesthetic and social as for its philosophical meanings.

As it condemned the contemporary abuses of nature, "New England on the Trapeze" also provided a clue about the type of landscape that Hartley sought. "What strange visions are these," he writes of the New Hampshire state parks, "for one who seeks to restore simple contacts with inherited old-fashioned things, things that were once a real part of one's earlier life, earlier cultivation, earlier faiths and aspirations."[37] In the year this article was published Hartley found the landscape he sought in the moraine of Dogtown Common in Gloucester, Massachusetts. The site so compelled him that he returned twice more, in 1934 and 1936, to record it in his art.[38]

He described the isolated place in a letter to Stieglitz—its history as a settlement established about 1650 and the unique forms of the rocky natural landscape, formed by prolonged glacial movement—and mentioned that he had seen Dogtown from afar some twelve years earlier. Hartley wrote enthusiastically, "I am sure I shall eventually be known as 'the' painter of Dogtown."[39] Because of his deep belief in the identity-forming interrelation of humans with the land they inhabit and the soil they till, he saw in Dogtown the perfect metaphor for the slow processes of adaptation and acculturation by which immigrants become Americans—processes much on the minds of circle members and others striving for a national culture.

The artistic self-discovery that Hartley's letter predicts appears in the Dogtown works themselves. Paintings such as *The Old Bars, Dogtown* (1936; plate 2) or *The Last Stone Walls, Dogtown* (1937, Yale University Art Museum, New Haven) underline all of Hartley's strengths as an image maker. In *The Old Bars, Dogtown*, for example, objects are strewn hither and yon with no central focus in a democratized composition that refuses hierarchies. The device may comment on the transplanted society at Dogtown, figuring the germ of American culture and society. The work also embodies, in its use of space, a keen awareness and appreciation of Giorgio de Chirico, the painter the contemporary European surrealist movement claimed as predecessor. And the attendant eeriness and haunting loneliness, which also recall de Chirico's, suggest both the ancestral bones that lie in the hallowed ground depicted and the old souls that still inhabit it: the ghosts of American history.

Hartley uses color experimentally in *The Old Bars, Dogtown:* there are vibrant forest green tones for the background trees and emerald greens for grasses in the foreground and midground, subtly blended. The dark shadows on rock and stone bear stern emphatic meanings. Green nature is in full array; it can rejuvenate itself. But the stones, the ruins of human-built structures—like the "bars" of the title, the posts that once supported the walls of dwellings—attest to the inevitable fate of human artifacts. There is a similar message in those serial city photographs by Stieglitz that avow the transience of human life and the ultimate failure of human intrusions on nature. The pines and evergreens will endure, Hartley reassures himself and viewers, and the green grasses return. But human makings are ephemeral; for all their craft and design, they will not survive the tests of nature and of time. Yet Hartley applied caressingly the broad passages of paint that compose this extraordinary horizontal landscape, evidently concerned that the work endure into the future, which alone can offer an artist genuine and lasting fame.

In the painting Hartley not only employs his knowledge of contemporary European ideas of form but also challenges the old masters successfully, demanding to be taken seriously as an artistic equal of such revered European predecessors as Claude Lorrain and Nicolas Poussin. The themes of the painting themselves work to this end: it is a weighty meditation on the powers of nature, on natural and human histories, and on the temper and meaning of human endeavors. More important, however, is the mode of address used: the lovingly labored surface, its paint laid on thick, especially in the evocative passage of sky that recalls Hartley's earliest works.

The reworking of the center midground records the process of the artist's thought and struggle, whose traces Hartley left deliberately as evidence. The strokes of paint bear much of his message: this is not the playful and cursory script of Marin, or the lighthearted celebration or puns of Demuth or Dove, but a brooding, sober, and pensive touch, clear and legible, that effectively conveys the instructive and moral tone of a poet-painter who urges viewers to collaborate in the search for a vital American culture. *The Old Bars, Dogtown* proves Waldo Frank's dictum that to seek American culture and identity is to create it.

Throughout the twenties and thirties, the Stieglitz circle attempted to support the native beliefs of American rural migrants to the city and to present democratic values in an intelligible, updated way for them, for their relatives left behind in the countryside, and for more recent emigrants from European nations. The circle's ideology, with its American socialist underpinning, certainly kept in mind lower-class viewers, but never exclusively. As members strove to gain and represent the broadest possible American audience for art and culture, they necessarily—and ironically—employed some design strategies similar to those of contemporaneous commercial artists. These early modernists viewed their artworks not as the means of division or social control that art has sometimes become at darker moments in Western history, but as potential mediators of class and sectarian interests.

6

THE CITY

THE WRITINGS OF THE STIEGLITZ CIRCLE, in striking agreement, praise all the moods of nature, whether rural or urban; but they both celebrate and damn the city. Each of these attitudes had a long genealogy, rooted in religious ideas: the powerful notion of the holy city and biblical descriptions of Babylon.

In faithfully recording their ambivalence about the city, the Stieglitz circle represented a transformation in the contemporary experience of the urban scene. Even as they saw possibilities for new models of social order and new kinds of human cooperation, they also recognized that cities threatened individuals with physical harm, confusion, and (at worst) loss of identity. The Janus-faced city invited paradoxical, contradictory interpretations. The opening paragraph of "The American Year," an essay Waldo Frank wrote in 1921 and included in his *Salvos* in 1924, superbly exemplifies how the early modernists use the rhetorical opposition:

> From my writing table I look south over the Hudson River. Cherry and plum and peach in bloom throw pelts of colored flame through the warm mist of the sun. The river rolls beside its western wall of palisading blue, down twenty miles within my sight. Here, it turns sharply and is gone. Another twenty miles, I know, and it is flowing free and serene beside the turmoil, beside the shrillness, beside the fevers of New York.
>
> There, millions of men and women live in a constant bout of jostling one another's souls. And among them, hundreds with sharp eyes and reaching minds paw over the mental and

> vocal products of each other . . . purr or snarl, nestle or claw in an agitation which they are sure sums up the cultural activity of the country.[1]

In cleverly juxtaposed paragraphs, the image of urban ferment slaps hard Frank's depiction of rural beauty and calm. The author's rural outpost betrays his desire to avoid the competitive compulsions of city life.

But in the next paragraph, Frank pictures New York as "the clearing house of the nation's intellectual products. There are other centers of exchange and valuation," he admits.

> But New York leads. . . . [I]f one takes note of these ranks of pundits, critics, popes, of these hierarchies of genius and of prophecy, one must recognize by all its sounds and odors the cultural Capital: the Metropolis: the sort of overnervous human complex which doubtless once was Jerusalem, Athens, Alexandria, Rome—and which today is Paris and Berlin.
>
> Add to your list: New York.[2]

New York thus is a New Jerusalem, a holy city. Frank's enthusiasm for the city was more specifically an interest in its artistic community, in which he participated actively. New York is hallowed for both Frank and Paul Rosenfeld, because it is filled with artistic saints, who have little relation to the urban environment per se. Cultural evolution relied more on how artists refigured that environment than on the attributes of the place. In Rosenfeld's *Port of New York* (1924), the city appears blessed by the presence and influence of fourteen artists. In his epilogue, he tells the astonishing results of that influence: "The city is a center like every other point upon the circumference of the globe. The circle of the globe commences here, too. The port of New York lies on a single plane with all the world to-day. . . . The sun is rising overhead, the sun which once shone brightly on Europe alone and threw slanting rays merely upon New York. The sun has moved across the Atlantic."[3] New York City was apotheosized by the talents of its artist "achievers," to use Whitman's term. Rosenfeld asserts that New York's redemption depends on the transformative powers of art, and his own prose provides an example of the very transformation he describes. He metaphorically creates a halo of cultural light where before there had been only "slanting rays," demonstrating both artistic virtuosity and the function of image making in a society. As far as Rosenfeld and Frank were concerned, New York had entered the spotlight of the international cultural scene.

Although Stieglitz's view of nature remained essentially the same, his perspective on the city surely changed. The differences can be traced in the alterations in tone and point of view in his New York photographic series. The transformation of the photographer's attitude toward urban areas in general seems to have changed his approach to New York scenes as well as the look of the photographs themselves. While his prewar views tend to be optimistic, the postwar photographs praise New York less. The shift to New Realism altered the content as well as the form of Stieglitz's work (just as paintings by other artists in the circle changed with the new mode of representation, even when the nominal subject remained constant).

Though visual artists and critics were proud of New York City's recent cultural progress, they judged other aspects of the city and its dwellers unacceptable. Even as these cultural workers strove to produce works that would better society, the impersonal forces of industrialism threatened their own moral and physical stamina. An especially relevant and poignant passage begins Waldo Frank's chapter on New York in *Our America* (1919). Anyone who has seen Fritz Lang's ingenious 1926 film *Metropolis* will find Frank's image familiar:

> New York is a resplendent city. Its high white towers are arrows of will: its streets are the plowings of passionate desire. A lofty, arrogant, lustful city, beaten through by an iron rhythm. But the men and women who have made this city and whose place it is, are lowly, are driven, are drab. Their feet shuffle, their voices are shrill, their eyes do not shine. They are different indeed from their superb creation. Life that should electrify their bodies, quicken them with high movement and high desire is gone from them. And if you seek that life, look to the flashing steel and stone that stands above them, look to the fierce beat of their material affairs.[4]

But these oppressed individuals are not workers, as in Lang: they are the middle-class owners and operators of the businesses and industries of the city. Frank saw the middle class's participation in uncreative, routinized, and mechanical processes of production as the ruin of their psyche and their creative potential.

Paul Rosenfeld, in "The City with a Glance at Honegger," one of the critical essays on visual and literary works in his book *By Way of Art* (1928), both describes and decries the city's effect on him. Here he condemns the urban experience as alienating:

> It was the city. . . . All day indeed it had been closing on me, the measly strait-jacket of self-feeling, binding me ever closer to myself until I touched myself and myself alone. Around me there had appeared hordes of hostile exclusive individuals. And in the midst of them I had felt solitary, defensive and oppositional. . . . Twenty-four hours had done it; twenty-four hours of the city and its rootless, jumbled being. Measly self-awareness, self-palpation, defensiveness, were the form of its disorder and alienation from earth and her cycles.[5]

After returning to New York City from one of his usual retreats (his own Connecticut farm or Stieglitz's family home at Lake George), he finds that it takes only a day of contact with city dwellers—people with no ties to him of family, support, or friendship—to make him feel solitary and distant.

Rosenfeld's "hostile exclusive individuals" are doubtless the same middle class described by Frank. Rosenfeld judged their particular individualism odious: a narrow, narcissistic self-interest (far from Whitman's "perfect individualism") in which shared interests or the good of the larger civic community had no part. Both Frank and Rosenfeld focused on the alienation that they believed cities fostered. The alternative notion of self to which circle members aspired was inclusive, to the point of being transnational.[6]

As Rosenfeld's criticism also suggests, circle members thought urbanites' "alienation from earth and her cycles"—their estrangement from the natural environment and the processes of nature—the source of all other baneful consequences of living in a city. Clearly, the antidote to the dispiriting effect of the city was nature. In "The City" Rosenfeld proposed specific solutions: "To avoid this disconnection from life, then I had hesitated coming to New York; not because of the oaks regal and ruddy over the fields! They had been mere symbols of the freedom of the heart where ragged chains of hills and out-spreading skies, and night and cold and color lift the burden of his life from the individual, and make him conscious of forces beyond himself" (p. 184). Sherwood Anderson's stories express the same faith in nature that prompts us humans to ponder our place in the broader scheme of things, gives us opportunities to see our role on a universal stage. Such an encounter leaves us with an expanded view of self. Indeed, Anderson asked Frank, "Is it not likely that when the country was new and men were often alone in the fields and forests, they got a sense of bigness outside themselves that has now in some way been lost?"[7]

Sherwood Anderson must figure large in any consideration of the Stieglitz circle's use of rural and urban imagery. In their own mythopoetic self-representations, he mediated between nature and the city. They could turn to him—born in a rural midwestern community—for firsthand knowledge of rural ways; he seemed at times (to Frank, Rosenfeld, and Stieglitz) to personify the social codes of the countryside. Like other circle members, Anderson held varying views of the city. He recognized that a metropolis such as New York, in its role as a cultural center, could be the vital core of the nation. He was not so quick, however, to place New York in that position—like Whitman, Anderson often expressed the belief that the future cultural mecca of America would be located in its heartland. But he agreed that the metropolis held America's cultural promise. He, at least, had seen enough of actual small-town ways and petty competitions to resist idealizing them. Anderson wrote in his memoir, "To me an American provincial, wandering occasionally to New York, always a mere guest there, New York is already beautiful." Coming to New York from the Midwest, Anderson, like any culturally minded tourist, was highly sensitive to the aesthetics of New York, in particular its strident early modern architecture. But like others of the circle, Anderson objected to the city's pace: "Faster and Faster. Faster and Faster. Speed. Speed. The life of buildings in New York became not nine years but nine days, nine hours, nine minutes, nine seconds."[8]

Although the height of New York's building boom (which both embodied and symbolized the growth of the city's businesses and industries) had occurred in the 1910s, during both the 1920s and 1930s routine city life was interrupted by periodic architectural assertiveness. In those times, the sense that "things" were getting out of control must have pressed especially hard on the engaged observer. Rosenfeld concludes "The City" with a passage that functions as a prayer, a traditional response to threatening cultural experiences with no intelligible historical analogues. Prayers seek aid for communities of believers who are trying to persevere in the face of uncertainty. Some, like Rosenfeld's, incorporate an imagined happy ending:

> Certainly, men would eventually live in cities as in nature, sympathetic to eternal rhythms and stretched beyond themselves. There were purplish rainbow nights when it was possible to look down on a New York waiting with prodigious building masses, Aztec man-made mountains like altars and like headless gods, and sign-illuminations floating loose in mid-heaven, and feel its summons to an individual able to think in terms transcending his own person. (pp. 184–85)

New York and other American urban centers, Rosenfeld hopes, might someday inspire in the human psyche feelings of sublimity like those imparted by the natural world. He awakens from this Whitmanian dream to the present moment and reflects: "But as I reembarked on my train for the hill and the lake under the mountains, and the old things favorable to man, I knew that for myself and most of my fellows in this generation between the old soil and the new, a day spent out of New York was a day of living music" (p. 185).

The visual artists of the Stieglitz circle, in their landscape images, also expressed deeply divided feelings about the modern American environment, most obviously in citing the disparity between city and country. After Whitman, the country was consistently seen as the most salubrious environment, benefiting the human mind and body. The city, however, especially New York, was both the holy city and New Jerusalem and the locus of greed, unbridled competition, and cultural profiteering. Like the sociocultural criticism of circle writers, their visual images of nature evoke a markedly constant tone and those of the city, a continuing ambivalence. Because the visual arts have no tradition of depicting the city as damned, early modern painters and photographers had to invent the means.

As we have seen in Rosenfeld's *By Way of Art*, the Stieglitz group strongly opposed the city for fostering a deficient sense of identity in the individual, an isolated and estranged self. As Paul Strand's photograph *Wall Street, New York* (1915; figure 31) demonstrates, in the city the human presence is diminished—by Big Business, specifically. Here the Morgan Guarantee Trust Building becomes an emblem of capitalist interests in the U.S. economy. Strand's photo inveighs against the corporate structure that, having supplanted a more communal economic system, now was dominant from Wall Street all the way to the uptown gallery district.[9]

Charles Demuth, in *Business* (1921; figure 32), comments more enigmatically on the same subject. In a sense the work is a landscape, although the dominant image is a calendar, with a sequence of numbers in a grid at the upper right and a list of the

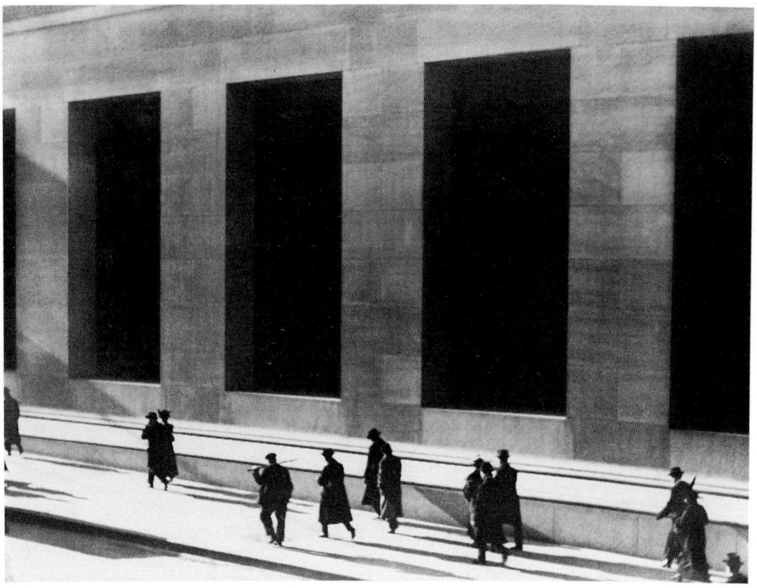

31. Paul Strand, *Wall Street, New York,* 1915, photograph. ©1971, Aperture Foundation, Inc., Paul Strand Archive.

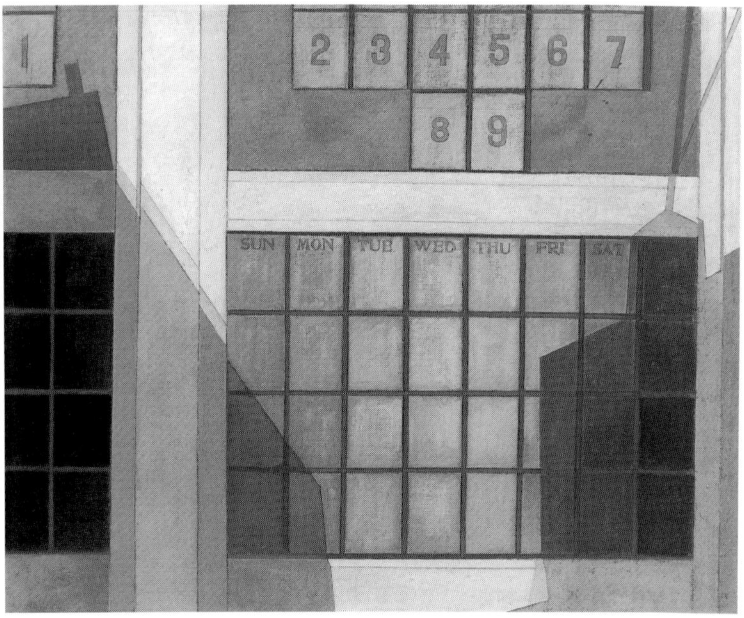

32. Charles Demuth, *Business,* 1921, oil on canvas, 20 × 24 ¼ in. Acquired 1949, The Art Institute of Chicago, Alfred Stieglitz Collection.

days of the week processing horizontally across the surface. The painting anticipates Jasper Johns's similarly inscrutable works of the 1960s featuring numerical sequences. Demuth also includes silhouettes of tall buildings with no architectural detail that give the illusion of being reflections on the picture surface, as if superimposed on the calendar. The shadows of buildings simultaneously call attention to and flatly deny the picture's traditional role of representing space.

But this painting (like much of Demuth's work) does more than make a statement about the subject identified in its title: it also makes a sarcastic remark. Viewers deduce the subtle content and meaning of *Business* only by piecing together the visual clues the artist provides for their amusement. The unusual colors that dominate the canvas—watermelon pink and gold—directly recall the colors of Renaissance religious frescoes, especially those of Fra Angelico, whose use of color, like Demuth's, was dulcet and poetic. To underscore this reference, the image of a cross, formed by the windowpanes through which the buildings of the industrial landscape are viewed, reminds us of the most potent emblem of the traditional church.

Business can be interpreted as mocking the exaltation of American business after the war. President Calvin Coolidge declared the mood at the time: "the man who builds a factory builds a temple. The man who works there, worships there."[10] Other works by Demuth, such as *Incense of a New Church* (see figure 50, discussed below), also make it their business to comment on America's newfound "religion." Rather than demonstrate Demuth's uncritical acceptance of the Coolidge ideology, they present homages that are tongue-in-cheek. To suggest the absurdity of the dominant American values, the paintings employ many of the formal devices of visual irony and satire introduced by Francis Picabia and Marcel Duchamp, who were involved with the Stieglitz circle gallery and publications in the 1910s.

Before further examining the visual images of the Stieglitz group that address the city and its economy, we must briefly consider another work of 1921, the year that Demuth created *Business:* the six-minute film *Manhatta,* collaboratively made by Paul Strand and Charles Sheeler. The film's title invokes a poem by Walt Whitman that is included in *Leaves of Grass,* the text strongly recommended by Waldo Frank as a model of social criticism. In fact, excerpts from the poem serve as subtitles to the visual imagery.[11]

Although we cannot be certain who was responsible for different segments of the film, the second half, which bears the unmistakable aesthetic stamp of Paul Strand, criticizes the effect of the urban environment on its human inhabitants. Not only does the sequence depict crushing swarms of humanity confined in urban thoroughfares, but the potent image of capitalist power, the Morgan Guarantee Trust, again surges up to dominate the American horizon. This comment on the forces controlling early-twentieth-century American life powerfully reiterates the view Strand expressed earlier in *Wall Street.* Surprisingly, this image in *Manhatta* contradicts Whitman's poem "Mannahatta," which celebrates the "million people—manners free and

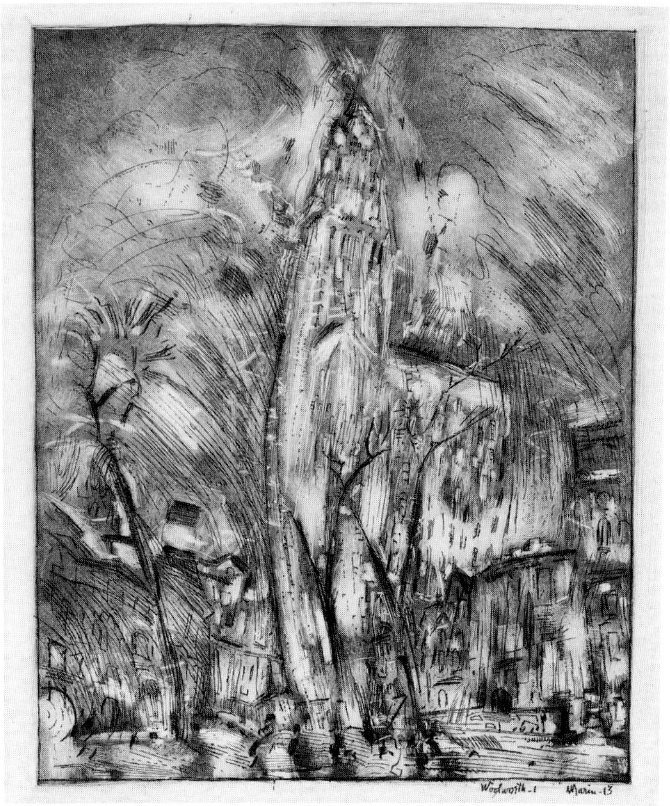

33. John Marin, *Woolworth, No. 1,* 1913, etching with monotype on japan paper, plate: 11 7/8 × 9 15/16 in. Avalon Fund, National Gallery of Art, Washington, D.C.

superb—open voices—hospitality—the most courageous and friendly young men."[12] In the film Whitman's happy citizens are long gone, their values seemingly laid to rest with their bones in the cemeteries depicted in one sequence. The early modern works of art, filmed or painted, democratically demand that viewers interpret them. *Manhatta,* like Demuth's *Business,* raises issues for public debate rather than presenting a dogmatic position of the artist.

Because John Marin's print of 1913 titled *Woolworth, No. 1* (figure 33)[13] is a prime example of the circle's prewar rhetoric, it provides an apt point of comparison for postwar works. Its mood is exuberant. The city is depicted as alive, its energy effectively conveyed by vigorous strokes of the stylus. Areas deliberately left unetched and unwashed on the plate complement the dark pen-strokes that form and highlight the swaying trees to each side of the protagonist, the Woolworth skyscraper. In this remarkable etching Marin undertakes not only to outdo his American predecessor James McNeill Whistler, but also to celebrate other American accomplishments. The skyscraper, after all, was America's unique contribution to early-twentieth-century art. Georgia O'Keeffe's oil painting *The Shelton with Sunspots* (1926; figure 34), created

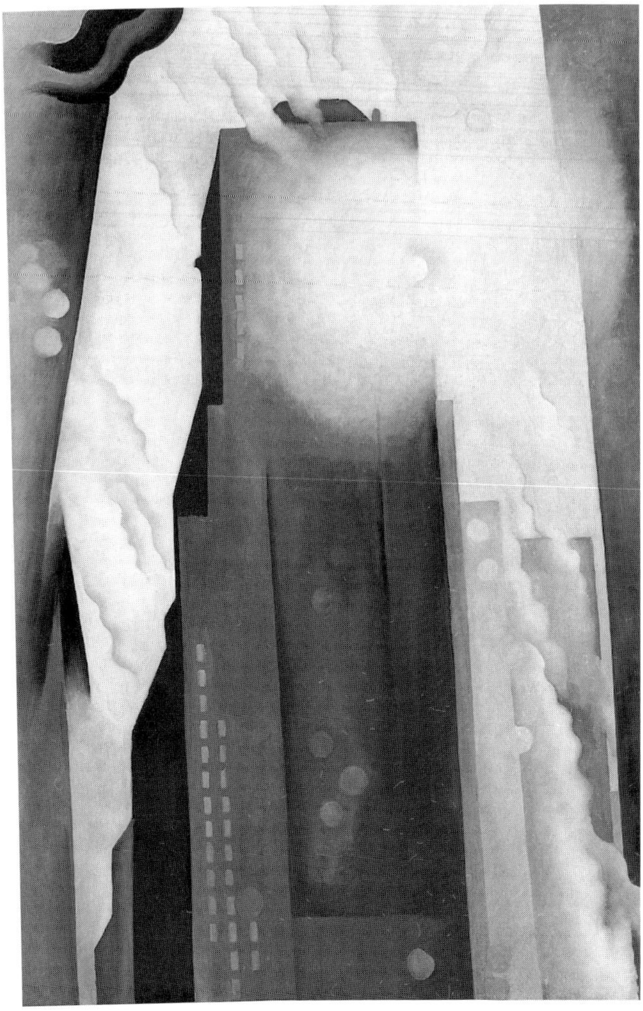

34. Georgia O'Keeffe, *The Shelton with Sunspots,* 1926, oil on canvas, 48 ½ × 30 ¼ in. Gift of Leigh B. Block, The Art Institute of Chicago.

a decade later, seems deliberately to recall, with its monochromatic palette of blacks, grays, and browns, Marin's early prints. The painting's viewpoint is an adjoining structure, about half the height of the Shelton Hotel. The tilted figure of the Shelton recalls an expressive device often used in Marin's early praises of urban architectural form.

O'Keeffe's work is a sober yet beautiful (and certainly novel and modern) rendition of "home." The Shelton Hotel served as the domicile-studio of the artist and her husband, Alfred Stieglitz, from 1925 to 1936.[14] An "aura," a halo marking the location of their small suite, appears at upper right. New York City's heat and fumes rise from the buildings to the sky, recalling how clouds hug mountainsides in more verdant locales. The vapors impart a sense of height and humanize the new cultural phenomenon of the modern building by suggesting its relation to nature. Like Marin's

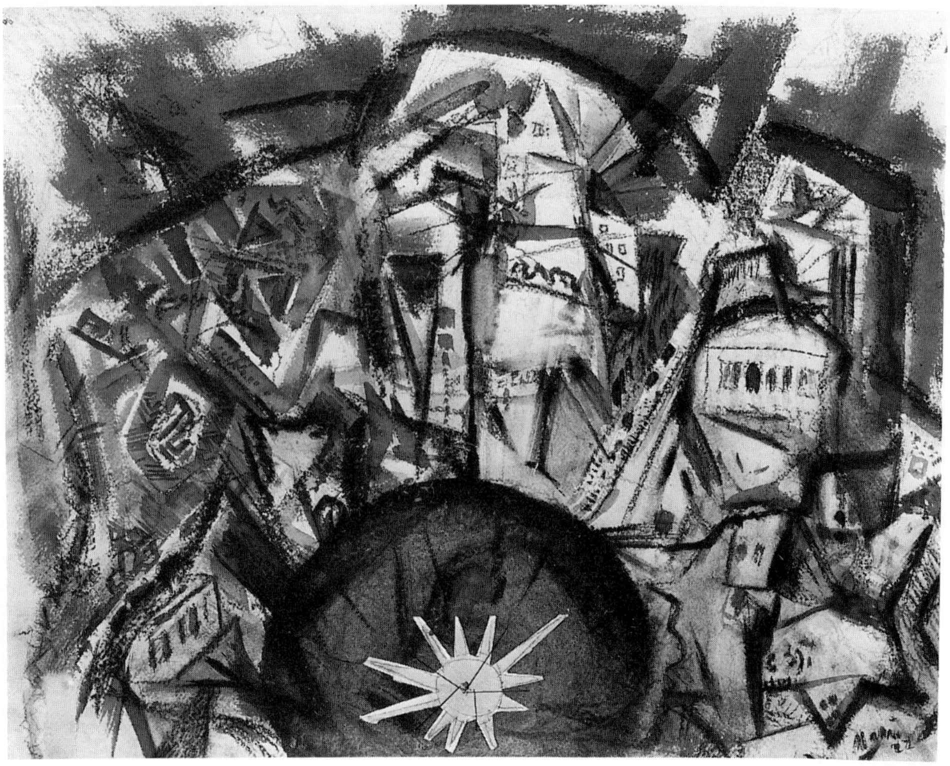

early investigations of the burgeoning New York scene that inspired O'Keeffe, *The Shelton with Sunspots* praises cultural creation. It also cleverly adds an autobiographical element, a reference to less publicly apparent cultural production: the city landscapes, both paintings and photographs, executed in suite 3003 of the Shelton.[15] While Marin's works of the 1910s were usually expressive, O'Keeffe's painting of the 1920s is less colored by subjective emotion, more sharp-focused and clear-sighted, as if the war had called forth the need for a new objective view.

Marin may have been the first to introduce the use of the unmixed colors red, white, and blue, a device that would become an important part of the circle's postwar repertoire. His *Lower Manhattan from the Top of the Woolworth Building* (1920; figure 35) is an early and especially well wrought example of this emblematic palette used effectively. Its depiction of two representative (yet anonymous) buildings of the New York City landscape is especially vibrant because the three colors are used in hot saturations, with red outlines and highlights that boldly defy the constraints often subscribed to by more conventional landscapists. The title explains the painting's message: Marin is looking down over "creation," over what human culture has wrought. The painter pronounces the urban scene both dynamic and worthy of interest and praise.

We might begin to think that Marin's paintings of urban architecture are uniformly

35. Opposite: John Marin, *Lower Manhattan from the Top of the Woolworth Building*, 1920, watercolor and charcoal on paper, 21 7/8 × 26 3/4 in. The Museum of Modern Art, New York, The Philip L. Goodwin Collection.

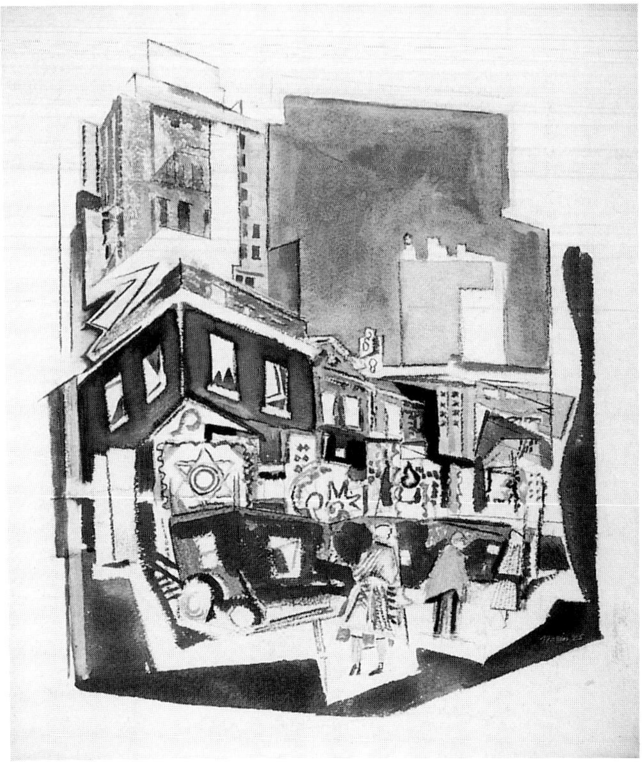

36. John Marin, *New York, 1925*, 1925, watercolor with charcoal, black crayon, and graphite, 20 5/8 × 17 1/4 in. Philadelphia Museum of Art, The Alfred Stieglitz Collection.

celebratory; but at least one contemporary art historian and critic suggested as early as 1924 that some cast New York City in a dim light. After viewing a number of Marin's watercolors at the Intimate Gallery (without, unfortunately, naming the specific works), Virgil Barker concluded: "Into his driving brush-slaps he concentrates all the confusion, all the noise, all the straining hurry with which New York assaults the nerves. Its buildings unite into a clanging paean of power run amuck."[16] Barker's interpretations depend heavily, no doubt, on his personal impressions of the city—but Marin depended on his viewers' bringing just that sort of experiential knowledge to his New York exhibitions. Barker's assessment does more than confirm our sense that Marin sometimes emphasizes the negative connotations of the modern city: it also demonstrates the critical participation through which Marin's meanings became accessible to contemporary viewers. While Marin could not expect a later generation of historians and critics to immerse themselves in the context of these works, most of his original audience had such knowledge at their feet.

Certain images that Marin produced in the mid- to late twenties also comment on early modern New York as undisputed capital of American advertising art. *New York, 1925* (1925; figure 36), a diagrammatic "map" of the urban landscape, is decorated with touches of red, yellow, and green that signify neither architectural embellish-

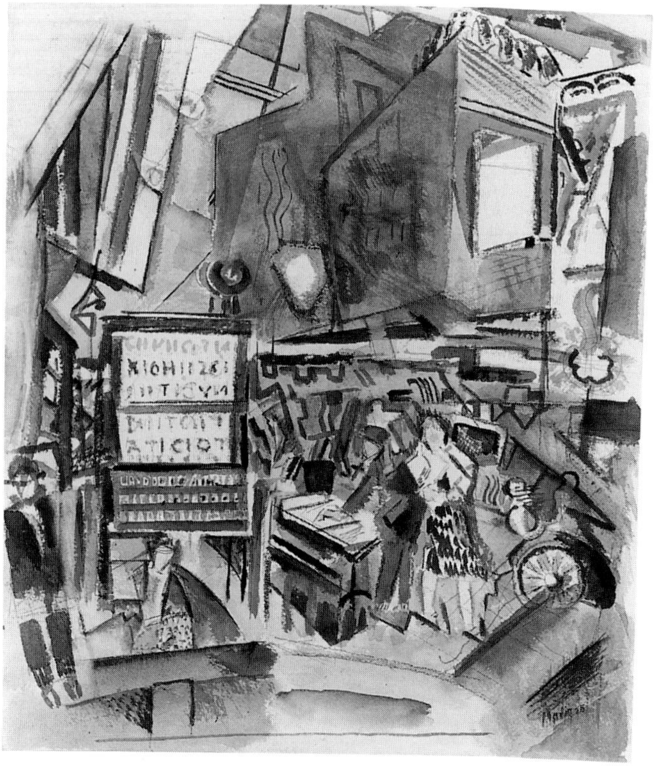

37. John Marin, *Street Crossing, New York,* 1928, watercolor and black chalk on paper, $26\frac{1}{4} \times 21\frac{3}{4}$ in. Acquired 1931, The Phillips Collection, Washington, D.C.

ment nor nature but advertising signs and goods on display. The watercolor deliberately mimics the style of contemporary graphic design; it could be a magazine cover illustration. Both the form and color of *New York, 1925* evoke New York's role as New World mecca of commercial art and the city's focus on commerce. Highly conceptual, the map declares that this is not a comfortably picturesque ethnic neighborhood. Postwar New York challenged landscape painters to invent new means of reporting and reacting to the changes they observed.

By 1928 Marin had found ways to incorporate more of his commentary on New York City into a single canvas. *Street Crossing, New York* (figure 37) also strikingly conceptualizes an urban landscape, but in a much less vibrant key. Below a passage of paint that cleverly suggests towering buildings, Marin presents the real subject of the work: three advertising signs whose deliberate indecipherability makes them generic emblems of graphic design. Unlike *New York, 1925,* which featured three static pedestrians, *Street Crossing* suggests the hustle and bustle that continues to impress visitors to New York. The impression of frenzied activity is sustained by numerous dashes, squiggles, and V-shapes in the right midground, a hieroglyphics the painter invented to suggest human movement (and perhaps city noise as well). Set against and thus

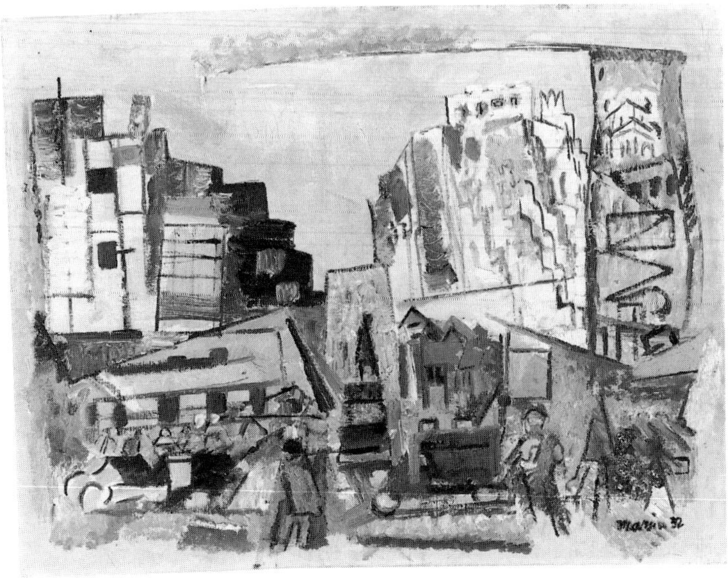

38. John Marin, *Bryant Square,* 1932, oil on canvas, 21 ⅝ × 26 ⅝ in. Acquired 1942, The Phillips Collection, Washington, D.C.

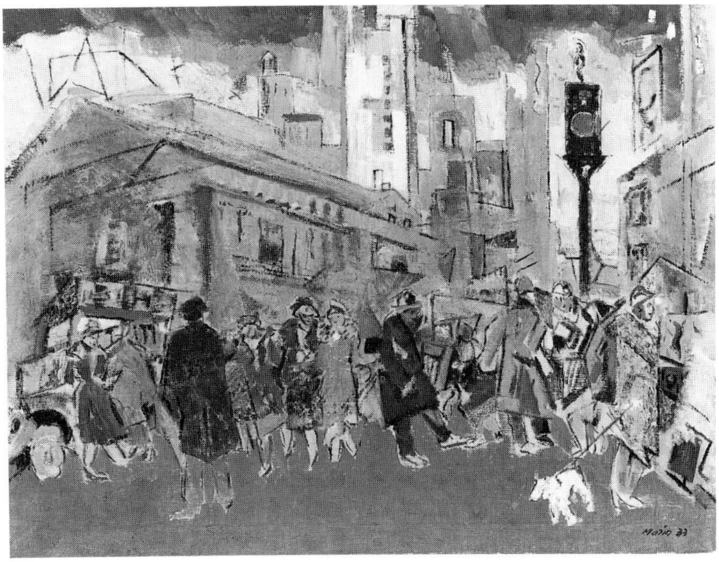

39. John Marin, *Pertaining to Fifth Avenue and Forty-second Street,* 1933, oil on canvas, 28 × 36 in. Acquired 1937, The Phillips Collection, Washington, D.C.

compared with the references to commercial art in the painting, these painterly glyphs constitute the virtuoso performance of a self-identified "fine" artist who nonetheless acknowledges the power, visibility, and accessibility of commercial art.

In paintings such as *Bryant Square* (1932; figure 38) and *Pertaining to Fifth Avenue and Forty-second Street* (1933; figure 39), Marin goes beyond speculations on the popular appeal of advertising art to consider the city as a place of human habitation.

Although the early critics took exception to the unaccustomed ugliness of Marin's pictures, when we examine the works closely we see that such anti-picturesqueness was quite deliberate. The unattractiveness accurately represents an idea of New York held by Marin and his colleagues from the late 1910s onward. In *Bryant Square,* for example, the dark tones connote lack of vitality. The suggestive "force" lines indicate the stress, the nervous energy, and by implication the imbalance of humans who inhabit the environment depicted, where architecture is not the crowning American achievement Marin celebrated in his earlier prints of the Woolworth and Singer buildings but a drab built environment (described with the acuity one finds in the contemporary writings of Lewis Mumford) that implies bleak life amid the crowded, homely forms whose antibeautiful shapes and unnatural colors Marin judges harshly. In his rural landscapes, he typically portrayed the mountains, islands, and ocean in balance at center stage. But in *Bryant Square* nothing is balanced: everything is on edge.

Similarly in *Pertaining to Fifth Avenue and Forty-second Street,* the tone, again exceptionally dark for Marin, gives clues to the content. Except for one fleeting glimpse of nature (a sun setting between the buildings in the background, right) the work is dominated by somber tones. A traffic light flashing green indicates that we are seeing New York on the go. And while the artist in his rural scenes applies paint thick and lush, here the surface texture mimics the lack of luster in the New York urban scene in 1933.

By taking a literal point of view in these works, Marin suggests that the towering, crowded city diminishes one's sense of identity and self-worth—as Rosenfeld had done in *By Way of Art.* The pedestrians included in the paintings strengthen this reading. Inhabitants of the city must move at a frenzied pace, always on the go. In the eyes of a painter who had chosen to live and work on a small private island off the coast of Maine, the modern city dweller led a diminished life. Marin's plain, unsensuous mode effectively conveys his negative impression of what the postwar city offered its inhabitants.

In addition to commenting on the alienation of the urban environment, Marin's works of the late twenties and early thirties document the pessimism brought on by the Depression. They record the effect of the 1929 crash on Americans, specifically on visual artists, whose incomes fell precipitously as almost everyone reduced purchases to essentials. But not all were downbeat in tone. One particularly fine example, *Region of Brooklyn Bridge Fantasy* (1932; figure 40), displays Marin's ability (which other circle members also demonstrate) to forget depressing circumstances in the process of making art. While New York and its inhabitants certainly appeared grim in the early thirties, older architecture still emblematized American achievement. And while Lewis Mumford criticized the current phase of American building in general, in *The Brown Decades* (1931) he singled out one historic structure, the Brooklyn Bridge, for high praise as a model of American artistry.[17] *Region of Brooklyn Bridge Fantasy* both seconds Mumford's view and acknowledges Whitman's earlier praise of Amer-

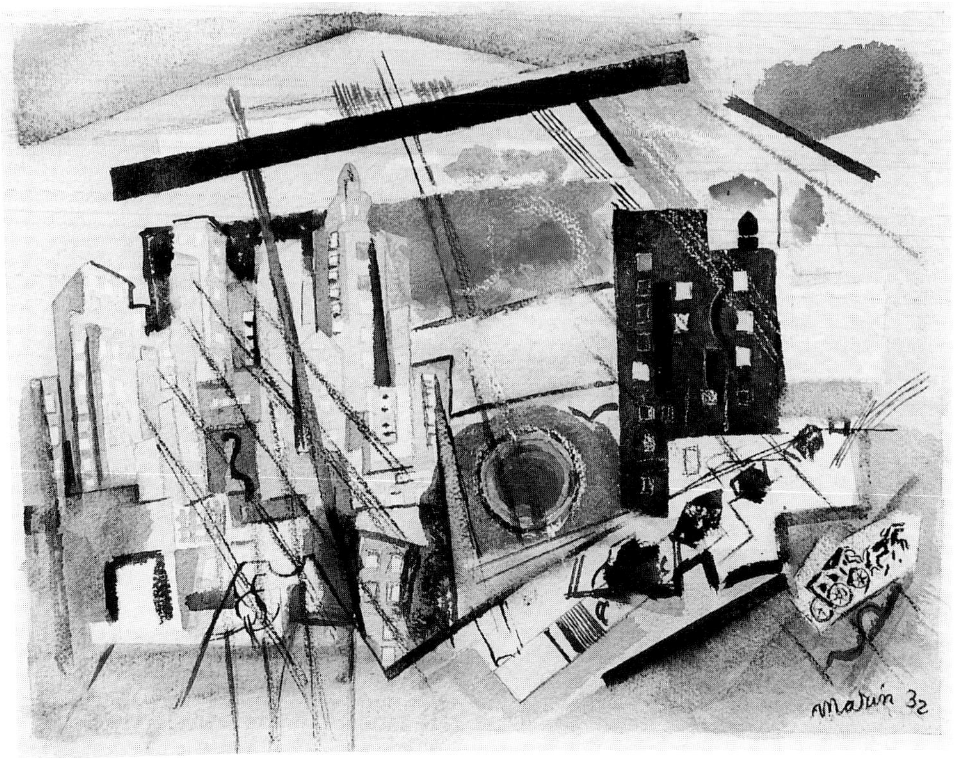

40. John Marin, *Region of Brooklyn Bridge Fantasy,* 1932, watercolor, sheet: 22 × 28 3⁄16 in. Purchase, Collection of the Whitney Museum of American Art, New York.

ican achievements (e.g., "Song of the Exposition" [1871]), including the bridge, which Marin himself had celebrated in artworks of the early 1910s. The watercolor is an energetic, multiperspectival view of the landscape of the bridge, with allusions to early European modernism in general and to the paintings by the French artists Sonia and Robert Delaunay in particular. The work's high color climaxes in the red solar orb depicted in the middle ground, near the center of the work. Its glow invigorates the whole composition.

At first it seems curious that Marin's vantage on the scene is distanced, with only spare reminiscences of the Brooklyn Bridge. This strongly suggests that the work is in fact a meditation on the past or, more accurately, pasts: both the time when the landmark was erected and the many times before when Marin had captured and celebrated the bridge in his art. Thus the horse and cart in the lower right of the picture are most likely included not because Marin saw them by the bridge in the 1930s but because they signify and memorialize more optimistic and simpler times in Amer-

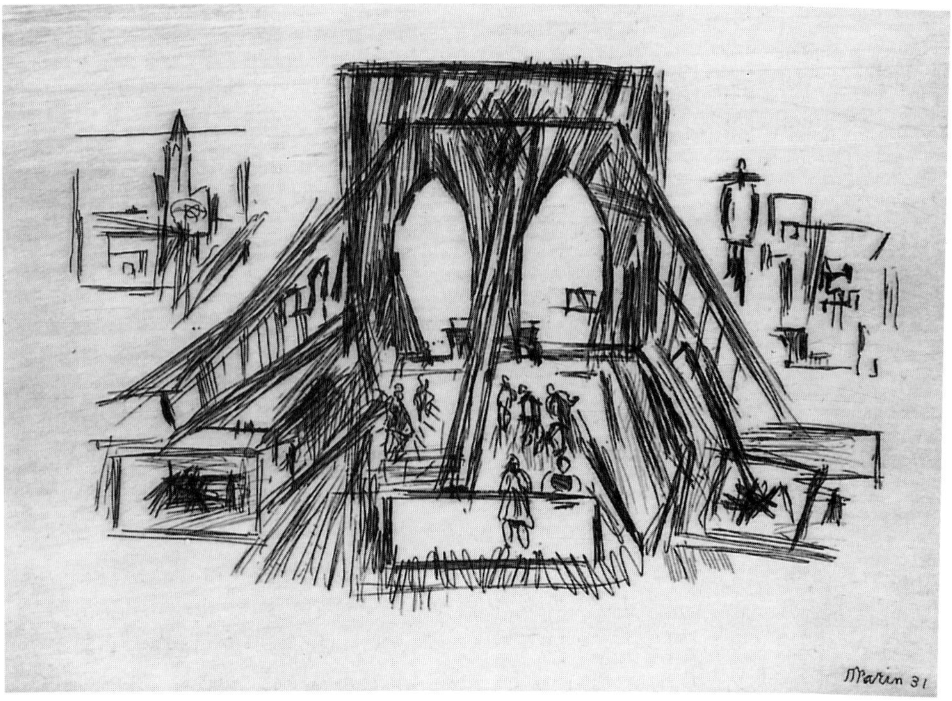

41. John Marin, *Approach to the Bridge*, 1931, etching printed in black, plate: 6 7/8 × 9 11/16 in. Gift of Abby Aldrich Rockefeller, The Museum of Modern Art, New York.

ica's past. In consciously reverting to the stylistic devices of early European modernism, Marin reflects on the development of his own creations, demonstrating the ascendancy of painting over architecture, now in eclipse. Such reflection, inspired in part by his early study of Whistler's Venetian prints, at times become overt. In some instances, Marin uses self-referential devices invented and employed by the nineteenth-century artist, in apparent homage. Thus the autobiographical content of the etching *Approach to the Bridge* (1931; figure 41) derives its subtle and understated tone from Whistler's late prints.

Hints to interpreting *Approach to the Bridge* are available on many levels. The average New Yorker seeing Marin's print would have had at least some familiarity with Whitman's treatment of the subject. Anyone who kept abreast of Mumford's reviews in the *New Yorker* or read his books of criticism would have brought that writer's views to bear on an interpretation, especially if the viewer knew of the critic's close relation to the Stieglitz galleries. Scholars with access to the correspondence between Stieglitz and the artists he regularly exhibited can note that "bridge" had special connotations for circle members. Stieglitz constantly assured his close associates that regardless of any turn of economic fortune, he would remain "on the bridge" supporting them—and "the bridge" became the group's private shorthand for whichever gallery Stieglitz was presently directing.[18]

The central image of the 1931 etching is the Brooklyn Bridge itself. And the permanency conveyed by the image of the bridge, so stable and prominent, is an element infrequently seen in the artist's oeuvre. The tone is especially solemn, for the image evokes a reverent mood more often associated with religious structures. Marin, like Lewis Mumford in *The Brown Decades,* on one level praises the architectural monument for its importance to American life. On a deeper level, also like Mumford, he celebrates the artistic achievement of yet another "builder," Stieglitz.[19] Both the private correspondence and published writings of the circle and its supporters suggest that this image records Marin's continuing reflection on his collaboration with Stieglitz and on their place as artists in Depression-era America. In the etching Marin judges his mentor's constructions (albeit in the realm of ideas and ideals, not steel and concrete) comparable to the physical bridge in their durability and their significance to American culture. Note that Marin includes small but important human figures in *Approach to the Bridge.* In the 1913 versions of the subject, Marin depicted two figures on the bridge; here seven fill the center of the image. These figures probably refer to the "Seven Americans" then exhibiting under the auspices of An American Place. The work's optimistic view rests on Marin's faith in the development of American art and his hopefulness about the role and status of the American artist in the modern world.

Art historians have charted the mood and content of Alfred Stieglitz's photographs of New York City along a simple trajectory from early celebratory prints to less optimistic later views,[20] but this account oversimplifies the photographer's engagement with the city. While an early work such as the acclaimed *City of Ambition* (1910) sustains the positive, energetic tone that the title suggests, precisely what is praised? Is it the city itself? If so, which aspect? If it is the architecture of the city, the emphasis is on human cultural achievement. Stieglitz in fact addresses all of these issues in his impressive production.

The correspondence of the circle during the twenties is useful for evaluating hypotheses about the works. Letters the members exchanged make clear that for all of them New York City was hell. In 1922 Rosenfeld wrote to Stieglitz: "The city is worse than futile. There is less than nothing doing, as far as I or anyone with whom I have spoken can see. We always seem to go deeper in a sort of Hades. . . . The world is breaking down, and there doesn't seem much of anything coming up." Three years later Stieglitz wrote to Anderson from Lake George: "I'm grateful for every moment that we are up here and not in that hellish place. New York."[21] Stieglitz's photographs reinforce this vision of the city.

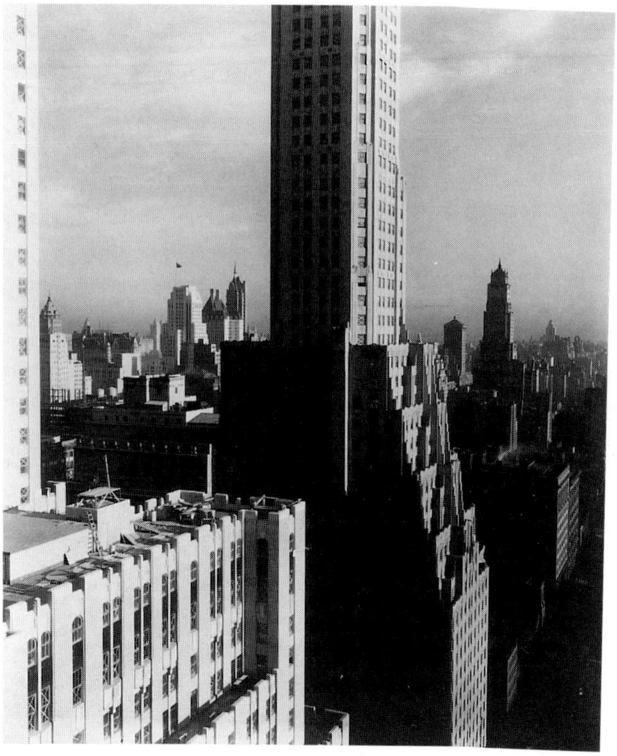

42. Alfred Stieglitz, *From the Shelton: Lower Part of the G.E. Building*, ca. 1931, gelatin silver photograph, 9 ½ × 7 ½ in. Philadelphia Museum of Art, The Alfred Stieglitz Collection.

Consider *From the Shelton: Lower Part of the G.E. Building* (ca. 1931; figure 42), a vertical city landscape. The subject is deliberately cut down to size, radically cropped; this reduction in stature directly opposes the artist's own earlier full views celebrating comparable urban structures. And the selective cropping of the central figure calls attention to the scale of New York City's buildings, demonstrating that they cannot be fully digested by the human eye or mind. In the photograph Stieglitz also reveals his own uncommon vantage point (in his home-cum-studio in the Shelton Hotel). This reading is buttressed by Stieglitz's correspondence, particularly a series of letters to Sherwood Anderson in 1925 that (like his photographs) record his evolving response to the contemporary urban scene. Stieglitz confided:

> New York is madder than ever. The pace ever increasing.—But Georgia and I somehow don't seem to be of New York—we live high up in the Shelton Hotel—for a while—maybe all winter—the wind howls and shakes the huge steel frame—We feel as if we were out at mid-ocean.
>
> We are indecently comfortable . . . warm rooms at will—hot water at all times—lots of air and beds that are dreams! And all with the feeling as if one were out at sea far away from all noises of City Life—and all its bustle and nervous tension.[22]

Admittedly the Shelton offered a privileged prospect. Stieglitz and O'Keeffe experienced the home-studio as a refuge as far removed from the hell of the city as Marin's island, conjuring up Marin's most familiar image of freedom, the sea.

Even when they are in their urban refuge, the image of Arcadia, of the soil, intrudes. Certain photographs, including *From the Shelton: Lower Part of the G.E. Building,* were taken not from the hotel suite but from its roof garden. Figuring the Shelton as a place of simple pleasure and quiet in the inferno of New York must have been irresistible to Stieglitz, who made every attempt to associate himself with various aspects of culture—even horticulture. Sherwood Anderson's and Jean Toomer's contributions to *America and Alfred Stieglitz,* the 1934 anthology celebrating the photographer and the circle, depict Stieglitz as a "City Plowman."[23] By literally stationing himself in the cultivated gardens high up in the Shelton Hotel, Stieglitz could claim, albeit with tongue in cheek, that his work came from the American earth.

By the late twenties it was not simply the attitudes of the artists but the face of the city itself that had changed. Sarah Greenough, in her catalogue *Alfred Stieglitz: Photographs and Writings,* perceptively sees in the later photographs Stieglitz's recognition

> that implicit in the constantly changing face of New York was a conflict, a tension, and an opposition of forces. A sense of conflict, or confrontation between man, nature, and the city had been an important element in his photographs of New York at the turn of the century. Although more subtly stated, it is still present in the 1930s photographs, in which the striking formal beauty of the skyscrapers seems at odds with their relentless growth, heedless of humanity. The skyscrapers are immaculate structures, but in Stieglitz's photographs they have little relationship to man, who is visible neither as their builder or inhabitant.[24]

Indeed Stieglitz's works (like the paintings of his colleagues), by omitting people, say much about the place of humans. Especially in the later photographs, this absence reads as a sense of loss. Numerous images of empty husks of pristine architecture mourn the loss of a community of feeling, of shared values. But Stieglitz's urban images contain much more. Greenough suggests that any analysis of the style of later Stieglitz photographs must acknowledge contemporary European modes, in particular de Stijl, as important influences.[25] One can see in the prints Stieglitz's intimate knowledge of European styles—but he adapted them for his own purposes. Certainly it seems highly unlikely that Stieglitz, so outspoken in sponsoring the postwar return to regional American subject matter, would uncritically embrace a theory of art like that of the de Stijl group, which advocated the reduction of nature's irregularities to geometric grids.

In the later Stieglitz photographic series, the choice of style itself becomes a main concern. The works clearly address the replacement of an old method of representation by a new one, especially in the pictures that have architecture as their subject. A stylistic shift took place in American architecture from 1927 to 1932 whose most visible change—and thus the change most accessible to the camera's lens—was the

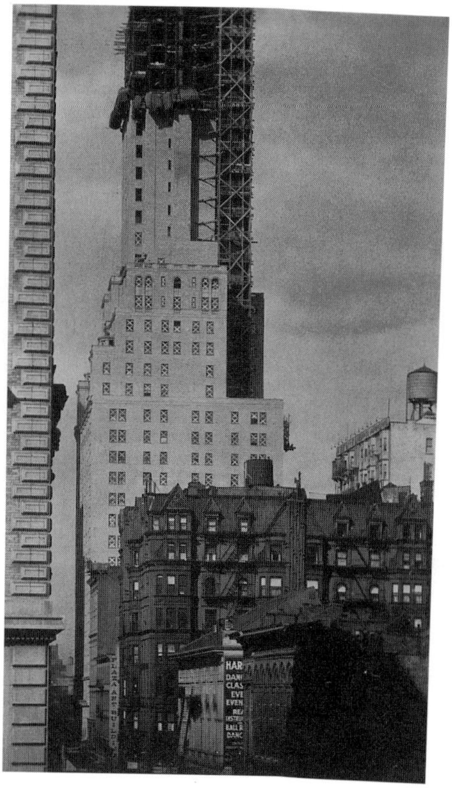

43. Alfred Stieglitz, *From Room "303" (Intimate Gallery), 489 Park Avenue, New York*, 1927, gelatin silver photograph. National Gallery of Art, Washington, D.C., Alfred Stieglitz Collection.

gradual move away from the elaborate ornamentation typical of early modern buildings, such as the Singer Tower (completed in 1907) or the Woolworth Building (completed in 1913), which had themselves supplanted romantic and classical forms. But more than style was changing, as one art historian has pointed out: "It was harsh economic reality—the fact that unornamented surfaces were considerably cheaper than those that required the additional labor of artisans—rather than the ideological triumph of reductivist modernism . . . that brought about the demise of Art Deco, the 'last of the decorated styles.'"[26] In his postwar photographs Stieglitz both documents these changes in architecture and meditates on their meaning for the arts. In studying new buildings on the rise, he ruminates not only on the art of architecture but also on photography and his own accomplishments in the arts.

We see such multilayered musings in Stieglitz's photograph titled *From Room "303" (Intimate Gallery), 489 Park Avenue, New York* of April 1927 (figure 43). In it an old, human-scale brownstone building, its edges rounded by hand carving, is compared with a towering modern skyscraper. The newer structure is so tall that it eludes framing. That the photographer preferred the older building is emphasized at the left edge by his careful inclusion of a row of timeworn bricks to frame his

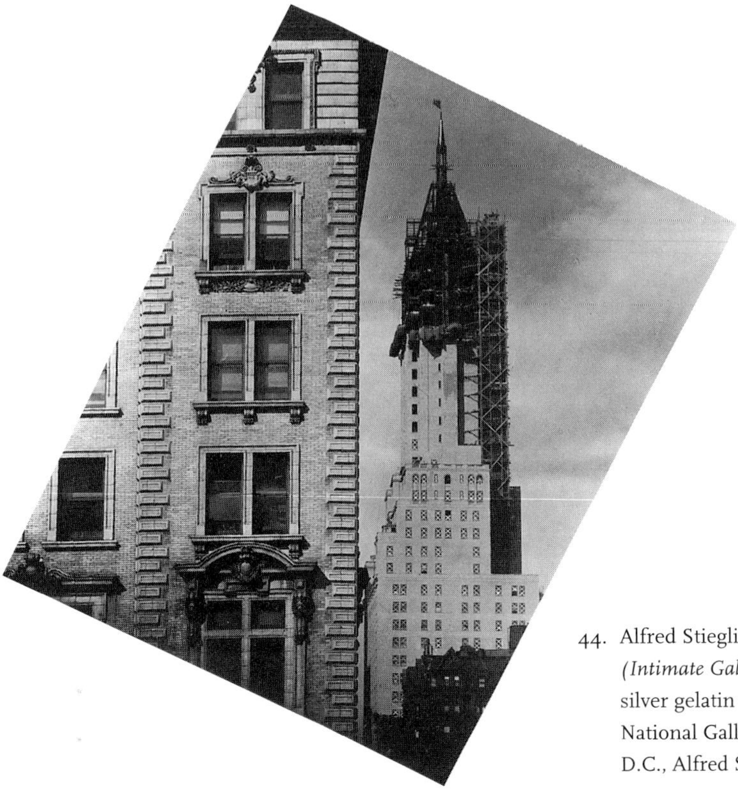

44. Alfred Stieglitz, *From Room "303" (Intimate Gallery), New York,* 1927, silver gelatin developed-out photograph. National Gallery of Art, Washington, D.C., Alfred Stieglitz Collection.

image, which would have been echoed by his customary handcrafted wooden frame.

From Room "303" (Intimate Gallery) pointedly refers to the stylistic battle raging in- and outside the Intimate Gallery. And (like some of Marin's paintings of New York) it also refers to the advertising signs that had begun to proliferate in the city. Stieglitz deliberately admits to his composition three such signs, telling ones. One of them, partially depicted in the foreground slightly left of center, announces dance classes at a ballroom and can be construed as a reference to that traditionally high-status art form. A second sign, which clearly spells out "up the street," could have referred to the Intimate Gallery, then the destination of the Stieglitz circle's art. Stieglitz's selected angle enabled him to include almost the entire wording of a third advertisement that, in its style of lettering, emphasized the last two words of the place-name "Plaza Art Building." In addition to offering visible proof that postwar New York is embellished with letters, Stieglitz transforms the commercial art forms into fine art by using the sign's proclamations for his own purposes. And he calls the viewer's attention punningly to his appropriations, his "building" of art. There is unquestionably more dada playfulness than de Stijl idealism in these views.

Certainly Stieglitz's *From Room "303" (Intimate Gallery), New York* (1927; figure 44) addressed the stylistic shift taking place in the art of architecture and the role of the de Stijl movement in that transition. The image is uniquely arresting in Stieglitz's oeuvre; by tipping the camera diagonally he framed a skyscraper under construction as a geometric subject. The resulting diamond-shaped image unmistakably refers to similarly structured paintings by de Stijl cofounder Piet Mondrian.[27] A U.S. flag flaps from the scaffolding of the building-in-progress, as if to alert viewers that a style native to the Netherlands is wielding its influence on American soil. But the photograph is hardly an homage to Mondrian or to the design aesthetic that he (to this day) represents. Conceived in an ironic and critical mode, it rejects the value of the new prefab building techniques that supplanted the one-of-a-kind, location-specific construction of the earliest skyscrapers lauded in the influential theories of Frank Lloyd Wright.

The older American architecture, represented as marginalized by its left-of-center placement in the photograph, is redeemed through a close reporting of every feature of the structure. The careful rendering of detail and the building's foreground placement show that it has not yet been superseded. Stieglitz's camera scrutinized most closely the older building's windows, with their beautifully hand-ornamented frames embellishing the flat surface with reminiscences of the natural world. The photograph effectively compares the lush, sensuous, eye-pleasing surface (comparable to that of a Marin painting) with the structure-in-progress. The new model, slender and unadorned by detail, looks unworthy to compete with the old. One cannot miss the photographer's implication that the circle's picture making—with its emphasis on nature, sensuosity, and craft—will withstand close scrutiny. These images impart an ethos of creative practice, not just a commentary on models of architecture.

Writers in the circle shared Stieglitz's and Marin's feeling that the modern city cannot sustain the desired quality of human life and, more particularly, Stieglitz's critique of the newest brand of European modernism infecting American urban architecture. The arguments were expressed most passionately and persuasively by Lewis Mumford, who bitterly opposed the new directions of urban architecture and city planning. Reinforcing the regionalist vision of the Stieglitz circle, Mumford prescribed the decentralizing of American cities in a series of articles titled "The Theory and Practice of Regionalism," published in the *Sociological Review* in 1927 and 1928.[28] As we have seen, in *The Brown Decades* Mumford celebrated Stieglitz as a "builder" of culture whose accomplishments in American art were comparable to those of Frank Lloyd Wright. Mumford elsewhere made the case that the urban crush in large American cities like New York not only deprived inhabitants of dignity but also, worse, made for depraved art.[29] It was just this type of cultural depravation that Stieglitz circle visual artists attempted to redress through their regular public exhibitions.

In such works as *From An American Place Looking Southwest* (1932; figure 45), Stieglitz dispelled the illusion that the latest vogue in building techniques had value. This photograph also refers to Stieglitz's art-making activity, itself a process of cul-

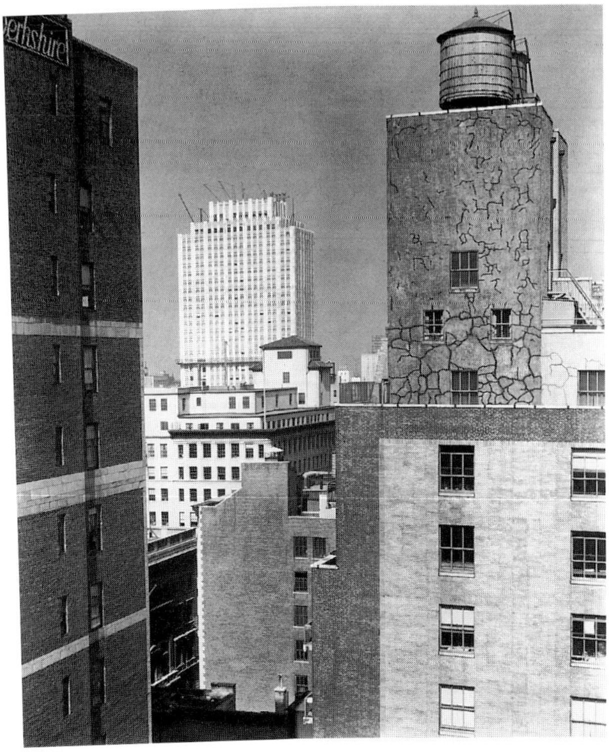

45. Alfred Stieglitz, *From An American Place Looking Southwest*, 1932, gelatin silver photograph. National Gallery of Art, Washington, D.C., Alfred Stieglitz Collection.

tural criticism. At the same time, the work seems to allude to certain paintings by Charles Demuth and John Marin. Three buildings, each with its own distinct character, inhabit this pictorial world. The building in the background, the least distinct, is nondescript. The one to the right is distinguished by a series of ugly cracks, like varicose veins. These signs of premature aging in the anthropomorphized structure lend credence to Stieglitz's belief that the new trend in urban architecture will fail the ultimate test of art: the test of time. The two water towers on its roof remind the viewer of Demuth's works, which frequently depict these forms that help conserve a natural resource (see below). Marin's landscapes are recalled by the building on the left, not just because it includes an advertising sign but also because that sign reads "Berkshire"; Marin often painted the image of the Berkshire mountains. Modern buildings that Stieglitz judged unworthy as art in themselves are thus reconstructed into art by his photograph, which transmutes them into city mountains.

From My Window at the Shelton Looking Southeast and *From the Shelton* (figures 46 and 47), both of 1931, share a different agenda. *From My Window*, a highly poetic version of New York City, deliberately recalls the tone of Stieglitz's early prints. Like his other works of the period, it speaks of the architecture of the city; but this time in praise. The protagonist of the photograph is a ziggurat-derived structure. We can guess

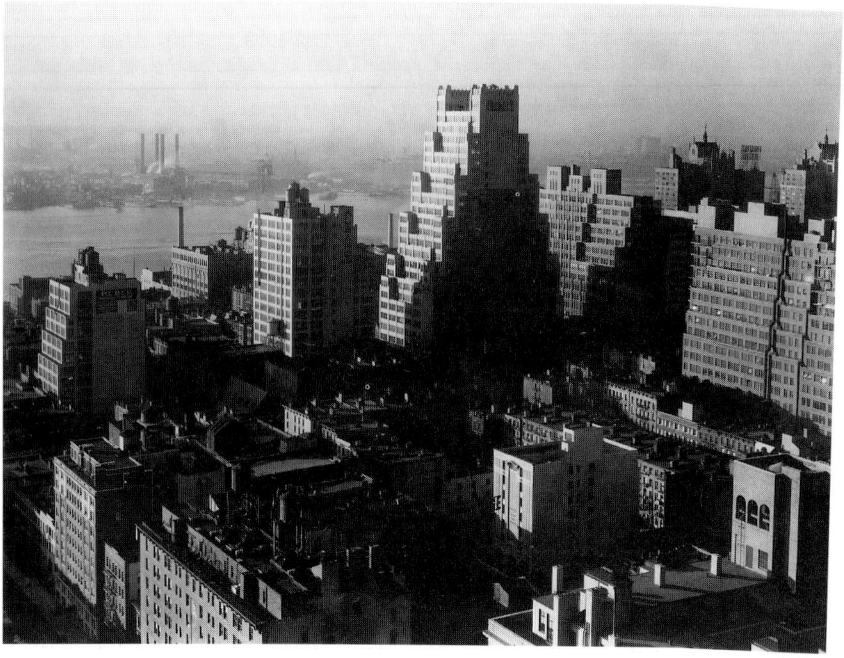

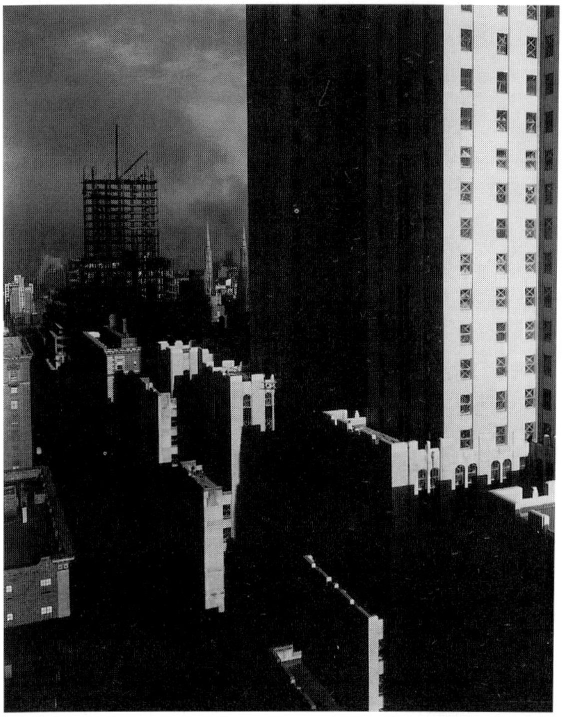

46. Alfred Stieglitz, *From My Window at the Shelton Looking Southeast,* 1931, gelatin silver photograph. National Gallery of Art, Washington, D.C., Alfred Stieglitz Collection.

47. Alfred Stieglitz, *From the Shelton,* 1931, silver gelatin developed-out photograph. National Gallery of Art, Washington, D.C., Alfred Stieglitz Collection.

that its form appealed to Stieglitz because the deliberate historical reference distinguishes it from the anonymous minimal shapes of the modern structures he disliked. A fraction of river landscape (in the left background) and a factory building boxed in by four majestic smokestacks, billowing plumes, are discernible. Even industry is rendered poetically here, as part of the vast energies of the metropolis shown under the control of art. Stieglitz's device of capturing the city at an angle humanizes the gridded pattern, turning Waldo Frank's abhorred "straight streets" into a lyrical statement.[30] Stieglitz claims, by his production of the photograph itself as much as by its highly selective view, that a photographer can create structure quite as successfully as the architect and city planner. And he addresses the issue of preservation: a well-conceived, insightful photographic style, like a good building style, will endure, be recognized, and be resurrected.

From the Shelton renders one of Stieglitz's overriding concerns in his postwar series in a uniquely beautiful fashion. The theatrical chiaroscuro of the buildings of the foreground, black shadows against bright sunlight, combine with the natural, spectacular lighting effects of the stormy sky—large, dark rain-bearing clouds circle the top of a skyscraper under construction in the left background—to create a highly dramatic moment. By conveying this impression so clearly, Stieglitz demonstrates that one must have a concrete scheme in mind before undertaking any design, whether of a building or a photograph. Another element in this photograph is the twin spires of an old church, rising just to the right of the large new building. The unfinished structure overwhelms the symbol of spiritual power and community in both mass and scale. But while dark clouds above the building-in-progress are threatening, the clouds above the spires are bright. Stieglitz's vision here recalls a famous nineteenth-century commentary, *The Course of Empire,* a series of works by the Hudson River School landscapist Thomas Cole on the fate of human structures made hubristically in the face of menacing nature. Although attracted to the historical narratives of the Old Testament,[31] Stieglitz does not employ an image of swift divine retribution. Rather (like Cole) he suggests that the punishment for a people gone astray will be slow but sure, as they fall under a natural process of decline.

John Marin similarly uses architectural construction to figure change itself, specifically one in the structure of the arts that Stieglitz and the circle were working to bring about. In *Skyscrapers in Construction, No. 1* (1930; figure 48), for example, an homage to the photographs of his friend and patron, the focus is divided, resulting in a more complex composition than is usually found in his earlier prints. These are not building "portraits"; and unlike in some of his other later landscapes, Marin neither vignettes the view nor angles the buildings. Instead, he refers to the "straight" approach of contemporary photographs by Stieglitz.

Charles Demuth's oil paintings of the architectural structures of his hometown of Lancaster, Pennsylvania, also reference and pay homage to Stieglitz's New York views, both in their subject (historic Lancaster buildings) and in their striking flatness. More-

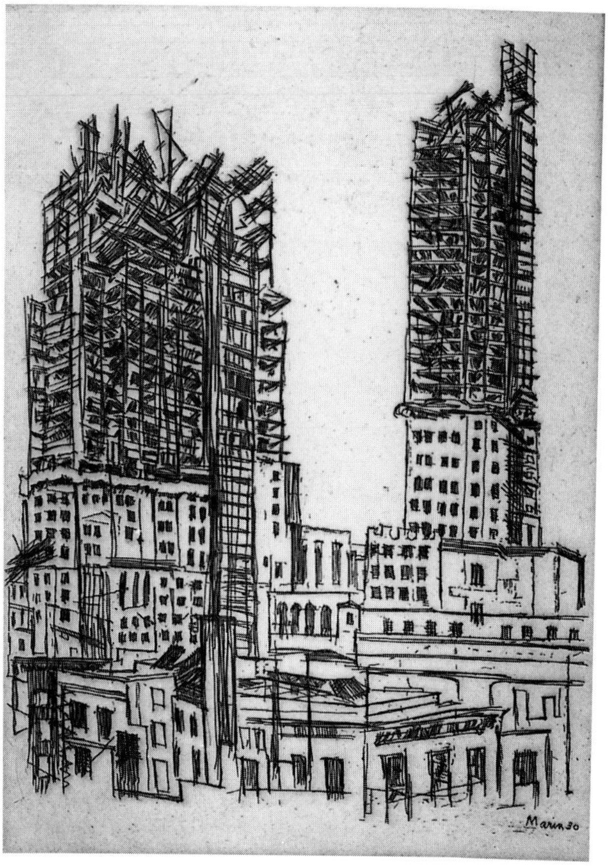

48. John Marin, *Skyscrapers in Construction, No. 1,* 1930, etching printed in black, plate: 9 15/16 × 6 13/16 in. Gift of Abby Aldrich Rockefeller, The Museum of Modern Art, New York.

over, Demuth's decision to inform his oils with properties of a different medium has another level of autobiographical significance: his father was an amateur photographer who documented Lancaster in a number of photographic series.

The Tower (After Sir Christopher Wren) (figure 49) was made about 1920, the year that marked Demuth's formal entry into the Stieglitz cooperative. The title leaves little doubt that the painting is about architecture per se as well as the history of architectural form. By comparing the rooftops of modern Lancaster dwellings with the prominent Wren-style tower of an old colonial church, Demuth celebrates the distinctiveness of the early form. He praises the ingenuity of its design in his equally ingeniously conceived composition. The painting established its own significance for the contemporary viewer by analogy, in much the same way that Stieglitz's photos promote the lasting value of the good design principles of early modern architectural styles. The painter, like the photographer, encouraged viewers to take a second look at earlier styles and rediscover the beauty in the cultural heritage left by indigenous (and often anonymous) artisans of previous generations. Marsden Hartley's essays prais-

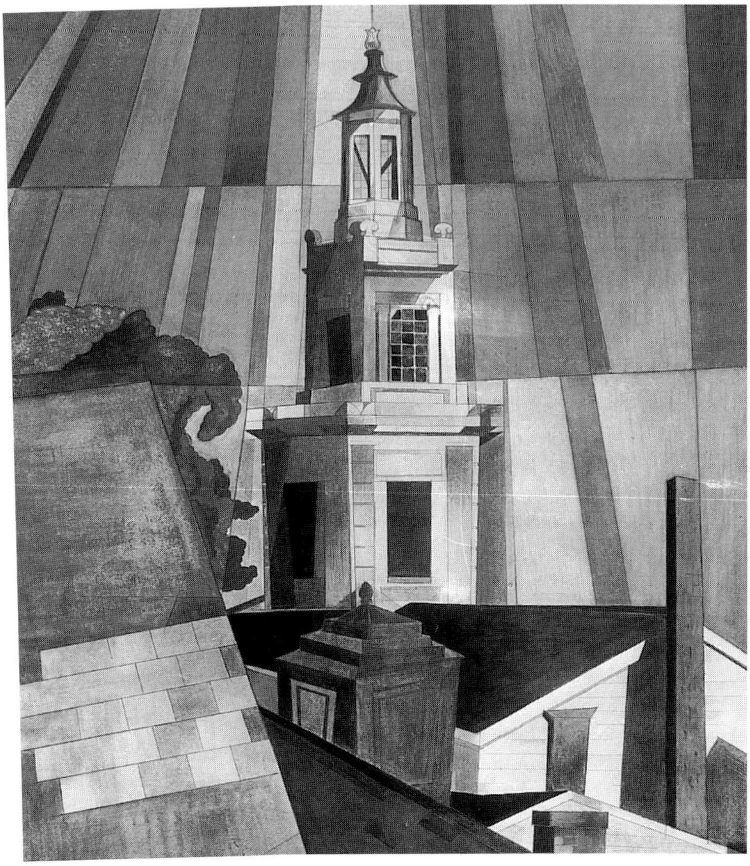

49. Charles Demuth, *The Tower (After Sir Christopher Wren)*, ca. 1920, tempera on pasteboard, 23 ¼ × 19 ½ in. Gift of Ferdinand Howald, Columbus Museum of Art, Columbus, Ohio.

ing American folk art and its meaning for contemporary culture had a similar purpose. And Demuth's chosen color scheme—red, white, and blue—reiterated and reinforced this metonymic device employed by other members of the exhibition group.

One of Demuth's most successful paintings of architecture is the eloquent *Chimney and Watertower* (1921), currently in a private collection. Here again he uses the colors of the U.S. flag to tell viewers that he was entering the unannounced competition among artists of the time to create "the great American artwork." The work's literal subject, the chimney and water tower of the Armstrong World Industry's Floor Plant building in Lancaster,[32] alluded to industry's important role in early-twentieth-century America. But Demuth was as worried as others in the circle about the harmful changes in American society caused by the dominance of industry, and these concerns are also prominent in this work. Because of its low point of view, for example, the vertical shapes depicted loom above the viewer. The composition admits no evidence of either human use or human craft, giving the effect of chilling precision. The New Realism is used here to criticize the mechanization of American

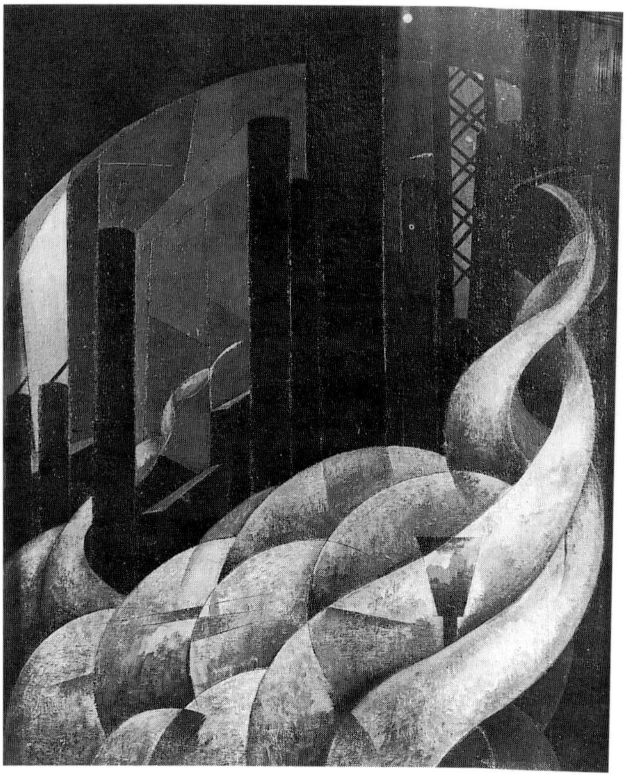

50. Charles Demuth, *Incense of a New Church,* 1921, oil on canvas, 26 × 20 ⅛ in. Gift of Ferdinand Howald, Columbus Museum of Art, Columbus, Ohio.

society. *Chimney and Watertower* shows that modern America had become a full-fledged industrialized society. The mechanical, rational, and inhuman elements of this transition that circle members attacked in books and essays are criticized in the painting as well, through both its reduced and flattened form and its spare realistic style. We are made to see that the unwanted societal changes have occurred not only in the city but also in "the province," Demuth's affectionate and joking epithet for his hometown.

In documenting Lancaster, Demuth plays the dual role of cultural anthropologist and artist, much as Hartley did in New Mexico. And like Stieglitz and Marin, he triumphs over the despised properties, quite intentionally and convincingly transforming them into artistic expression. These paintings speak out clearly in favor of American artistry, not industry. In conveying the same message, *Incense of a New Church* (1921; figure 50) depends, like some Stieglitz photos, on the church as a symbol of traditional values. But here the reference is verbal, not visual. The figure of speech had a more private meaning as well, since circle insiders often called their co-op galleries "a new church," to which they contributed icons. Indeed, though its overt subject is the Lukens Steel factory,[33] the work refers to the New York gallery.

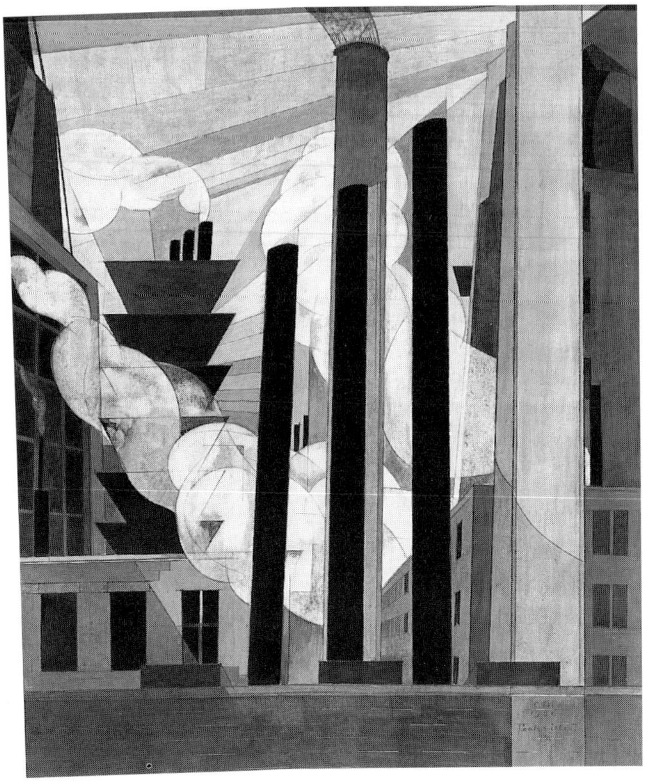

51. Charles Demuth, *The End of the Parade,* 1920, tempera and pencil on composition board, 19 7/8 × 15 3/4 in. Curtis Galleries, Inc., Minneapolis, Minnesota.

Rather than make a statement about the relationship between industry and religion, Demuth's painting, like *Chimney and Watertower,* demonstrates that the true new American church is art, not industry.

In *Incense of a New Church* Demuth transforms Lukens Steel, a nineteenth-century industrial plant, into an object of great interest and beauty by representing it from a provocative angle. The composition also frames the steel plant with a black arch that crowns the tops of the smokestacks and wittily recalls Renaissance religious icons, as if to underscore the artist's belief in America's cultural rebirth. The face of industry is altered most by Demuth's memorable handling of the clouds of smoke billowing from the dark stacks—the title's incense, wafting to perfume the painted air. Of course, only painted air could be perfumed by factory smoke: Demuth's sarcastic metaphor is extremely clever. Through humor, one of the primary weapons of the modern visual artist, he undercuts the seriousness of American industry.

In *The End of the Parade* (1920; figure 51), related to the later *Incense of a New Church,* Demuth can be seen sharpening his wit in preparation for his definitive statement on industry. Here too the ostensible subject is the Lukens Steel factory, and the title is even more important to understanding Demuth's point. By tradition, the Fourth of July parade held in the small Pennsylvania town of Coatesville ended at the steel factory, which in fact ended the parade's real significance, for the coming of twentieth-century industry to the small rural community meant the end of the independence that had so long been celebrated.

In these works Demuth borrowed from dada both its characteristic use of understatement and the cryptic titles that force the viewer to actively participate in the making of meaning. Demuth could have subverted industry's status in a more obvious fashion, but like other circle members, he wished to produce multivalent, enduring artistic statements that demand slow, careful, and informed readings. Such challenging artwork reflects not the desire for a limited audience, as some have concluded, but faith in the American public. The circle members hoped and believed that through their galleries and other public programs, a broad audience could learn to appreciate the complex ideas they presented and recognize the cultural value of their work.

In paintings and photographs of New York City, the Stieglitz circle used recognizable architectural monuments to emblematize the absent countryside, the tacit foil to urban subjects. Yet the views they presented were by no means nostalgic; instead, they offered incisive and often critical comments about contemporary America, focusing on how the metropolis was affected by the influx of peoples from both the American provinces and foreign shores.

In singling out architecture and advertising, the circle artists represented powerful forces of the city's economy, in which the cooperative galleries where they exhibited played a small but important part. Their competition for lasting renown and economic parity with European contemporaries and past masters was a major topic of conversation, correspondence, publications, paintings. Sometimes the visual artists and writers borrowed from one another in treating the theme. Thus in a passage from *Port of New York* quoted at the beginning of this chapter—"The sun is rising overhead, the sun which once shone brightly on Europe alone and threw slanting rays merely on New York"—Paul Rosenfeld may be alluding to a particularly striking watercolor painted about 1922 by John Marin. What immediately rivets the attention of the viewer of *Red Sun, Brooklyn Bridge* (plate 3) is the brilliant crimson orb in the upper left. The watercolor is intense, with a luscious raspberry hue in the foreground and a building in the right midground that echoes the same hot exotic color against a light aqua ground dotted with cobalt. The spirited colors sing in electric, Whitmanian praise of American architects and engineers who conceived and laborers who raised the Brooklyn Bridge. The monument itself is depicted in a remarkable passage, its forms scratched out as if in an etching, in the left midground. At the same time, Marin's original color demonstrates and celebrates the inventiveness and conscious skill of early-twentieth-century American artists, whom he implicitly compares with the bridge builders.

Rosenfeld's 1924 description in turn engendered a later work of art. Georgia O'Keeffe could have painted *East River from the Shelton* (1927–28; plate 4) with Rosenfeld's book balanced on one knee. Certainly while executing the work she had in mind the implications of his heady assertion. Dark silhouettes of urban architecture crowd the foreground of O'Keeffe's powerful depiction. The abstract pattern of the Hudson River ripples across the near midground, while in the far midground the buildings on the opposite bank dissolve into blurred shapes of fog, fume, and cloud. At absolute center, at the top of the canvas, the round shape of the sun is haloed in white and yellow. White sunspots shoot from it, and long, abstracted rays of pure light strike groundward from its center. As in Rosenfeld's passage, the sun is the protagonist: the emblem of prosperity for the city and for the Americans on whom it beats down.

The colors O'Keeffe selected also relate her painting to Rosenfeld's prose. For while the foreground silhouette of the city is dour black and slate gray, the river of the near midground is luminous red, with emphatic blue shading at either side. Glowing blue smoke rises from the tallest chimney, just left of center in the foreground, leading the eye of the viewer into an intense blue sky that takes up most of the composition's surface area. Unusual, eye-catching, and effective, the deep blue core of the sun holds the viewer's attention. Not only are the resplendent red, white, and blue tones of the work inventive and poetic but they also—once again—signify American-made art, whose production and prestige Rosenfeld addressed eloquently in his influential work of theory and criticism. Produced during a gallery season that was O'Keeffe's most profitable to date, *East River from the Shelton* reiterates the ambition of American artists to gain their rightful place in the international cultural marketplace. This painting, like Rosenfeld's book, constitutes part of the critical democratic ideology that the group created and disseminated in the postwar years.

Another urban landscape, also in patriotic hues, presents a final word on the new place of American artists in the transnational cultural scene and their relation to native and foreign pasts. In *After All* (1935; plate 5), his final oil painting (and his final major treatment of an architectural subject), Charles Demuth sums up the ideology he had been formulating in collaboration with other circle members since just after the war. This vertical landscape depicts a portion of the Armstrong Flooring Plant that still exists in the artist's native Lancaster, Pennsylvania.[34] Demuth, much like Stieglitz in his New York photographs, cropped one of the buildings. The composition is framed at left by a partial view of a redbrick facade. Before it a telephone pole stands erect, sporting two bright blue trapezoids backed by rhyming black geometric foils, which playfully suggest a bow tie. The repository of electrical power, wittily personified, has a comical presence. The sky is a neutral silvery blue, slightly graduated (a homogenous tone that also recalls Stieglitz's photographs). The combination of red brick, blue bow tie, and silver-white sky evokes the national emblem, as the image of an American flag rises from the viewer's subconscious. Surely, the artist jokes ironically, this is "the great American artwork"!

In the middle ground is a second redbrick building of the industrial complex, with white water towers at the top. Two majestic smokestacks are portrayed at right in pale

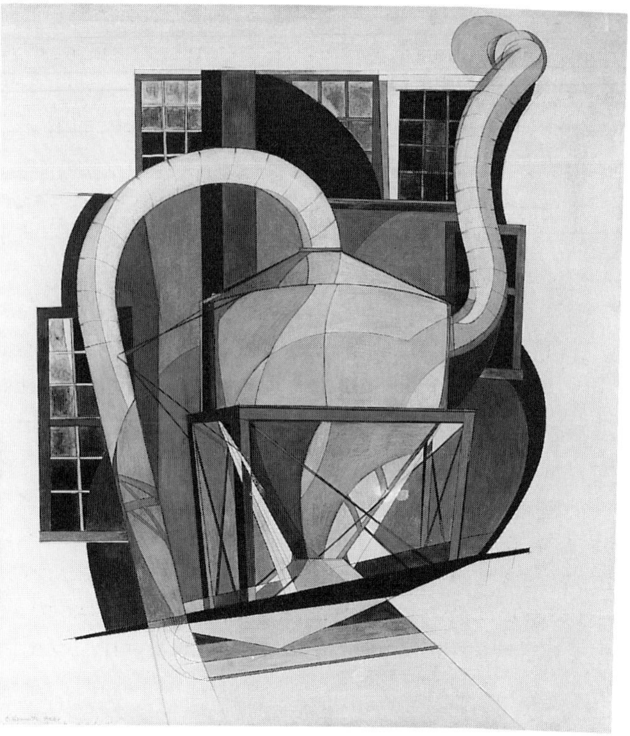

52. Charles Demuth, *Machinery (For W. Carlos Williams)*, 1920, tempera and pencil on cardboard, 24 × 19 7/8 in. Acquired 1949, The Metropolitan Museum of Art, Alfred Stieglitz Collection.

gold. The stacks rhyme poetically with each other while balancing the entire composition. Perhaps the most interesting feature in this complex painting appears in a light blue tone in the right midground: a cyclone separator, a type of centrifuge then widely used in American industry. The same image had formed the dominant motif in Demuth's painting *Machinery (For W. Carlos Williams)* (1920; figure 52).[35] The reference to this earlier work, and thus to an earlier stage in his development, helps the viewer discover Demuth's meaning.

Machinery, a tongue-in-cheek homage to his friend the poet William Carlos Williams, was executed at a time when European modernists, most prominently the dadaists and Marcel Duchamp, were praising America's modernity. They argued that because America lacked a history, Americans could become exceptional artists. European modernists visiting America in the middle and late 1910s insisted that by focusing on the present Machine Age and its apparatus, American artists would win fame. Among other things, Demuth's *Machinery* questions the validity of those assertions and the stereotype of America as a techno-Eden devoid of history and thus of genuine culture. So did William Carlos Williams (celebrated by Demuth in a famous poster-portrait), who challenged this view of America as early as 1920. He later codified his provocative beliefs about the value of local subject matter, the capturing of a sense of place beyond nationalism, progress, or science, and the importance of history—specifically American history—in *Spring and All* (1923).[36] Williams's ideas on these issues were evolving along lines so close to those of the Stieglitz group that his book *In the American Grain* (1925) convinced the circle to name its last gallery in his honor when they changed locations in 1929.[37]

In 1933, with the benefit of over a decade of hindsight, Demuth commented again on the dominant European view—this time taking the same representative of modern industrial apparatus, the separator, and setting it back into its original context of local forms that retain their historical resonance. No matter how modern the industrial plant might be, one could not deny that the forms of the buildings themselves—and of their fire escapes, water towers, and smokestacks—were as much a part of the European heritage as the form of communication, the painting, in which the image appears.

As is often the case, Demuth's title provides another clue that the work is an amused meditation on the continuing vitality and inescapability of the past. *After All* derives from a stanza of "Song of the Exposition" from *Leaves of Grass,* a poem in which Whitman (like Demuth after him) reflects on the uses to which European ideologies and material cultures have been put—though with none of the painter's irony.

> After all not to create only, or found only,
> But to bring perhaps from afar what is already founded,
> To give it our own identity, average, limitless, free,
> To fill the gross the torpid bulk with vital religious fire,
> Not to repel or destroy so much as accept, fuse, rehabilitate,
> To obey as well as command, to follow more than to lead,
> These also are the lessons of our New World;
> While how little the New after all, how much the Old, Old, World![38]

The image and title of Demuth's *After All* acknowledge Whitman's prescience. That American artists can best win status through a shared past and common knowledge—including the antique Mediterranean heritage—was accepted by Demuth and his colleagues of the Stieglitz circle, after all. This democratically inclusive definition of the particular past to be valued and preserved distinguished their regionalism or localism from the nativist versions of Thomas Hart Benton and his adherents.

The city views by the Stieglitz circle take account of the demographic changes still in progress as they aspire to break free of the traditional definition of landscape as property, with its emphasis on pedigree and ownership. The circle attempted to judge the effects of the new urban space and its modern aesthetics (the billboard, the highrise) on the human psyche. They aimed to render the city and its novel sights intelligible as homeland for the masses of folk who were continuing to pour into the metropolis in search of fresh beginnings and new perspectives.

7

"THE MOST AMERICAN PLACE"

New Mexico

SINCE THE TURN OF THE CENTURY, a particular portion of America's unspoiled landscape had been attracting the attention of visual artists and artisans from around the world: New Mexico. In 1912 the New Mexican territories achieved statehood, accelerating the development and acquisition of land by nonlocals. Art makers of all persuasions played a prominent role in reshaping the communities of Taos and Santa Fe, if only by their conspicuous presence. They arrived in the hundreds; some settled permanently, while others only escaped harsh winters elsewhere.

Several members of the Stieglitz circle were lured by the attractions of the Southwest. Marsden Hartley made his way to Taos on a grant from the art dealer Charles Daniel in 1918. His visit continued into the following year, briefly interrupted by an exploration of southern California. New Mexico inspired Hartley to formulate the first postwar appeal for American artists to pursue indigenous expression. As we saw in chapter 4, in his Southwest articles he insisted that "[t]he fetish of Paris . . . has been destroyed by the war."[1] Hartley believed that Americans could overthrow the cultural dominance of France if they would redefine the terms of their identity, and he sought the roots of that identity in the Southwest. Both the theories and the artworks that he created there had lasting consequences for other circle members. During his first trip to Taos, Paul Strand admitted to Stieglitz that Hartley was "the only one who has penetrated the spirit of the place."[2] Paul Rosenfeld seconded the opinion, observing of the

Southwest that "everything marvelous and sensational about the spot reminds me of a Hartley painting. There is no doubt that he has gotten farther with the locality than any other painter[;] . . . as far as the depths of colors go, the extraordinary differentiation of planes, the tapestry-like look of the earth, Hartley is highly realistic."[3]

On Hartley's recommendation, Strand and Rosenfeld simultaneously visited the northern New Mexico artist colonies in 1926, and they rendezvoused as guests of the art patron Mabel Dodge Luhan.[4] In 1929 both Georgia O'Keeffe and John Marin accepted the hospitality of Luhan, living and working at her compound in the center of Taos. Three of the later visitors—Strand, Marin, and O'Keeffe—returned to the area again. O'Keeffe began living there alone each winter after 1930, eventually purchasing the property she had been renting; after Stieglitz's death in 1946, she became a permanent resident. Although the circle members' written testimonies about the place include scant information about what first inspired their visits, the 1920 edition of a popular guidebook of the period, *Clason's Green Guide,* helps us reconstruct the area's early-twentieth-century cultural meanings.

Even at that early date the image of the "Land of Enchantment" (the boast of the state's license plates) had been struck, no doubt created in part by residents of the Taos and Santa Fe art communities. *Clason's Guide* characterizes New Mexico as "a land of undeveloped resources, a land of big opportunities and a land of romance." In a small reproduction a young Native American woman raises her right hand in a customary gesture of welcome (imitating that of the Statue of Liberty) to herald the next claim: "Here dwelt the first Americans, members of those vanished races, the Cliff Dwellers and their contemporaries."[5] Thus New Mexico is valued most for its history: a history of true native non-Anglo peoples that stretches back thousands of years before the arrival of the Puritans whom Van Wyck Brooks so reviled. This positive image of genuine Native American communities with a traditional way of life gave the state a unique pedigree. But while the state of New Mexico may have profited from the image, the native peoples themselves—here as throughout modern America—continued to suffer racial stereotyping and economic exile.

Marsden Hartley executed most of his works in oil of New Mexico subjects after he had left the state.[6] One biographer counts four series of such works, all landscapes: one done in pastel, in California, in the winter of 1918 during a brief absence from New Mexico and three done in oils, one in New York in 1919, one in Germany in April 1923, and one in Paris in the midsummer of 1924.[7] Thus although Hartley's Southwest works are primarily (and somewhat ironically) studio works, the image of the New Mexican land haunted the artist for some seven years. Hartley's characteristic compositional device in his Southwest productions, which appears in the New Mexico works of 1919, is to frame the landscape view with a window, something he first tried in Bermuda in 1918.[8] This device can be interpreted as a comment on the Renaissance notion of a painting as "a window on the world." In using it, Hartley aligned himself with contemporary European modernists, from whom he appropriated it, thereby advancing American art practice beyond its traditional concerns to those of a developing modernist avant-garde.

It also reflects Baudelaire's equation of painting with poetry, which inspired Hartley's own critical and theoretical text, *Adventures in the Arts*. In a famous review of 1859, Baudelaire attempted to win for landscape painting and its practitioners a loftier rank in the artistic hierarchy. Landscape painters, he wrote, "open a window, and the whole space included in the frame of it, trees, sky, and house, take on for them the value of a poem, ready-made."[9] Perhaps no other member of the Stieglitz circle could appreciate this equivalency of poetry and painting as well as the painter-poet Hartley. In his Southwest writings, as he makes the case for a New Realist mode, he invokes this powerful idea. Thus his New Mexican windowscapes offer a novel response to the traditional dictum *ut pictura poesis*. A picture, for Hartley, can be a concrete poem.

Hartley's framing device, furthermore, posits a distanced observer. In his 1924 critique of the New Mexico works, Paul Rosenfeld stressed that Hartley seemed to take in the land at a remove. That was his choice, inevitable if he was to represent his position honestly. As in his articles, Hartley in his Southwest paintings—particularly those executed on site—took the perspective of an objective anthropological observer. By including the window, Hartley acknowledged that as a white nonresident, he was necessarily reporting at a distance.

Window, New Mexico (1919; figure 53) can serve as an example. The characteristic vertical format includes the image of a windowsill in the foreground; in front of it is a bowl of fruit, as well as the billowing fabric of drapes at the right and left edges of the canvas that poetically echo the external frame. By including the sill and curtain, Hartley sets himself apart from the impressionists, who often chose to record their landscape subjects from "studio" windows—but without specifying the position of the artist so precisely. Hartley's limited palette of greens and browns and grays, combined with the very rich paint texture and handling, produces the desirable earthiness and sensuousness that Hartley ascribed, in his articles, to the Southwest terrain and to its native inhabitants.[10] As Brooks would have agreed, these properties distinguished nonwhite from Anglo cultures.

Other Southwest landscapes by Hartley in a more traditional format not only celebrate the regional landscape (and the opportunity it provided to create visual poems to give shape to the information his articles conveyed) but are also homages to the writings of Walt Whitman. In these landscapes Hartley depicted a peculiarly American world, the Southwest, and a particular nature Whitman thought best suited to representation. As we noted in chapter 3, Whitman had demanded not "the smooth walks, trimm'd hedges, poseys and nightingales of the English poets, but the whole orb, with its geologic history, the kosmos, carrying fire and snow."[11] In New Mexico the painter discovered a landscape that was both untrimmed and awesome, and thus uniquely suited to Whitman's call for the sublime. Such an environment could re-

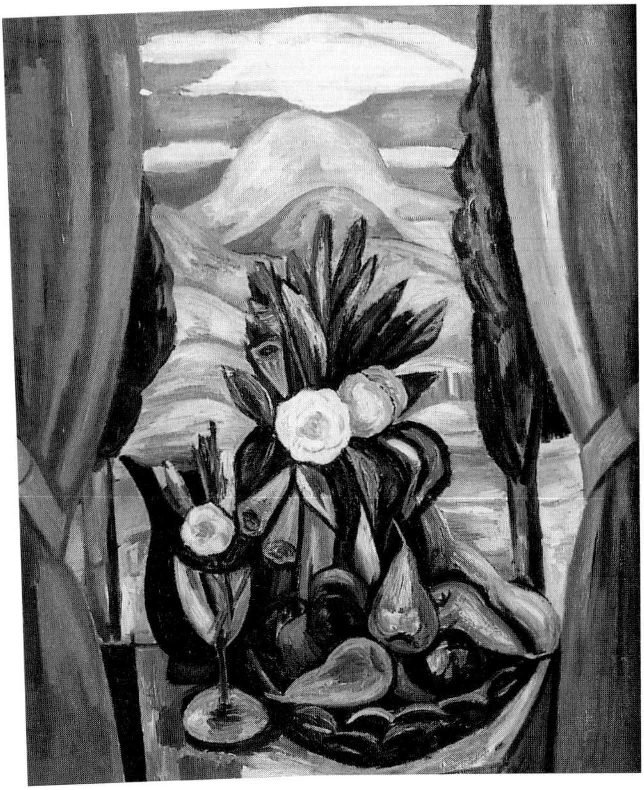

53. Marsden Hartley, *Window, New Mexico,* 1919, oil on canvas, 37 1/8 × 29 in. Gift of Joseph H. Hirshhorn, 1966, Hirshhorn Museum and Sculpture Garden, Smithsonian Institution, Washington, D.C.; photography by Lee Stalsworth.

make Anglo culture from the ground up. Hartley's early painted reports about the new state, such as the oil painting *Landscape No. 3, Cash Entry Mines* (1920, Art Institute of Chicago), fill Whitman's prescription and praise the natural resources of the region. This horizontal landscape in exotic tones of green, flesh, blue, and red conveys the general outlines of a mining operation in the domed hillside of characteristically mountainous terrain. The colors used to describe the wildness and distinctiveness of the land are also ordered to impart a sense of depth that does not rely on traditional conventions of Renaissance perspective. At the same time, the visible strokes of color allow the surface plane to retain its integrity as flat surface, denying (like Hartley's window landscapes) the illusionism of the European old masters.

Moreover, the distanced perspective in these works fits Hartley's own theories of New Realism, as well as the tone in which he presents those theories. In the case of *Cash Entry Mines,* the selection of a vantage point far enough from the subject to obliterate details of the mining operation once more underscores the artist's position as a nonresident, an "outside" observer. The painting does not comment critically on the purpose and methods of the mining operation, which is only cursorily suggested,

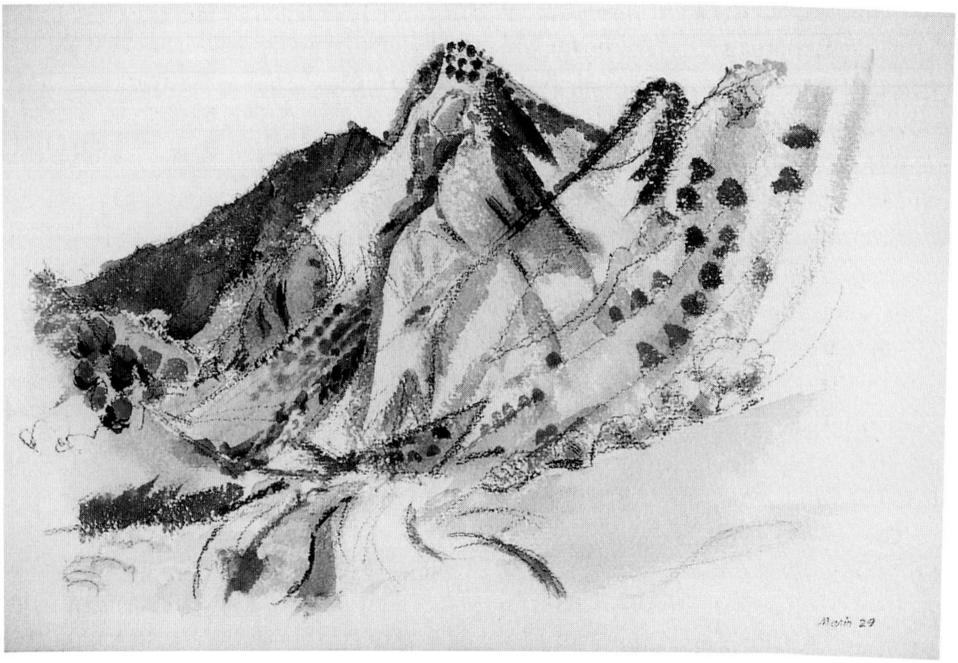

54. John Marin, *Taos and Vicinity, New Mexico, No. 1,* 1929, watercolor and black crayon, 13 7/8 × 19 7/8 in. Philadelphia Museum of Art, The Alfred Stieglitz Collection.

but—in line with what his articles propose as the real job of the American modernist—celebrates the country's natural resources. But the reserves on which he mainly focuses are metaphorical, not literal. The work demonstrates just how artists mine their own nature to unearth what Hartley, in words and pictures, proclaimed America's most valuable resource: the artistic talent native to American soil.

Strand and Rosenfeld were not alone in thinking immediately of Hartley's paintings at their first sight of New Mexico. John Marin, who spent several months there in 1929 and 1930, recalled both Hartley's images and his theories. In watercolors such as *Taos and Vicinity, New Mexico, No. 1* (1929; figure 54), Marin invoked the memory of Hartley in his subject and composition: here, the sacred mountain is protagonist. A large portion of the heavy rippled surface of the paper support is bare, as it often is in Marin's works. But the color—terra-cottas, grays, olive greens (different from his usual Maine palette)—recalls several of Hartley's renditions of the Southwest, especially the subtle blend of the earthen colors of *Window, New Mexico.* The horizontal landscape painting is a superb example of the naturalistic rendering of a specific place Hartley called for in his manifestos. The mood is sober, intimating the respect for the majestic site that contemporary anthropologists attributed to the local

Pueblo Indians. *Taos and Vicinity* reproduces a specific secluded area that viewers are encouraged to imagine is unknown and unappreciated by any but the respectful artist and Native Americans. Yet all this is subtly suggested; Marin has not dramatized or glamorized the locale. The naturalistic rendering communicates instead the sense of taking a very hard look at a particular American place, conveying not merely a love of land but a love of beholding land.

Although Marin, unlike Hartley, did not revise his theory and practice after encountering New Mexico's landscape or, like Strand, invent new ways to reproduce regional social histories, he clearly depicted the Southwest with greater attention to nature than in his New England landscapes of the same period. Perhaps his unfamiliarity with the terrain called forth a more studied approach. Marin confided to the New Mexico artist Ward Lockwood, "when the country is new I can't take liberties with it at the start," and apparently he didn't; Lockwood claimed that the exact sites of Marin's New Mexico landscape depictions were easily recognizable.[12]

The works themselves indicate the influence on Marin of Hartley's appeal in 1918 for indigenous styles of representation grounded in specific landscapes. Most of the more than one hundred watercolors Marin produced in New Mexico are landscapes.[13] In fact, in the Southwest Marin introduced a new element to his oeuvre: the sublime awe of an expansive, nearly uninhabited countryside racked by thunder and lightning. Apparently his true object was to paint a modern Western creation myth that would parallel the nature legends of the Southwest Indians. In July 1929 Marin wrote: "The One who made this country, this big level seeming desert table land cut out slices. They are the canyons. Then here and there he put mountains atop. Astanding here you can see six or seven thunder storms going on at the same time."[14] The mountains were thus created as platforms from which the fearless could witness the pyrotechnic displays of nature. Many of Marin's paintings give structure to unfamiliar southwestern nature, simultaneously redefining sublimity and making it accessible to eastern urban audiences. These works illustrate how the New Realism could be made to serve important communal functions.

Another of Marin's watercolors of the region, *Storm over Taos* (1930; figure 55), also captures a sense of place, but more histrionically. Again the color is subtle: a coordinated surface of browns, grays, and yellow ochers. The immediate foreground is striated in both color and form, lending an uncommon vibrancy to the image. A striking hieroglyph—a Native American design element with no referent in the natural world—enlivens the sky. The tone is strong and vital, imparted by the classic balance and the marked distinctiveness of form and color. By including not just the flat forms and subdued tones of landscape under darkened skies but also a tiny human village, Marin powerfully conveys awed respect for nature's changing moods. The hamlet is dwarfed by the background mountains and the overhanging storm, a dark and threatening passage of sky with rain-bearing clouds portrayed in idiosyncratic, abstract notation. Nature is posited as triumphant over humankind—much as we saw in

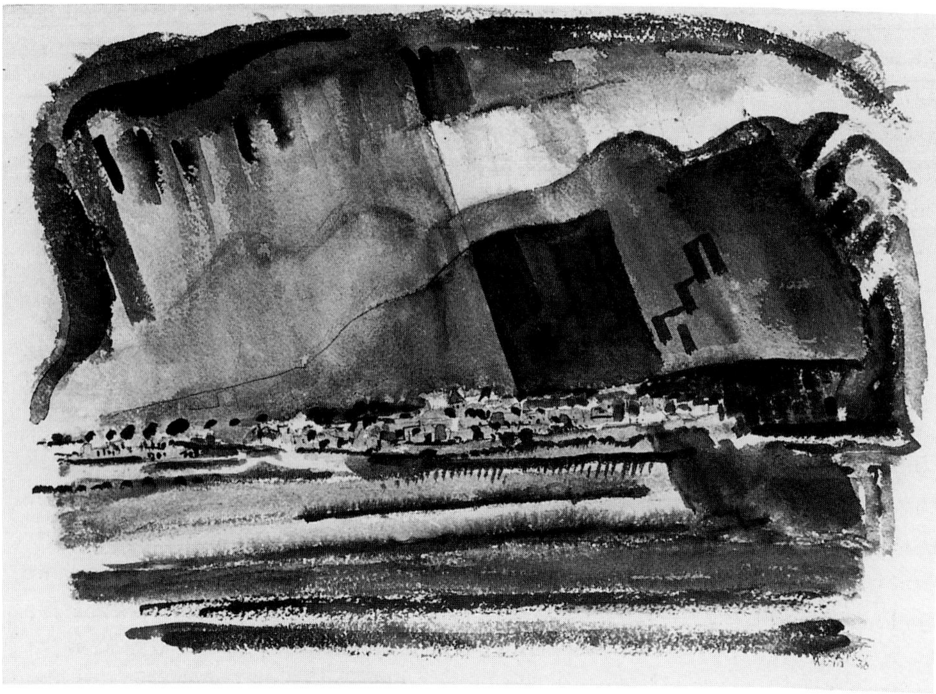

55. John Marin, *Storm over Taos,* 1930, watercolor over graphite, 15 1/16 × 20 15/16 in. National Gallery of Art, Washington, D.C., Alfred Stieglitz Collection.

Stieglitz's New York landscape photographs. The French impressionists were interested in displaying weather in its various forms, but in *Storm over Taos* (and other paintings of New Mexico that celebrate nature's spectacular displays) Marin had another tradition in mind as well: the landscapes of the great nineteenth-century romantic painters like Washington Allston, the first American artist to suffuse his views with imagination rather than rely wholly on literal appearances. In this image and others, Marin both acknowledges their artistry and attempts to outstrip them.

Experiences in New Mexico led Marin, like Hartley, to experiment with ways to frame images. Indeed, Marin pushed Hartley's device of a window frame even further. Especially in rain or extreme heat, he often painted in his borrowed Ford—a practice that may well have promoted some of the fragmentation of image customarily attributed to cubist influence. The device wittily responds to the visible panes of Hartley's works and suggests that mobility had something to do with their distancing effect. In making his car the ultimate modern mobile studio, Marin wryly comments on the earliest phases of an American propensity for relocation that still shows no signs of abating.

Doubtless influenced by the earlier firsthand accounts of his friends Hartley and Rosenfeld, on August 4, 1929, Marin attended the annual performance of the Corn Dance at Santo Domingo Pueblo, an Indian village located near the Rio Grande, midway between Santa Fe and Albuquerque. In the painting that records the event, *The Dance of the Santo Domingo Indians* or *The Corn Dance* (1929; plate 6), Marin (like his literary colleagues) focused on the Native American dance form as a metaphor for a vigorous indigenous culture. The watercolor, now in the collection of the Metropolitan Museum of Art in New York City, is a thoughtful recollection—executed in the studio—of the splendor of the annual dance. "A big Indian dance I attended—I feel my greatest human Experience," Marin wrote from the Southwest to Stieglitz's gallery assistant.[15]

Marin's visual rendition of the dance has more in common with what Hartley wrote in *Adventures in the Arts* (1921) than with Rosenfeld's account in *By Way of Art* (1928).[16] Marin in fact seems challenged to duplicate in paint Hartley's precise description of the intricate details of movement and costuming. *The Dance of the Santo Domingo Indians* carefully differentiates the functions and appearances of the different participants. Using interpenetrating angular forms throughout the composition, Marin also communicates the same vitality and energy that Hartley had reported. Here, as in Hartley's southwestern theory, the American Indian becomes the model of indigenous art maker and dance itself an analogue for harmonious social relations. Marin's insistence on acute angles also recalls Frank's "Straight Streets" of 1925 (see chapter 4),[17] which emphasized the types of lines—ubiquitous in Native American culture—that signal unity with the environment.

The allover patterning of the paper surface creates a convincing sense of the high energy that Marin wished to ascribe to the native dancers. Form and content blur to create the desired effect. And the red, white, and blue edges of the composition suggest that he considered this particular work as possibly the "great American painting" that members of the circle were consciously striving to produce. The metonymic device also accords with Hartley's early understanding of Native Americans as the "real" Americans. But the painting is not especially colorful: only a few bright touches mark the surface here and there. Marin wanted his viewers to take the ritual event seriously; this is not the atmosphere he created for later series on circuses. Most of the dancers are painted in subdued grays and browns, but a shamanic figure in the center foreground is set off from the crowd in scale and direction of movement. This compelling protagonist is depicted as empowered by and empowering a disk that glows fiery red, radiating as if with supernatural energy, in the right midground. The shaman can be taken on one level as a surrogate for "the artist": the respected position and the ritual function of the shaman in the native community correspond to the status and role that Stieglitz circle members wanted the American artist to occupy in the national community. Here, however, the American artist is a distanced observer, an outsider recording the activities of initiates.

In fact, Marin's is not a literal depiction, at least not of the landscape. A visitor to the still extant pueblo of Santo Domingo will note that while Marin could only have viewed the performance from the north or south sides of the plaza, the landscape background he depicted could not have been seen from either of those vantage points.[18] Marin selected prominent regional landmarks—flat-topped mesas to the east of the pueblo—to frame the composition. His interpretations of Indian designs compose the interior frame. Native American craftwork, which Frank praised in "Straight Streets" as a manifestation of a harmonious culture, inspired this graphic improvisation. Clearly, the New Realism demanded that the visual artist go beyond mirroring surfaces to record the sociocultural meanings of what is perceived.

In addition, Marin confirmed visual art's vital role in creating new forms for American culture, a role that Rosenfeld had urged in his reflections on the Corn Dance. *The Dance of the Santo Domingo Indians* is significant not for providing an accurate copy of an event but rather for thoughtfully synthesizing a particular view of a real event in a rich social context with the art theory and cultural criticism of the circle. Indeed the painting itself constitutes a socially engaged cultural criticism unique in America of the period. Through positive images of Native Americans, the visual artists Hartley and Marin together with the critics Rosenfeld and Frank argued powerfully that American culture would benefit from reconfirming its historical commitment to pluralism. Opposing the Progressives' ideal of "Americanization," these more radical thinkers wanted white culture to embrace Native American values. To Stieglitz circle members, the fluid, interdependent communal forms of the Southwest pueblo dwellers seemed an early, and enduring, American model of socialistic structure.

Hartley's vivid recollections in oil and in print of the New Mexico landscape and of the state's distinctive folk art forms convinced Paul Strand to go there in 1926. Even without the evidence of Strand's letters to Stieglitz from the Southwest, we would be certain that Hartley's vision strongly colored his. The dramatic chiaroscuro of many of Strand's New Mexico landscape photographs recalls Hartley's deliberately Ryderesque recollections of the place. Strand adopted other Hartley New Mexico subjects as well as Hartley's tone, photographing southwestern and Mexican *santos* and *retablos,* the folk forms of traditional religious icons that Hartley had painted earlier. And with Hartley's maxims for postwar painting in mind, Strand began to devise a new approach to his own art. According to one of Strand's biographers, Naomi Rosenblum, "Strand's Western experiences resulted in a new concept of photographic activity"; Strand himself names 1926 a transitional year.[19]

Strand's "new concept" also owed much to Edgar Lee Masters's collection of free-verse epitaphs, *Spoon River Anthology,* first published in 1915 but reprinted several times in the late 1910s and the 1920s (including a new edition in 1924). Masters's anthology, like many of Sherwood Anderson's tales, explores the interdependence of rural people with their environment. Strand's debt to this poetry links his photographic efforts even more tightly to Hartley's theories of a new democratic and popular art.

Rosenblum views Strand's Southwest endeavors as a search "for structures that suggested the traditions and the life of the area."[20] While Hartley (and Rosenfeld and Frank after him) discovered the locus of communal life in the form of the dance, Strand's photographs place it in the art of architecture: abandoned edifices of rural ghost towns, pueblos. These buildings embody and reveal the specific regional cultural histories that bore special meaning for his circle. Between 1920 and 1932 he (like his mentor, Stieglitz) favored a new objectivity, a New Realism, characterized by extreme clarity, sharpness, and renewed interest in "the object." This approach is related to postwar European "realisms," such as German Neue Sachlichkeit and Russian suprematism (which ultimately led to social realism), as well as to the new uses of realism in works produced after the war by Italian artists of the Novecento group and French artists such as Picasso, Derain, and Matisse. Despite all their theorizing about indigenous practices of representation, in reformulating realism the Stieglitz circle was responding to an impulse felt around the world, as they too tried to cope with the changes wrought by the war.

One of photography's great contributions to the new mode was the serial format. The artists produced multiple images of the same subject with minor alterations or sometimes fragmentation of the subject and with changes in point of view or weather. The French impressionists, with their interest in changing atmospheric conditions, had also found serial images useful. But now the Stieglitz circle artists used the format, in which the individual part can stand for the whole series, as an emblem of American democracy, a social ordering in which each individual can stand for, or represent, a larger whole.

For example, Paul Strand photographed and Georgia O'Keeffe painted the church at Ranchos de Taos, New Mexico, many times. If we compare one of Strand's 1931 photographs (figure 56) with O'Keeffe's earlier *Ranchos Church* (1930; figure 57), we clearly see the differences in expression between photography and painting.[21] The tone of Strand's print depends on the extremely subtle gradation of shifting light and shadow captured in an instant. Each part of the irregular massing of the indigenous architecture is described in a different value of gray. Strand waited for and caught the moment when the subject's shape was most clearly articulated by natural light.

In this case Strand stepped far back from the church in order to capture nearly its entire form, compressing a great deal of information into the small frame of the photographic image. There is almost a *horror vacui* in the composition, which lends the architectural structure an illusion of closeness, of intimacy. The highly "natural" look of the adobe building's rounded edges plainly bespeaks the craft of the human hands that patted it into shape. Strand's view includes all the details of aging, most prominently the cracking of the buttress portrayed in the center foreground. Through this image of the solitary church the artist proposes that human cultural achievements are both rare and vulnerable to nature and time. The sandy soil, punctuated only by sparse grasses in the foreground, suggests the arid and somewhat forbidding native

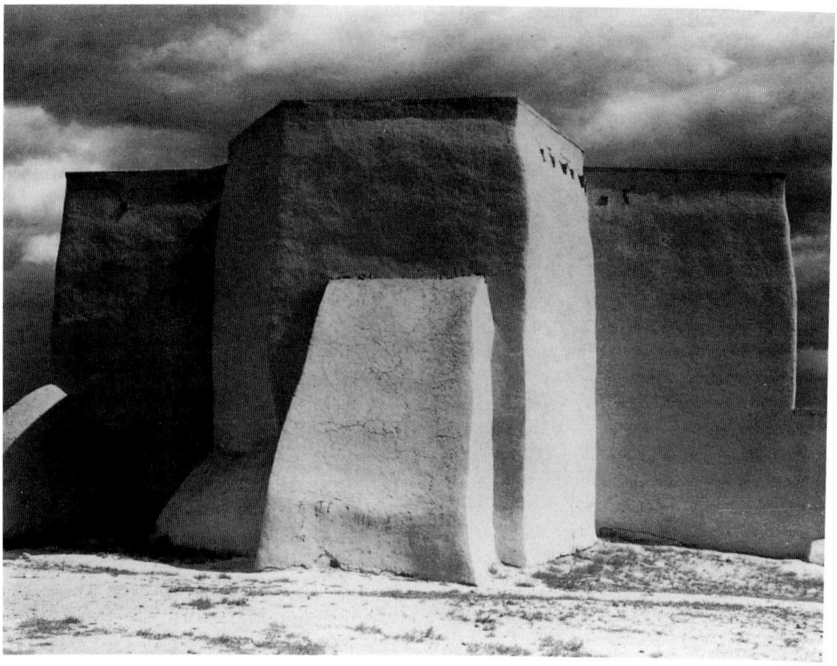

56. Paul Strand, *Church, Ranchos de Taos, New Mexico,* 1931, photograph. ©1971, Aperture Foundation, Inc., Paul Strand Archive.

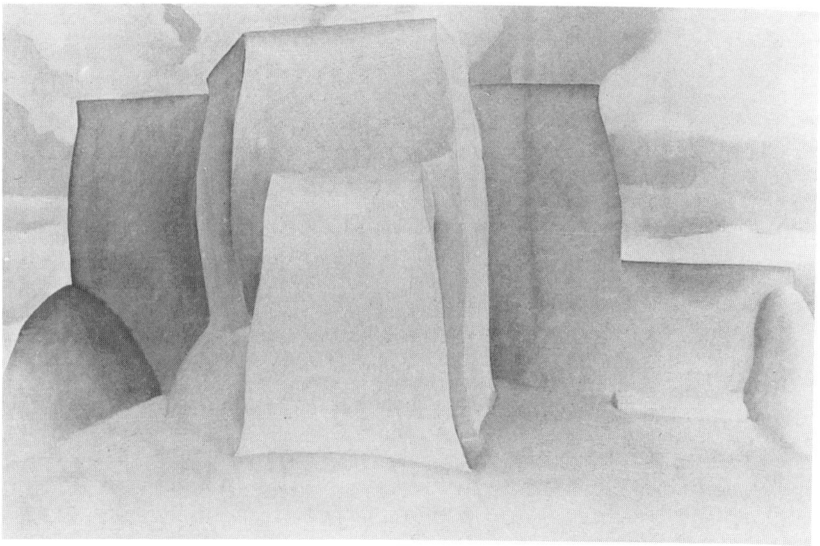

57. Georgia O'Keeffe, *Ranchos Church,* 1930, oil on canvas, 24 × 36 in. Acquired 1949, The Metropolitan Museum of Art, Alfred Stieglitz Collection.

environment. This soil, the tone and composition insinuate, is intimately related to the architectural structure; the connection suggests an "ashes to ashes, dust to dust" philosophy, especially appropriate to a depiction of an old church. The photograph as a whole meditates on the fragility and transience of human makings. The dark rain-bearing clouds above the church cast foreboding shadows on its left side that remind us of nature's effect on humans and human achievements.

Georgia O'Keeffe takes a nearly identical vantage point in painting the church, capturing the shadows of clouds on the structure and its reflection of light in a strikingly similar way. But although Strand's image both recalls and pays homage to the work of his colleague, its purpose could hardly be more different. While dark clouds also threaten in O'Keeffe's painting, the church they surround is a consummate image of permanence, durability, and solidity: all signs of aging and wear are erased. Its flawless facade rhymes with the faultless surface of the painting, which was built up, like the church, by the strong strokes of a human hand. Rather than address the ephemeral nature of human cultural makings, O'Keeffe presents architectural evidence of a productive human history and—as in all her New Realist depictions of the Church of St. Francis of Assisi at Ranchos de Taos, complete and partial, in storm or calm—celebrates the cultural accomplishment of two indigenous groups of artists: the Native Americans, from whom the Spanish learned to build with the soil beneath their feet, and modernists. (She herself, in keeping with the original spirit of the Arts and Crafts movement, sometimes used pigments ground from the New Mexican soil.) Both the photograph and the painting of the church explicitly address the essential nature of their different media. A painting, because of the medium's long history, is the appropriate vehicle for imparting a sense of longevity; a photograph, because of its recent appearance and unstable status among the arts, aptly expresses impermanence.

It is useful to consider the images of New Mexico fabricated by the Stieglitz circle in their broader social and historical context. The circle's enthusiasm for the Native American and Spanish-Indian hybrid cultures they encountered in the Southwest was in fact part of a widespread sociocultural trend. For members of New York's intellectual community—mostly white and male—populations of nonwhites compellingly modeled other manners of expression, as well as alternative communal structures. Closer to home, the processes of cultural self-discovery and self-representation in the 1920s known as the Harlem Renaissance did not go unnoticed; urban whites provided much of the financial support that enabled the arts to flourish in that community. Its artifacts and customs were also observed, recorded, and interpreted by sociologists (in research similar to that being done in the Southwest). "Primitivism" and its values were seen by a young, questioning generation as a barrier against a return to pragmatism. They hoped that by adopting alternative cosmologies and lifestyles, American elite culture could escape selfish individualism and avarice. Sherwood Anderson, whom literary critics often labeled a primitivist, declared in *A Story*

Teller's Story (1924), a biographical work dedicated to Alfred Stieglitz: "I had always been drawn toward horses dogs and other animals and among people had cared most for simple folk who made no pretense of having an intellect[,] . . . who followed instinctively a force outside themselves—they felt to be greater and more worthy than themselves."[22]

The position the Stieglitz circle assumed toward America's nonwhite populations inverted the notions of Progressive reformers.[23] Rather than desiring to "Americanize" Indians, blacks, or other minority groups—that is, to resocialize them to conform with the standards of the dominant white culture—artists and critics of the circle called for a broader and more inclusive sense of "American." In part, they went to the Southwest to find it. By supporting the work of the black author Jean Toomer, and welcoming him and the Taos Indian Tony Luhan (the husband of their patron Mabel Dodge) into their intimate company, they demonstrated more than an abstract receptivity to differing attitudes, behaviors, and values: they affirmed their belief in a common human nature, a belief that has ethical, social, and political implications. With the rise of postmodern theories this Whitmanian faith in the binding power of a common nature has fallen out of fashion.

At the same time, the exodus of these artists to the Southwest was also a form of escape. In *Exile's Return* (1934), Malcolm Cowley outlined two possible ways for artists in the early decades of the twentieth century to cope with American society: one could either shut oneself up in a private world of inner fantasy or attempt to leave the twentieth century behind.[24] The flight continued even as Cowley was writing: the search for a refuge from the industrial centers, with their claustrophobic architecture and street plans, their neurosis-breeding crowds, led to the Southwest more frequently than to Gauguinesque island paradises. The artists who found healthier climes irreversibly transformed them, for better and worse.

Thomas Hart Benton's autobiography, *An Artist in America* (1937), offers a barbed critique of the transformation of Santa Fe in which he broadcasts his conservative bent and prejudices against women and homosexuals. Unlike Hartley, who maintained a respectful distance in the face of the unfamiliar or foreign, Benton presumptuously speaks for the New Mexican locals:

> There is nothing quite so offensive as a clique or colony which, living economically independent of people, takes superior or patronizing airs towards them. During the twenties, when eastern artists began coming in great herds to New Mexico, they were under the influence of an exotic purism which was calculated to set them off and keep them off the ordinary behavior patterns of New Mexico society. Their productions were wholly incomprehensible to plain people and their talk borrowed from the jargon of Parisian aesthetes was outrageous in the environment. Lots of the artist emigrants were to my knowledge perfectly sane democratic-minded fellows but they were under technical and aesthetic influences which worked against their participation in the normal activities of their new background. The prewar "genius" complex was still very strong among them and that alone

would be sufficient to provide a marked queerness of character. It is no great wonder that the ordinary run of New Mexico people lumped the artists all together as nuts. I imagine it will be quite a time before artistic New Mexico lives down the influx of gabbling and vain women, of priggish aesthetes, minor poets, and fairies which followed the War.[25]

Benton criticizes the social stance of Santa Fe's most recent emigrant class as alienated (and indeed alienating). That artists did not participate in "the normal activities" of their new community strikes him as offensive.

Paul Rosenfeld, who was far more sympathetic to the artists, also noticed this social disjuncture. In a long letter to Stieglitz of July 1926, he interrupts a rapturous account of the charming "primitive" effect of the multicolored dwellings of downtown Santa Fe to acknowledge that among these houses

> there are some pretentious ones: Sloan has a pink affair which looks like the palace of the Princesse de Sagan on the Avenue du Bois de Boulogne, and up on the Camin del Monte Sol, where Dasburg and some of the other daubers live, there are writhing would-be Aztec effects . . . and Greenwich Village has painted many of their doorways and windows blue. In a way, the place is terribly funny. I am living on the unpaved Canyon Road opposite an apple orchard, and all day there pass artists in immense sombreros in Ford cars.[26]

While Rosenfeld ends on a comic rather than a vituperative note, he, like Benton, disparages the artists who had gone to New Mexico and set themselves apart, erecting prominent markers of their social difference from the existing community (the aesthetic equivalents of the gaudy posturings of the nouveaux riches). He objects to some artists' thrusting themselves forward in their adopted communities, competing for admiration and notice very much as they had done in their urban neighborhoods in the East. Acting inappropriately in the environment and, worse, blind to cultural differences, they repeat the original sin of the first Anglo settlers.

It is ironic that the same new social mobility that made it easier for artists to try alternatives to industrial society made it more difficult for them to establish meaningful relations with their new neighbors and their new environments. The rootedness that Stieglitz circle members and other contemporary American artists sought—the reintegration into communities with common values to which they could contribute and from which they could draw strength—would have to be painstakingly won through time, thought, and effort, as Georgia O'Keeffe's transplanting demonstrates.

Unlike Waldo Frank, Paul Rosenfeld felt compelled to see the Southwest before writing about it; in 1926 he took the train from New York to Santa Fe. He recorded the journey and his subsequent experiences in detail in "Turning to America: The Corn Dance," an essay included in *By Way of Art*. At first sight New Mexico looked to Rosenfeld like a landscape painting come alive: "The painted canvas stretched on a jagged low frame-work, and prepared for the sudden tower of a gigantic show-man come to juggle oranges, was the remote Hamos range! . . . The whole world, the petrified past and vague future, was present, or visible from this eagles' eyrie."[27] Such were the landscapes in which the circle encoded America's history. Rosenfeld's first experience of a new landscape is a "revelation," with all its traditional spiritual connotations. "I knew this country," he intones solemnly, acutely conscious of his prophetic mission, "and feeling the grasp and order of the perspective, my churned feeling brought up the name 'America.' Midmost the continent, New Mexico lay about me, its penetralia; at once the sacred essential point of the land, where it was most itself; and the mysterious projection of a long dormant idea. I kept repeating, 'The most American place.'"[28] Rosenfeld recognized that New Mexico could be an icon of a new sociocultural order. Because its earlier cultural mixing had apparently succeeded, the new state could serve as a metonym of a revitalized America.

For these passages Rosenfeld only slightly revised the letter he wrote to Stieglitz from Santa Fe immediately after his arrival.[29] The essay thus offers a re-presentation of the land based on fresh impressions and reworked "in the studio," so to speak. We see the importance of fresh impressions in Rosenfeld's 1924 discussion of Hartley's New Mexico paintings (themselves constructed by a parallel method), which appeared in *Port of New York:* "And New Mexico, with its strange depraved topography: earth-forms fitting into each other like coupling organs; strawberry-pink mountains dotted by fuzzy-poison-shrubs, recalling breasts and wombs of clay; clouds like sky-sailing featherbeds, is in the pastels and the oils done in the Southwest."[30] Before his own visit to New Mexico, Rosenfeld falls back on a literary convention—the sexualized landscape, a style popularized by the British author and painter D. H. Lawrence (a sojourner in New Mexico who was Alfred Stieglitz's friend and correspondent). Afterward, affected much like his colleagues working in visual media, he was inspired to take a fresh approach to representing the Southwest.

None of the circle responded to the region more strongly than Georgia O'Keeffe, who said she had journeyed to New Mexico in 1929 in fulfillment of a promise she had made to herself twelve years earlier when she and her younger sister, Claudia, spent a few days in Santa Fe on their way back from the Colorado Rockies.[31] The story of her productive annual visits and eventual residence is better known than the stories of other Stieglitz circle members who explored the region. Since the 1930s she has become identified with New Mexico and its desert environment; conversely, the state has become identified with her. One can easily understand how the artist whom circle members (especially Stieglitz) saw as the personification of the promise of America could be represented by images of New Mexican land, which was itself "the most American place." "Georgia IS America," Stieglitz was fond of repeating. Members of the circle rhetorically figured her as an icon of the rebirth of American cultural identity: the New Woman (who, as representative American citizen, ultimately derived from Whitman's poetry and prose). The rhetorical and imagistic casting of

O'Keeffe as New Woman and as New Mexico profoundly affected both her work and Stieglitz's portrayals of her.

In the mythopoetic thinking of her circle, O'Keeffe's attraction to the Southwest fulfilled her destiny. Her New Mexican paintings present an intimate view of the process of working out a relationship to a beloved countryside. Many of the sites she rendered repeatedly in her New Mexico series are, as she often proudly put it, views of her "own backyard." By acquiring property in the Southwest, O'Keeffe ensured that her artworks would have a particular perspective; Sherwood Anderson did much the same thing in the South. In both cases, "their" land came to possess them. In her own life, O'Keeffe worked out the circle's concept of the American landscape reconfigured as the homeland of migrants instead of the property of the wealthy.

Soft Gray, Alcalde Hill (1929–30, Hirshhorn Museum and Sculpture Garden) represents one southwestern landscape in Georgia O'Keeffe's New Mexican repertoire. The work deliberately refuses the dramatic vertical emphasis of her cityscapes, presenting instead a horizontal format that alludes to the spaciousness of the terrain depicted. The subject is a stretch of hillside that dominates the background of the composition and is poetically echoed by a hillock of lesser height and width in the left foreground. The hills are muted and soft in color, predominantly silver-gray with a glowing band of semimetallic paint in the center foreground. The surface of this canvas, like that of nearly all of O'Keeffe's productions, is carefully rendered. The image, in its scale and radiance, pointedly recalls the intimacy of a silver photographic print. Like a Stieglitz photograph, O'Keeffe's slender painting seems a precious ritual object. Her concern, however, is not only the precious art object per se but also the intrinsic value of the untouched American landscape, which for the circle was a powerful metaphor for the similarly endangered production of American modernist art makers.

The softly rounded landforms of *Soft Gray, Alcalde Hills* invite anthropomorphic readings. Stieglitz appropriated such O'Keeffe landscape images in his portrayals of her, thereby inverting the process. Stieglitz's serial photographic portrait of O'Keeffe (comprising over three hundred photographs) has been enormously influential in structuring her complex, persuasive, and enduring public image. In the series O'Keeffe often stands for America. Her body, especially when nude, is represented as a topography of America reborn. Indeed, owing in part to these photographs of her, first shown in 1921, O'Keeffe is still America's most notorious cultural reproducer of the period.

In photographs such as *Georgia O'Keeffe: A Portrait—Torso* (1932), Stieglitz turns the nude image of the landscape painter itself into a landscape, multiplying its layers of significance. The work functions on one level as an homage to O'Keeffe's accomplishments, referring to her corpus of Southwest paintings. At the same time it sustains the metaphorical identification of the female body with nature, and of

O'Keeffe's body in particular with undespoiled American land. In this and other portrait photographs Stieglitz lovingly describes a terrain intimately known. Here the body of O'Keeffe is shown horizontally in a three-quarter frontal view distinctly unlike that of the traditional portrait. Her breasts are cropped in the background and foreground of the left edge, and her gaunt hips inscribe convex peaks at the center of the composition at top and bottom. Her pubic area, a dark triangle, is slightly right of center. The uniformly tanned skin of the subject, with its small dark patches of hair and of shade, recalls nothing so much as her own depictions of the shading and forms of southwestern terrain: O'Keeffe looks as angular and spare as the desert itself. Stieglitz suggests a new standard of female beauty to replace the voluptuous forms favored by the Victorians. The image celebrates the New Woman as a representative of modern America, while praising the new, clean lines of O'Keeffe's own New Realist paintings.

It is not clear who invented the image of woman as desert, but women authors and artists from 1880 through 1980 used the figure widely in portraying southwestern landscapes.[32] It cannot be dismissed as a view of female nature contrived by men. In any case, Stieglitz used this representation of O'Keeffe to sustain the conventional portrayal of the American Republic as a powerful woman. By associating the traditional mythic figure with a specific regional landscape, he transforms the soil of the continent into sacred ground, treating it with an awe similar to that of Native American pueblo dwellers toward their environment. Although earlier landscapes had made claims about America's sacredness, they had done so in essentially Western terms. Works of art such as O'Keeffe's and Stieglitz's conflate Western imagery (often literary) with that drawn from Native American oral traditions to relocate the Holy Land in the contemporary moment and the New World.

If many desert landscapes by O'Keeffe in subtle opalescent tones appear to be in dialogue with the nineteenth-century American luminist school, most of them derive their impact from the more torrid local colors and exotic landforms of the Southwest. Several—for example, *Cow's Skull: Red, White, and Blue* (1931; figure 58) and *Red Hills with the Pedernal* (1936; plate 7)—transplant onto southwestern subject matter the patriotic palette of the eastern seaboard and its meanings.

The bleached bone in *Cow's Skull* stands for O'Keeffe's personal experience of the arid yet hauntingly magnetic landscape of New Mexico. It also constitutes O'Keeffe's solution to a problem all members of the circle faced: how to create symbols of the vast expanses of America that lay beyond the American intellectual and cultural nucleus of New York City. In 1976 O'Keeffe recalled her thoughts as she painted it:

> As I was working I thought of the city men I had been seeing in the East. . . . I knew the middle of the country—knew quite a bit of the South—I knew the cattle country—and I knew that our country was lush and rich. I had driven across the country many times. I

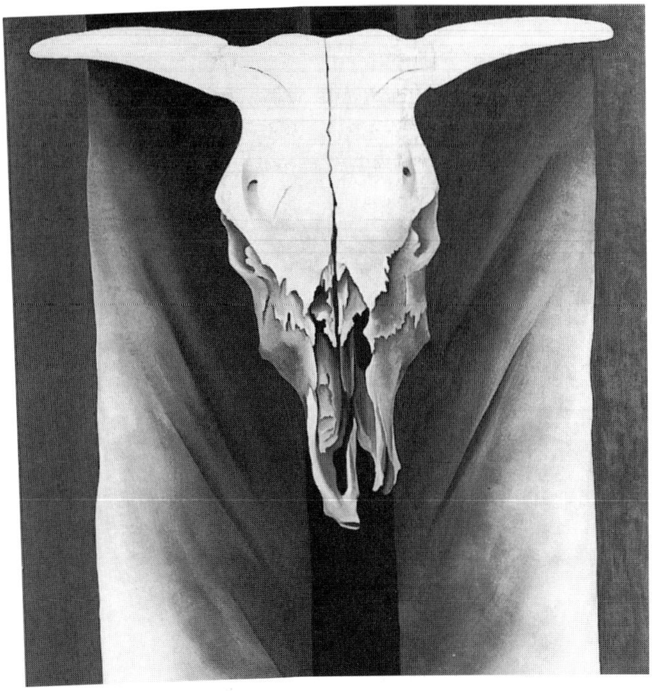

58. Georgia O'Keeffe, *Cow's Skull: Red, White, and Blue,* 1931, oil on canvas, 39 ⅞ × 35 ⅞ in. Acquired 1949, The Metropolitan Museum of Art, Alfred Stieglitz Collection.

> was quite excited over our country and I knew that at that time almost any one of those great minds would have been living in Europe if it had been possible for them. They didn't even want to live in New York—how was the Great American Thing going to happen? So as I painted along on my cow's skull on blue I thought to myself, "I'll make it an American painting."[33]

Thus *Cow's Skull: Red, White, and Blue* is also an admittedly tongue-in-cheek claim to victory in the contemporary competition to create "the Great American Thing."[34] O'Keeffe consciously differentiates her painting from those of other artists, even those of her own circle, by expressing personal experience rather than distanced reflection. She concretely enacted the circle's idea of creating art "from the American earth," from a position of rootedness and belonging.

O'Keeffe makes especially potent metonymic use of the colors of the U.S. flag in *Red Hills with the Pedernal.* It depicts the particular expanse of New Mexican land that the artist claimed as her home, symbolically appropriating it through devotional acts of representation. In purchasing the property, she established only a legal relationship to it; to gain the more important spiritual relation required repeated symbolic acts.

In this vibrant and memorable painting on linen, three vivid red-pink smoothly surfaced hills sweep gracefully up into the midground from the (light) purplish clay and sand-toned desert of the foreground. Patches of brightly leafed cottonwoods depicted in the far midground, right, announce the time of year and suggest the large scale of the red hills. The majestic flat-topped mountain depicted in bright blue, the Pedernal, presides over this desert landscape—the backyard of the painter's Abiquiu farmhouse. The sky, like that of a platinum print photograph, is silvery-white, emphasizing the unusual red and blue of the hills below. The smooth surface of these geological formations appears sculpted and polished by the elements over time. Nature itself has assisted in creating a work suitable for the artist to portray; and the artist should use all the natural resources provided, earthen pigment and talent alike. Like Hartley's *Landscape No. 3, Cash Entry Mines* (1920, Art Institute of Chicago), O'Keeffe's *Red Hills with the Pedernal* suggests that America's most important resource is the talent of its artists. Through the artwork O'Keeffe also demonstrates the truth of Frank's claim (see chapter 2); in the process of her search for America, she created its image. In a catalogue accompanying an exhibition of her Southwest works at An American Place, O'Keeffe commented: "A red hill doesn't touch everyone's heart as it touches mine, and I suppose there is no reason why it should. The red hill is a piece of the bad lands where even the grass is gone. Bad lands roll away from my door, hill after hill—red hills of apparently the same sort of earth that you mix with oil to make paint. All the earth colors of the painter's palette are out there in the many miles of bad lands."[35]

Taken together, O'Keeffe's New Mexico paintings work out Whitman's notion of rootedness, exploring her own personal mythos in relation to that of a particular place where human social history stretches back beyond the relatively brief life of the new nation. They reveal New Mexico, "the most American place," as a timeless landscape that supports an ever-continuing historical process of human acculturation. While Hartley, Strand, Marin, and Rosenfeld remained distanced observers of the new state, O'Keeffe chose instead to be an active, engaged resident, staying on year-round and participating in community activities and local politics. In these ways she put her socialist and feminist beliefs into action. And at the same time that she cultivated her art, this daughter of a failed independent farmer tended her own garden in Abiquiu for sustenance in a region where produce could rarely be bought. In this way, too, she maintained a real connection to her agrarian roots.

By one simple measure O'Keeffe's attempts to forge a relation of belonging, to represent her status as citizen, can be judged a great success. In 1996, eighty years after her debut at 291, and ten years after her death, the U.S. Postal Service issued a commemorative stamp featuring O'Keeffe's *Red Poppy* (1927); each sheet included a 1960 photograph of the artist. Thus O'Keeffe's cultural productions have been officially recognized as icons of post–World War I America; her legible, accessible art has become nationally famous and internationally recognized as part of the iconography of the modern United States.

None of this would have surprised O'Keeffe or others in the Stieglitz circle, who believed not only that an individual must work out a personal destiny but also that the transformed, communitarian American future predicted by Walt Whitman would soon arrive. Indeed, following Van Wyck Brooks, they imagined that the poet had laid down sure guidelines to achieve it. As we have seen, in "Democratic Vistas" Whitman had prophesied a "Third stage" of American intellectual, cultural, and social development that would transcend business and corporate power: it was to be signaled and spurred by native expression in all the arts.[36]

New Mexico provided O'Keeffe with a fresh sense of space where she could experiment with more innovative and open forms and create metaphors of an open, freer society to come. In response to Whitman's and his followers' clarion calls to find democratic modes of artistic representation, members of the Stieglitz circle imagined an America renewed by way of art. Though they never stopped fighting against the capitalism that controlled the marketing of their works, they managed to fashion, out of alternative economic structures that themselves persist, an art that still powerfully represents alternative and radically democratic visions of America.

NOTES

INTRODUCTION

1. *Democracy* has no single definition; the participatory model associated with Whitman emphasizes the need for solidarity and community created by a common culture. Its followers view politics as the search for public interests. Liberal democracy, perhaps associated most strongly with John Stuart Mill, emphasizes negative and exclusive liberties and assumes that politics is necessarily an interminable clash among private interests. By examining how the participatory model was taken up by the Stieglitz circle in particular historical and cultural contexts, we see what I call the radical aspect of the poet's vision of America.
2. See William Innes Homer, *Alfred Stieglitz and the American Avant-Garde* (Boston: New York Graphic Society, 1977), pp. 260–68 (six pages of text with large plates).
3. Michael Lind, in "Where Have You Gone, Louis Sullivan?" (*Harper's Magazine,* February 1998, pp. 53–59), describes the dominant view: that in art and architectural history, intellectual and cultural history, literary history, and even foreign policy, America's genuine innovations did not occur until the stimulating influx of European intellectuals after World War II.
4. Serge Guilbaut, *How New York Stole the Idea of Modern Art* (Chicago: University of Chicago Press, 1983), p. 3 n. 2.
5. A good example of how the later achievements of the Stieglitz circle were downplayed is provided by the catalogue of a joint exhibition of watercolors by Charles Demuth and Arthur

Dove held at Edith Halpert's Modern Gallery in 1954. Two MoMA curators, Alfred Barr and Andrew Ritchie, provided commentaries that associated these artists exclusively with the period that closed with the end of World War I and labeled them simply "pioneers." Barr in particular had a strong interest in keeping intact his canon of modernists—exclusively European—as clearly spelled out in his influential book *Cubism and Abstract Art* (New York: Museum of Modern Art, 1936). Barr did have an interest in and respect for the art produced by the Stieglitz circle, according to Peter Selz, who was curator of exhibitions of the Department of Painting and Sculpture at MoMA from 1959 to 1965. Yet his choice to exclude them from his widely accepted account of the development of important modern styles influenced art historians and critics for decades.

6. Theodore E. Stebbins, Jr., and Carol Troyen, *The Lane Collection: Twentieth-Century Paintings in the American Tradition,* exhibition catalogue (Boston: Museum of Fine Arts, 1983), pp. 51–55. The influence of the Stieglitz circle in the forties and fifties deserves much more attention. According to Irving Sandler (*The Triumph of American Painting: A History of Abstract Expressionism* [New York: Harper and Row, 1970], p. 15), John Marin was admired by the younger painters. And Susan Klein has found that Mark Rothko's letters at Yale's Beinecke Library attest to his great interest in Arthur Dove's work (conversation with author, 1984). The painter Theodoros Stamos was also very interested in the work of Arthur Dove and, as Rothko told Peter Selz in 1966, first drew Rothko's attention to Dove's work (Selz, conversation with author, September 1985).
7. In *Art and Culture: Critical Essays* ([Boston: Beacon Press, 1961], pp. 181–83), and elsewhere, Clement Greenberg figured Marin as a link between the first and second American avant-gardes and as a direct ancestor of Jackson Pollock. Marin himself rejected any such connection; in a brief catalogue published by An American Place in 1946, he insisted that a truly abstract art was impossible, claiming that "There never was or never will be a non-objective art" (reprinted in John Marin, *Selected Writings,* ed. Dorothy Norman [New York: Pelligrini and Cudahy, 1949], p. 216).
8. Notable exceptions to this failure to move beyond biography to address social context and theoretical issues include Barbara Buhler Lynes, *O'Keeffe, Stieglitz, and the Critics, 1916–1929* (Chicago: University of Chicago Press, 1989), and Jonathan Weinberg, *Speaking for Vice: Homosexuality in the Art of Charles Demuth, Marsden Hartley, and the First American Avant-Garde* (New Haven: Yale University Press, 1993).
9. Paul Rosenfeld, "When New York Became Central," *Modern Music,* summer 1946, p. 84. I think it no coincidence that he made this comment shortly after Stieglitz's death.
10. Walt Whitman, "Democratic Vistas," in *Complete Poetry and Collected Prose,* ed. Justin Kaplan, Library of America (New York: Literary Classics of the United States, 1982), p. 929. In the early 1920s and again in the late 1960s, Whitman's prose and poetry were seen as a powerful medium of political reeducation.
11. In their socialist phase (in the late 1910s to mid-1930s) members of the circle were in part reacting against artists and critics who called for simpler, more "popular" art—first the Ashcan school and later the Regionalists and social realists. They presented New Realism, with its selective infusion of modernist strategies, as a more authentic depiction of modern life than overtly didactic forms like social realism and also as more truthful than traditional American naturalism.

12. See Steven Watson, *Strange Bedfellows: The First American Avant-Garde* (New York: Abbeville Press, 1991) for a comprehensive and anecdotal who's who of cultural innovators from 1913 to 1917.

13. Warren I. Susman, "The Thirties," in *The Development of an American Culture*, ed. Stanley Coben and Lorman Ratner (Englewood Cliffs, N.J.: Prentice-Hall, 1970), p. 189.

14. See Marsden Hartley, "The Importance of Being 'Dada,'" in *Adventures in the Arts: Informal Chapters on Painters, Vaudeville, and Poets* (New York: Boni and Liveright, 1921), pp. 247–53. Earlier, the collaborative periodical *291*, produced in twelve numbers from March 1915 to February 1916 by gallery 291, included contributions from Francis Picabia, a dadaist friend of Marcel Duchamp.

15. The San Francisco exhibition was *Images of America: Precisionist Painting and Modern Photography*, organized by Karen Tsujimoto, to whom I am forever grateful for providing the occasion for my (inadvertent) discovery of this rich topic. Georgia O'Keeffe's *Barn with Snow* (1933) and Stieglitz's *New York in 1932*, both featured in the show, introduced me to the city-country dialogue that I later found explored in the writings of members of the circle as well.

16. I do not mean to imply that any work has a single meaning nor that interpretations are necessarily so tendentious as to be useless and distorting. Different viewers (or one viewer at different times) might discover different messages, but these messages derive from a core of meanings in the work itself.

17. Raymond Williams, *The Country and the City* (New York: Oxford University Press, 1973), pp. 5–6.

18. Malcolm Cowley, *Exile's Return: A Narrative of Ideas* (New York: W. W. Norton, 1934), p. 298.

19. Lewis Mumford to Alfred Stieglitz, December 31, 1940, Alfred Stieglitz Papers, Collection of American Literature, Beinecke Rare Book and Manuscript Library, Yale University, New Haven, Connecticut.

20. Edward Abrahams, *The Lyrical Left: Randolph Bourne, Alfred Stieglitz, and the Origins of Cultural Radicalism in America* (Charlottesville: University Press of Virginia, 1986), pp. 205–9.

21. The ideas of radical thinkers such as Theodore Roszak and Charles Reich commanded a much broader audience in the sixties than did those of the members of the Stieglitz circle or the *Seven Arts* group in the twenties.

22. American postmodernist critics have been reluctant to trace their lineage. See Brian Wallis, introduction to *Art after Modernism: Rethinking Representation*, ed. Wallis (New York: New Museum of Contemporary Art; Boston: David R. Godine, 1985), pp. xi–xvii.

CHAPTER 1. TOWARD A DEMOCRATIC ART

1. As I use the term, *democracy* (whether describing the American past or pointing toward a desired future) entails an assertion of the public good over private interests. The privileging of the public (*res publica*) is a fundamental legacy of the American Revolution, one that was cherished and reasserted by a generation of reform-minded politicians and social critics and theorists that included Theodore Roosevelt, John Dewey,

and William James. Their Madisonian ideas concerning disinterested service for the common good were inherited and reworked by the socially engaged critics of the Stieglitz group.

2. The sentiment of the subtitle seems an unmistakable foreshadowing of "community-based" conceptions of the 1990s.
3. Stickley is quoted in Donald Drew Egbert, *Socialism and American Art in the Light of European Utopianism, Marxism, and Anarchism* (Princeton: Princeton University Press, 1967), p. 86.
4. Gustav Stickley, "The Craftsman Movement: Its Origins and Growth," *Craftsman,* no. 25 (October 1913): 18.
5. Egbert, *Socialism and American Art,* p. 86.
6. Susan Fillin-Yeh, "Innovative Moderns: Arthur G. Dove and Georgia O'Keeffe," *Arts* 56 (June 1982): 68–72.
7. Egbert, *Socialism and American Art,* p. 88.
8. Ibid., pp. 97–98.
9. Alfred Stieglitz to Lewis Mumford, September 10, 1925, Alfred Stieglitz Papers, Collection of American Literature, Beinecke Rare Book and Manuscript Library, Yale University, New Haven, Connecticut. Unless otherwise noted, all letters cited are from this collection.
10. Paul Rosenfeld to Alfred Stieglitz, July 7, 1922.
11. Van Wyck Brooks, "Amor Fati," in *The Freeman Book: Typical Editorials, Critiques, and Other Selections from the Eight Volumes of the "Freeman," 1920–1924* (New York: B. W. Huebsch, 1924), p. 108.
12. Waldo Frank, "The American Year," in *Salvos: An Informal Book about Books and Plays* (New York: Boni and Liveright, 1924), p. 207.
13. A letter to Waldo Frank from Alfred Stieglitz dated September 26, 1926, documents that the photographer purchased one of the first subscriptions to *New Masses.* See also Sue Davidson Lowe, *Stieglitz: A Memoir/Biography* (New York: Farrar, Straus and Giroux, 1983), pp. 178, 237; Anne Tucker, "Strand as Mentor," in *Paul Strand Essays on His Life and Work,* ed. Maren Stange (New York: Aperture, 1990), pp. 123–24.
14. Laurie Lisle, *Portrait of an Artist: A Biography of Georgia O'Keeffe* (New York: Washington Square Press, 1981), p. 240.
15. The account of the debate and the quotations from it are provided by Gladys Oaks, "Radical Writer and Woman Artist Class on Propaganda and Its Uses," *New York World,* March 16, 1930, women's section I, p. 3.
16. For a thorough consideration of the failure of Marxism to consider aesthetic and gender issues, see Janet Wolff, *Aesthetics and the Sociology of Art,* 2d ed. (Ann Arbor: University of Michigan Press, 1993).
17. In a typewritten note to the Artists' Committee of Action, dated May 24, 1934, and addressed to Lionel S. Reiss, Alfred Stieglitz called the recent occasion of his publicly speaking on behalf of the committee at City Hall in New York "one of the Red Letter Days in my life." In addition, he requested that his honorarium for that appearance be added to the organization's funds.
18. Orozco is quoted in Patricia Hills, *Social Concern and Urban Realism: American Painting*

of the 1930s, exhibition catalogue (Boston: Boston University Art Gallery, 1983), p. 16. On *Art Front,* see pp. 16, 18.

19. Paul Rosenfeld, *Port of New York: Essays on Fourteen American Moderns,* with camera portraits by Alfred Stieglitz, Alice Boughton, Paul Strand, and Dana Desboro (New York: Harcourt, Brace, 1924), p. 47.
20. Brian Wallis, "What's Wrong with This Picture," introduction to *Art after Modernism: Rethinking Representation,* ed. Wallis (New York: New Museum of Contemporary Art; Boston: David R. Godine, 1985), pp. xi–xii.
21. Similarly, in the *Freeman* Brooks attacked the muckrakers out of his opposition not to the *politicization* of writers or writing but to the particular type of politics that muckrakers espoused: Progressivism.
22. Van Wyck Brooks, *The Wine of the Puritans: A Study of Present-Day America* (New York: M. Kennerley, 1908), p. 113.
23. Walt Whitman, "Democratic Vistas," in *Complete Poetry and Collected Prose,* ed. Justin Kaplan, Library of America (New York: Literary Classics of the United States, 1982), pp. 978–79. This work is hereafter cited parenthetically in the text.
24. Van Wyck Brooks, *America's Coming-of-Age* (New York: B. W. Huebsch, 1915), p. 74. This work is hereafter cited parenthetically in the text.
25. While Brooks tries to synthesize James's and Dewey's disparate notions of mind and body, Waldo Frank (and especially Paul Rosenfeld) shifted the pragmatists' emphasis on *doing*—the necessity for the human to perform a function—to a stress on *being.*
26. Terry Eagleton's *Illusions of Postmodernism* (Oxford: Blackwell, 1996) powerfully and creatively reconsiders traditional socialist assumptions, critiquing how they have been misused (wittingly and unwittingly) by the fashionable varieties of postmodern thought currently disseminated in many colleges and universities.
27. Lowe, *Stieglitz,* pp. 178–79; quotation, p. 178.
28. Henry F. May, *The End of American Innocence* (New York: Knopf, 1959); see in particular pp. 280–300, on "the Young Intellectuals."
29. Ibid., p. ix.
30. Alfred Stieglitz to Paul Rosenfeld, September 5, 1923.
31. Alfred Stieglitz to Sherwood Anderson, December 28, 1925.
32. Waldo Frank, *Our America* (New York: Boni and Liveright, 1919), p. 195.
33. Walt Whitman, "Crossing Brooklyn Ferry," in *Complete Poetry and Collected Prose,* pp. 312–13.
34. Rosenfeld, *Port of New York,* pp. 168–69.
35. "Nonhierarchical" does not here mean "nonpatriarchal"; even contemporary critics noted the primacy of phallic form in works by members of the Stieglitz circle (except O'Keeffe).
36. Alfred Stieglitz to Paul Rosenfeld, November 14, 1923.
37. Waldo Frank, *In the American Jungle [1925–1936]* (New York: Farrar and Rinehart, 1937), p. 93.
38. On 1990s factionalism, see Terry Eagleton, "Fallacies," chapter 5 of *Illusions of Postmodernism,* pp. 93–130.
39. I am referring in particular to Robert Hughes's ambitious reevaluation of American art from the colonial period to the present in *American Visions: The Epic History of Art in*

America (New York: Alfred A. Knopf, 1997), and in the companion eight-hour television series, originally broadcast on PBS from May 28 to June 18, 1997.

CHAPTER 2. RECYCLING WHITMAN

1. In his unpublished essay ("Peter Doyle and the Whitman Group," Hartley-Berger Collection, Collection of American Literature, Beinecke Rare Book and Manuscript Library, Yale University, New Haven, Connecticut), Marsden Hartley refers to his two paintings of Whitman's home (dated by scholars to around 1905). Hartley had already been exposed to European modernism in 1903 (as is well known, he saw the Segantini "stitch"—the overlapping and interweaving of small, bright-colored strokes of paint distinctive to the works of the contemporary Italian painter Giovanni Segantini—reproduced in the January 1903 issue of *Jugend*), but he may have felt that his homages to such a deeply American subject were most appropriately expressed in a realist mode. The better known is an oil-on-board work reproduced in Gail Scott, *Marsden Hartley* (New York: Abbeville Press, 1988), plate 5, and also in Jeanne Hokin, *Pinnacles and Pyramids: The Art of Marsden Hartley* (Albuquerque: University of New Mexico Press, 1993), figure 5.
2. Elizabeth Hutton Turner, *American Artists in Paris, 1919–1929* (Ann Arbor, Mich.: UMI Research Press, 1988), pp. 49–52.
3. Waldo Frank, *Salvos: An Informal Book about Books and Plays* (New York: Boni and Liveright, 1924), p. 278; his ellipses.
4. Walt Whitman, "Democratic Vistas," in *Complete Poetry and Collected Prose,* ed. Justin Kaplan, Library of America (New York: Literary Classics of the United States, 1982), p. 991; this work is hereafter cited parenthetically in the text. These aims are very much akin to those of European reformers such as the Fourierists and the Utopian socialists.
5. See Paul Oskar Kristeller, "The Modern System of the Arts," in *Renaissance Thought II: Papers on Humanism and the Arts* (New York: Harper and Row, 1965), pp. 163–227.
6. Waldo Frank, *Our America* (New York: Boni and Liveright, 1919), pp. 13–15, 7–8. This work is hereafter cited parenthetically in the text.
7. It also matters little whether Frank's claims were true. They are important because of what they do: i.e., challenge the perceived European cultural hegemony and help gain international acclaim for American artists.
8. Waldo Frank, introduction to *Adventures in the Arts,* by Marsden Hartley (New York: Boni and Liveright, 1921), p. xv. Frank's developmental "stages" present a historical progression; in the final, ideal stage, the solitariness or alienation of the artist ends with his or her return to the community.
9. Marsden Hartley, *Adventures in the Arts* (New York: Boni and Liveright, 1921), p. 57. This work is hereafter cited parenthetically in the text.
10. Marsden Hartley, "Aesthetic Sincerity" and "America as Landscape," *El Palacio* 5, no. 20 (December 9, 1918): 332–33, 340–42, discussed in chapter 4.
11. In the late 1910s and 1920s, the term "national" was used by artists, theorists, and critics as a synonym for "native"—that is, without the negative connotations often attached to "nationalism" and even more to "nativism" in the 1930s.
12. Malcolm Cowley, *Exile's Return: A Narrative of Ideas* (New York: W. W. Norton, 1934), p. 67.

13. Raymond Williams, *The Country and the City* (New York: Oxford University Press, 1973), p. 234.
14. Cowley, *Exile's Return*, p. 223.
15. Waldo Frank, *The Re-discovery of America: An Introduction to a Philosophy of American Life* (New York: Charles Scribner's Sons, 1929), p. 134.
16. See, e.g., Alfred Stieglitz to Sherwood Anderson, June 22, 1925, and Stieglitz to Waldo Frank, November 5, 1928, Alfred Stieglitz Papers, Collection of American Literature, Beinecke Rare Book and Manuscript Library, Yale University, New Haven, Connecticut. Unless otherwise noted, all letters cited are from this collection. The letters also show that in addition to speculating whether the circle had an audience, members did anecdotal research. Some show particular interest in what working-class Americans thought of their visual artworks. Stieglitz recorded in some of his letters the reactions of their maids at the lake to his work or O'Keeffe's, and Paul Rosenfeld (in a letter dated July 8, 1923) reported that a friend's servant, "a sturdy intelligent hard-working girl," has "gone into ecstasies over the Marins and O'Keeffes."
17. Waldo Frank, "The Art of Arthur Dove," *New Republic*, January 27, 1926, p. 269.
18. Joseph Shiffman, "The Alienation of the Artist: Alfred Stieglitz," *American Quarterly* 3 (fall 1951): 244–58.
19. Alfred Stieglitz to Sherwood Anderson, June 22, 1925.
20. Alfred Stieglitz to Waldo Frank, June 19, 1925.
21. Sherwood Anderson to Dwight McDonald, April 1929, in Sherwood Anderson, *Letters of Sherwood Anderson*, ed. Howard Mumford Jones (New York: Kraus Reprint, 1969), p. 192.
22. For a contemporary instance of socially engaged art that is class-blind even in the 1990s, see my "Rooftop T.E.A.M.-Building," *Public Art Review* 7, no. 1 (fall/winter 1995): 34–35.
23. Ironically, it was the issue of alienation that forced the split between Stieglitz circle critics and Van Wyck Brooks, whom they acknowledged as an important influence. Both Rosenfeld and Frank interpreted Brooks's shift of focus from literature of the present to that of the past as exemplifying just the kind of alienation from vital social issues that Brooks himself had initially condemned.
24. Robert Morss Lovett, "Emotional Sincerity," review of *By Way of Art*, by Paul Rosenfeld, *Dial*, April 1929, p. 334.
25. Waldo Frank, "Emerging Greatness," in *Salvos*, p. 31.
26. Waldo Frank, "A Letter to the Annual Whitman Celebration," in *Salvos*, pp. 276–79; quotation, p. 277.
27. Waldo Frank, "For a Declaration of War," in *Salvos*, p. 15. This work is hereafter cited parenthetically in the text.
28. Sherwood Anderson, *Sherwood Anderson's Notebook* (New York: Boni and Liveright, 1926), p. 195.
29. Paul Rosenfeld, *Port of New York: Essays on Fourteen American Moderns*, with camera portraits by Alfred Stieglitz, Alice Boughton, Paul Strand, and Dana Desboro (New York: Harcourt, Brace, 1924), p. v. This work is hereafter cited parenthetically in the text.
30. See also Sarah E. Greenough, "From the American Earth: Alfred Stieglitz's Photographs of Apples," *Art Journal* 41, no. 1 (spring 1981): 46–54, for further use of the apple tree metaphor in the work (textual and visual) of the Stieglitz circle.

31. The painter willingly assumed and heightened his "identity" as Marin the Ancient Mariner (even signing letters to circle members with the epithet). Just as Hartley is the native son of Maine, so Marin is figured in *Port of New York* as an old New England salt: "there is a nervousness, a fine dash and roughness of edge, in him, that is Yankee" (p. 162). This fabrication of a persona for Marin is, of course, as much a fiction as are his paintings. And Marin's eventual ownership and habitation of a small island off the Maine coast were largely an attempt to enact an ideal.
32. What matters here is not Anderson's "realism"—his fiction is no more or less "real" than any other genre, including literary and art criticism—but the terms in which this claim is made. Suddenly the vernacular (the vocabulary of "the folk," as it were) was becoming acceptable to critical discourse. Rosenfeld himself moves in this direction, and consciously away from the devalued refinement of the genteel tradition. In so doing he also fulfills the dictates of his model critic, Brooks.
33. See Barbara Buhler Lynes, *O'Keeffe, Stieglitz, and the Critics, 1916–1929* (Ann Arbor, Mich.: UMI Research Press, 1989), pp. 44–88.

CHAPTER 3. "A DIRECT POINT OF CONTACT": THE INTIMATE GALLERY AND AN AMERICAN PLACE

1. Linda Henefield Skalet, "The Market for American Painting in New York: 1870–1915" (Ph.D. diss., Johns Hopkins University, 1980), p. 39.
2. E. P. Richardson, *A Short History of American Painting* (New York: Harper and Row, 1963), p. 210.
3. George E. Mowry and Blaine A. Brownell, *The Urban Nation, 1920–1980,* rev. ed. (New York: Hill and Wang, 1981), p. 8.
4. Paul Rosenfeld, *Port of New York: Essays on Fourteen American Moderns,* with camera portraits by Alfred Stieglitz, Alice Boughton, Paul Strand, and Dana Desboro (New York: Harcourt, Brace, 1924), p. 266.
5. Alfred Stieglitz to Charles Demuth, January 1930, Alfred Stieglitz Papers, Collection of American Literature, Beinecke Rare Book and Manuscript Library, Yale University, New Haven, Connecticut. Unless otherwise noted, all letters cited are from this collection.
6. Rosenfeld, *Port of New York,* p. 266.
7. Waldo Frank, *Our America* (New York: Boni and Liveright, 1919), pp. 200–201.
8. Ibid., pp. 228–29.
9. Stieglitz's active engagement in the socialist movement during the early twenties, documented by Susan Davidson Lowe (*Stieglitz: A Memoir/Biography* [New York: Farrar, Straus and Giroux, 1983], pp. 177–79), lends credence to the idea that he structured his three galleries on the model of profit-sharing provided by William Morris, whose theories he surely knew. During his student years in Berlin (1887 and 1888), Stieglitz was actively submitting his works to numerous exhibition societies, particularly in England; he probably had contact with members of the Arts and Crafts Exhibition Society, which was founded in 1887 to promote Morris's ideas. At the very least he would have known of the society's novel methods and ideas, since fin de siècle Germany was itself caught up in the reform ethic first promulgated by Morris. The most complete account of Stieglitz's

student years and his support of American photography on his return to New York City in 1890 is found in William Innes Homer, *Alfred Stieglitz and the Photo-Secession* (Boston: Little, Brown, 1983).

Stieglitz's notions of art were closely aligned to the ideas that Morris expressed in his first public lecture, "The Decorative Arts" (delivered in April 1877): in particular, that "works of art" are all things made by humans and that "art making" is a social activity. In addition, Morris's early renunciation of industrial capitalism growing from his concern for the devastation of vast areas of rural land is remarkably close to the prescient proto-ecological awareness voiced by the Stieglitz circle and embodied in their landscape paintings. Even the circle's challenge to the dominance of the French modes of representation through the medium of the minor art of photography was a strategy borrowed from Morris and his group of decorative artists, who had initiated a new phase in Western art production by challenging the French Beaux Arts tradition with minor arts such as wallpaper and furniture. Members of the circle, like their Arts and Crafts predecessors, found circumventing capitalist means of production and distribution their most difficult task.

10. Eileen Boris, "Art and Labor: John Ruskin, William Morris, and the Craftsman Ideal in America, 1876–1915" (Ph.D. diss., Brown University, 1981), p. 54.
11. Hugh McClellan Potter, "The 'Romantic Nationalists' of the 1920s" (Ph.D. diss., University of Minnesota, 1964), pp. 156–57.
12. Alfred Stieglitz to Arthur Dove, March 30, 1936. In this letter, Stieglitz relates that he has just sold a Dove seascape that he owned to the University of Minnesota; as was his customary practice, only a personal letter records the terms of the sale: "As soon as Minnesota sends the check . . . 250 goes to the Dorothy Norman Rent Fund—& the $250 which goes to me for the original outlay I am also turning over to The Place!!" If Stieglitz in any way separated himself out from other group members, it was in his unflagging patronage of his colleagues.
13. Alfred Stieglitz to the unnamed purchaser of a Marin oil painting, April 7, 1941.
14. In "Georgia O'Keeffe in Love" (*Art and Antiques*, September 1987, p. 104), Jeffrey Schaire quotes the artist on her fellow group members: "I got on with them very well because I did all the hard work. I was quite a useful citizen."
15. "An Invitation to the Friends of John Marin," a plea for subscription funds issued by Alfred Stieglitz in 1923, in the Stieglitz Papers, Beinecke Rare Book and Manuscript Library, Yale University.
16. "Membership List of the Friends of John Marin," a document showing the total amount as of March 1924 each member had contributed toward Marin's support, in the Stieglitz Papers, Beinecke Rare Book and Manuscript Library, Yale University.
17. Whitman's own "difference" (i.e., his homosexuality) was made plain to any close reader of his work (as is also true of the visual productions of Hartley and Demuth). One could persuasively argue that Whitman's style was appropriated by artists and writers of the liberal-minded circle precisely because it was an obvious marker of such difference. For a thought-provoking discussion of Whitman's style, see Karl Keller's "Walt Whitman Camping," in *Camp Grounds: Style and Homosexuality*, ed. David Bergman (Amherst: University of Massachusetts Press, 1993), pp. 113–20.

18. Alfred Stieglitz to Waldo Frank, undated.
19. Alfred Stieglitz to the State Tax Commission, June 22, 1928.
20. Alfred Stieglitz to Charles Demuth, undated. Emily Farnham, *Charles Demuth: Behind a Laughing Mask* (Norman: University of Oklahoma Press, 1971), quotes the same letter and dates it to "not long after the doors of the Intimate Gallery opened" (p. 151). Its contents suggest, however, that it was written before the gallery opened in December 1925.
21. For a complete list of exhibitions hung at all three cooperative galleries through 1934, see "List of Exhibitions," in *America and Alfred Stieglitz: A Collective Portrait,* ed. Waldo Frank et al., rev. ed. (Millerton, N.Y.: Aperture, 1979), pp. 150–52. A complete list of exhibitions at An American Place from 1929 to 1934 is included in a catalogue by Ronald G. Pisano, *An American Place* (Southampton, N.Y.: Parrish Art Museum, 1981), n.p.
22. The catalogue for the 1921 show at Anderson Galleries; copies of the catalogue can be examined at the Library of the Museum of Modern Art (MoMA), New York, and in the Mitchell Kennerly Papers at the New York Public Library.
23. Marsden Hartley, "The Importance of Being 'Dada,'" in *Adventures in the Arts: Informal Chapters on Painters, Vaudeville, and Poets* (New York: Boni and Liveright, 1921), pp. 247–53.
24. Unpaginated catalogue prepared by Alfred Stieglitz: *Alfred Stieglitz Presents Seven Americans: 159 Paintings, Photographs, and Things, Recent and Never before Publicly Shown,* exhibition catalogue, Anderson Galleries, March 9–28, 1925 (New York: Anderson Galleries, 1925). The show included all the artists who would become part of the re-formed Stieglitz circle of the 1920s, 1930s, and 1940s. A number of copies of the various exhibition catalogues of those years exist; the Stieglitz Papers in Yale's Beinecke Library has the most complete set I have found.
25. See Marsden Hartley, "Aesthetic Sincerity" and "America as Landscape," *El Palacio* 5, no. 20 (December 9, 1918): 332–33, 340–42.
26. Georgia O'Keeffe's presence in the group was also a statement about inclusion. Before he discovered O'Keeffe, Stieglitz had scouted for years for a woman painter to join the circle. His earlier coterie, the Photo-Secession, had from its founding included significant numbers of women photographers.
27. Frank, *Our America,* p. 10.
28. Kenneth E. Silver, *Esprit de Corps: The Art of the Parisian Avant-Garde and the First World War, 1914–1925* (Princeton: Princeton University Press, 1989).
29. Alfred Stieglitz to Charles Demuth, January 1930. Stieglitz's question is highly ironic, since the American photographer Man Ray had been an informal member of Stieglitz's circle before he moved to Paris in July 1921. For a complete account of Stieglitz's role as Ray's mentor and model, see Neil Baldwin, *Man Ray: American Artist* (New York: Da Capo Press, 1988). It is interesting to consider the influence of Stieglitz's early, surreal photographic images on Ray—e.g., the New York night scenes of the 1890s and the inventive use of superimposition in *Dorothy True* (1919).
30. Skalet, "The Market for American Painting."
31. Judith Collins, *The Omega Workshops* (Chicago: University of Chicago Press, 1984).
32. I examined a copy of the catalogue for *Seven Americans* with reproductions (another version has text only), in a folder of correspondence and documents on Stieglitz's associa-

tion with Anderson Galleries in the Mitchell Kennerly Papers at the New York Public Library.

33. "Seven Alive," in *Alfred Stieglitz Presents Seven Americans*, n.p.

34. Walt Whitman, "Democratic Vistas," in *Complete Poetry and Collected Prose*, ed. Justin Kaplan, Library of America (New York: Literary Classics of the United States, 1982), pp. 983–84. This work is hereafter cited parenthetically in the text.

35. This use of the natural landscape in Anderson's work begins early. See in particular *Winesburg, Ohio* (1919).

36. Hilton Kramer, "Marin's Romance with New York City," *New York Times*, October 23, 1981, C:23.

37. Harold Clurman, "Alfred Stieglitz and the Group Ideal," in *America and Alfred Stieglitz*, ed. Frank et al., pp. 130–35.

38. Alfred Stieglitz to Sherwood Anderson, July 5, 1924.

39. Theodore E. Stebbins, Jr., and Carol Troyen, *The Lane Collection: Twentieth-Century Paintings in the American Tradition*, exhibition catalogue (Boston: Museum of Fine Arts, 1983), p. 39.

40. In a letter to Alfred Stieglitz dated August 31, 1921, Charles Demuth calls Daniel "a crook."

41. Elizabeth McCausland, "The Daniel Gallery and Modern American Art," *Magazine of Art* 44, no. 7 (November 1951): 280–83. Stieglitz's 291 did more than educate Charles Daniel about modern art; it was there that he met Alanson Hartpence, generally thought to have attracted to the Daniel Gallery its most important client—Ferdinand Howald, a collector from Ohio. It has also been suggested that Hartpence, a poet, painter, and friend of Marsden Hartley who became Daniel's gallery assistant, was responsible for the exhibition hangings and decor at the gallery (see Susan Noyes Platt, "Responses to Modern Art in New York in the 1920s" [Ph.D. diss., University of Texas, Austin, 1981], p. 60).

42. Archives of American Art, *Collection of Exhibition Catalogues Index* (Boston: G. K. Hall, 1979), pp. 227–28; Archives of American Art, Smithsonian Institution, roll D-160, pp. 297–98; Archives of American Art, Smithsonian Institution, roll NAAA-1.

43. Herbert J. Seligmann, *Alfred Stieglitz Talking: Notes on Some of His Conversations, 1925–1931* (New Haven: Yale University Library, 1966), p. 104.

44. Opening announcement of the Intimate Gallery, dated December 1925. Copies are in the Stieglitz Papers at Yale and in files on the Stieglitz circle in MoMA's library.

45. Thomas C. Cochran and William Miller, *The Age of Enterprise: A Social History of Industrial America* (New York: Macmillan, 1942), p. 258.

46. Roy A. Kotynek, "291: Alfred Stieglitz and the Introduction of Modern Art to America" (Ph.D. diss., Northwestern University, 1970), p. 167. Kotynek documents and supports the impressive attendance figures of Intimate Gallery exhibitions (pp. 282–83).

47. Roland Marchand, *Advertising the American Dream: Making Way for Modernity, 1920–1940* (Berkeley: University of California Press, 1985), pp. 140, 26. Also see the illustrations (pp. 141–43) showing how approaches to noncommercial art (and particularly that of Charles Demuth) were rapidly absorbed by the ad industry.

48. A photograph of Ayer and Son is reproduced in ibid., p. 27, fig. 2.1.

49. Malcolm Gee, *Dealers, Critics, and Collectors of Modern Painting: Aspects of the Parisian Art Market between 1910 and 1930* (New York: Garland, 1981), p. 125.
50. In a letter dated August 31, 1921, Waldo Frank wrote to Alfred Stieglitz from Paris, denouncing the city's "too fixed achievement" and "the static mood of its spirit, despite constant experimentation." The only exception was to be found in the gallery of Léonce Rosenberg, where "the painters are still creating." Stieglitz could rely on more than secondhand descriptions for his knowledge of contemporary European painting; Frank took care to send him photographic reproductions of the Parisian works he judged significant.
51. Gee, *Dealers, Critics, and Collectors of Modern Painting*, pp. 115–21.
52. Ibid., pp. 68–69.
53. Ibid., p. 274.
54. Waldo Frank to Alfred Stieglitz, April 18, 1927.
55. Alfred Stieglitz to Duncan Phillips, April 16, 1943.
56. Lowe, *Stieglitz*, p. 302.
57. Dorothy Norman, "An American Place," in *America and Alfred Stieglitz*, ed. Frank et al., pp. 67, 75.
58. On A.I.R., see Judith K. Brodsky, "Exhibition Galleries, and Alternative Spaces," in *The Power of Feminist Art: The American Movement of the 1970s, History and Impact*, ed. Norma Broude and Mary D. Garrard (New York: Harry N. Abrams, 1994), pp. 108–9, 118; in the same collection, see also Yolanda M. López and Moira Roth, "Social Protest: Racism and Sexism," pp. 146, 155, and Laura Cottingham, "The Feminist Continuum: Art after 1970," pp. 282–83. On Noho, see Kathy O'Dell, *Kate Millett, Sculptor: The First Thirty-eight Years*, exhibition catalogue (Catonsville, Md.: Fine Arts Gallery, University of Maryland Baltimore County, 1997). Renny Pritikin's analysis "The Port Huron Statement and the Origin of Artist's Organizations," in *New Writing in Arts Criticism*, ed. Anne Marie MacDonald, Kathy Brew, Peter Saidel, and Maureen Keefe (San Francisco: San Francisco Artspace, 1988), pp. 37–40, is an early recognition of the important resurgence of the cooperative idea and its political underpinnings in America in the 1960s.

CHAPTER 4. RECONFIGURING REALISM

1. Marsden Hartley, "Aesthetic Sincerity," *El Palacio* 5, no. 20 (December 9, 1918): 332. This work is hereafter cited parenthetically in the text. The spelling of "aesthetic" changes in the body of the essay.
2. Waldo Frank, *Our America* (New York: Boni and Liveright, 1919), p. 27. This work is hereafter cited parenthetically in the text.
3. Marsden Hartley, "America as Landscape," *El Palacio* 5, no. 20 (December 9, 1918): 341, 340, 341.
4. Marsden Hartley, *Adventures in the Arts: Informal Chapters on Painters, Vaudeville, and Poets* (New York: Boni and Liveright, 1921), p. 135. This work is hereafter cited parenthetically in the text.
5. In *Der Blaue Reiter*, a book produced by contemporary German artists with whom Hartley had exhibited abroad, approximately half the illustrations are of tribal and folk art; see Wassily Kandinsky and Franz Marc, eds., *Der Blau Reiter* (Munich: R. Piper, 1912).

6. Hartley here appropriates both the form and content of his criticism from Charles Baudelaire, emphasizing "the primitive" (he calls Rousseau "the great modern primitive"), "the naive," and the subject of death, just as the French critic did in his well-known "Salon of 1855" (Baudelaire's review of the government-sponsored Salon held in Paris that year). Moreover, an unknown amateur (Jennie Vanvleet Cowdery) becomes Hartley's central focus as the minor figure Constantine Guys did for Baudelaire. In both cases, the examples are secondary to the point being made.
7. William Homer, *Alfred Stieglitz and the American Avant-Garde* (Boston: New York Graphic Society, 1977), pp. 198, 298.
8. Jean Lipman and Thomas Armstrong, *American Folk Painters of Three Centuries* (New York: Hudson Hills Press, in association with the Whitney Museum of American Art, 1966), p. 220.
9. Lincoln Kirstein, *The Sculpture of Eli Nadelman* (New York: Museum of Modern Art, 1948), p. 52.
10. Ibid.
11. Marsden Hartley, undated manuscript, "American Primitives," 5 pp. long, p. 1, Alfred Stieglitz Papers, Collection of American Literature, Beinecke Rare Book and Manuscript Library, Yale University, New Haven, Connecticut.
12. Ibid., pp. 3, 5.
13. Ibid., p. 2.
14. During the 1910s Robert Henri had called for the expression of "the American spirit" in painting. See, e.g., Henri, "The New York Independent Artists," *Craftsman*, no. 18 (May 1910): 161.
15. Hartley, "American Primitives," p. 5.
16. Dorothy Rylander Johnson, *Arthur Dove: The Years of Collage*, exhibition catalogue (College Park: [University of Maryland Art Gallery], 1967), pp. 9–13; reprinted in part in Johnson, "The Collages of Arthur Dove," *Art Forum*, May 1, 1967, pp. 40–41.
17. Barbara Haskell, *Arthur Dove*, exhibition catalogue, San Francisco Museum of Modern Art (Boston: New York Graphic Society, 1974), p. 49.
18. Henry May, *The End of American Innocence: A Study of the First Years of Our Own Time, 1912–1917* (New York: Knopf, 1959), pp. 261, 281–94.
19. Indigenous folk art forms were also very important to contemporary European modernist production in France, Germany, and the nascent Soviet Union.
20. John Marin file, Archives of American Art, Smithsonian Institution, Washington, D.C.
21. Paul Rosenfeld, "The World of Arthur Dove," *Creative Art* 10, no. 6 (June 1932): 427–30; quotation, 428.
22. *Clason's New Mexico Green Guide* (Chicago: Clason Map Company, 1920), pp. 6, 7. A copy is available in the Map Collection of the Doe Library, University of California at Berkeley.
23. Ibid., p. 11.
24. Hartley, "America as Landscape," p. 341.
25. Hartley, "Aesthetic Sincerity," p. 332.
26. Marsden Hartley, "Red Man Ceremonials: An American Plea for American Esthetics," *Art and Archaeology*, January 1920, p. 7. This work is hereafter cited parenthetically in the text.

27. In "Red Man Ceremonials," Hartley names the Taos Indians as well as the Tesuque, San Ildefonso, Santo Domingo, and San Felipe tribes. There was a great deal of trading among tribes, so he and circle members would undoubtedly have seen some Hopi, Navaho, and Zuni works in addition to the local pottery (each pueblo with a distinct type), jewelry, beadwork, Kachina dolls, and rugs; they probably also saw some painted works and some cave pictographs (Adisa Willmer, conversations with author, August 14 and 20, 1999).
28. Marsden Hartley, "The Scientific Esthetic of the Redman," *Art and Archaeology,* September 1922, p. 137.
29. Ibid., p. 138.
30. Frank, *Our America,* p. 114.
31. Waldo Frank, *The Re-discovery of America: An Introduction to a Philosophy of American Life* (New York: Charles Scribner's Sons, 1929), p. 230.
32. Waldo Frank, "Straight Streets," in *In the American Jungle [1925–1936]* (New York: Farrar and Rinehart, 1937), pp. 125–26.
33. Ibid., pp. 124–26. This work is hereafter cited parenthetically in the text.
34. Paul Rosenfeld, "Turning to America: The Corn Dance," in *By Way of Art: Criticisms of Music, Literature, Painting, Sculpture, and the Dance* (New York: Coward-McCann, 1928), pp. 228–29. This work is hereafter cited parenthetically in the text.
35. Elizabeth McCausland, *Marsden Hartley* (Minneapolis: University of Minnesota Press, 1952), p. 30.
36. Ibid., p. 19.
37. Forbes Watson, "The Star-Spangled Banner," *Arts* 18, no. 1 (October 1931): 43–56; quotation, 45.
38. Matthew Baigell, *The American Scene: American Painting of the 1930s* (New York: Praeger, 1974), p. 19.
39. Ibid., pp. 38–41.
40. As Baigell points out, the term *Regionalism* was often originally used as a pejorative, and it has never proved well suited to any particular body of artwork of the period: "Critics never succeeded in finding truly Regionalist painting in America during the 1930s. They saw plenty of localized subject matter, but they never discovered styles typical of particular sections of the country" (ibid., p. 55). Perhaps *localism,* a term used by Marsden Hartley during the period, might be more useful in classifying many of the important American paintings of the 1920s and 1930s.
41. Matthew Baigell, "The Beginnings of the 'American Wave' and the Depression," *Art Journal,* summer 1968, pp. 394–95.
42. Marsden Hartley, "Is There an American Art?" undated manuscript [early 1930s], 10 pp. long, pp. 2, 4, in the Stieglitz Papers, Beinecke Library, Yale University.
43. Lewis Mumford, exhibition review, "A Group of Americans," *New Yorker,* May 11, 1935, pp. 31–32.
44. Baigell, *American Scene,* p. 111.
45. Ibid.
46. Ibid., p. 61.
47. Thomas Craven, *Modern Art: The Men, the Movements, the Meaning* (New York: Simon and Schuster, 1934), p. 312.

48. Alfred Stieglitz to Kopman, May 29, 1934, Stieglitz Papers, Beinecke Library, Yale University. Unless otherwise noted, all letters cited are from this collection.
49. Lewis Mumford to Alfred Stieglitz, May 15, 1934.
50. Craven, *Modern Art,* p. 315. This work is hereafter cited parenthetically in the text.
51. Paul Rosenfeld to Alfred Stieglitz, September 4, 1924.
52. Cited in Craven, *Modern Art,* p. 342.
53. Walt Whitman, "By Blue Ontario's Shore," from *Leaves of Grass,* in *Complete Poetry and Collected Prose,* ed. Justin Kaplan, Library of America (New York: Literary Classics of the United States, 1982), p. 471.

CHAPTER 5. THE COUNTRY

1. Don S. Kirschner, *City and Country: Rural Responses to Urbanization in the 1920s* (Westport, Conn.: Greenwood, 1970), p. 20.
2. William E. Leuchtenburg, *The Perils of Prosperity, 1914–1932* (Chicago: University of Chicago Press, 1958), p. 229.
3. Loren Baristz, "The Culture of the Twenties," in *The Development of an American Culture,* ed. Stanley Coben and Lorman Ratner (Englewood Cliffs, N.J.: Prentice-Hall, 1970), p. 155.
4. Ibid.
5. Kirschner, *City and Country,* pp. 23–24.
6. Ibid., pp. 24, 25.
7. Lewis Mumford to Alfred Stieglitz, March 25, 1940, Alfred Stieglitz Papers, Collection of American Literature, Beinecke Rare Book and Manuscript Library, Yale University, New Haven, Connecticut. Unless otherwise noted, all letters cited are from this collection.
8. Kirschner, *City and Country,* p. 57.
9. Quotation from the *Goshen Democrat,* July 20, 1922; cited in Kirschner, *City and Country,* p. 58.
10. Paul Rosenfeld, *Port of New York: Essays on Fourteen American Moderns,* with camera portraits by Alfred Stieglitz, Alice Boughton, Paul Strand, and Dana Desboro (New York: Harcourt, Brace, 1924), p. 266.
11. Leuchtenburg, *Perils of Prosperity,* p. 225.
12. George E. Mowry and Blaine A. Brownell, *The Urban Nation, 1920–1980,* rev. ed. (New York: Hill and Wang, 1981), p. 21.
13. Ibid., p. 22.
14. For a full account of how Anderson selected and acquired land and then constructed his rural retreat, see Sherwood Anderson, *Sherwood Anderson's Memoirs: A Critical Edition,* ed. Ray Lewis White (Chapel Hill: University of North Carolina Press, 1969), pp. 485–505.
15. Paul Rosenfeld to Alfred Stieglitz, July 18, 1926.
16. Malcolm Cowley, *Exile's Return: A Narrative of Ideas* (New York: W. W. Norton, 1934), p. 223.
17. Sue Davidson Lowe, *Stieglitz: A Memoir/Biography* (New York: Farrar, Straus and Giroux, 1983).
18. Van Wyck Brooks, *America's Coming-of-Age* (New York: B. W. Huebsch, 1915), p. 163.

19. Alfred Stieglitz to Sherwood Anderson, August 7, 1924.
20. Lowe, *Stieglitz,* passim. John Szarkowski has opened the door to such studies with his exhibition catalogue *Alfred Stieglitz at Lake George* (New York: Museum of Modern Art, 1995).
21. Alfred Stieglitz to Waldo Frank, August 6, 1927.
22. John Ruskin, "Of the Pathetic Fallacy," in *Modern Painters* (New York: J. Wiley, 1858), vol. 3, part 4, chap. 12, p. 158.
23. Alfred Stieglitz to Sherwood Anderson, May 21, 1924.
24. Stieglitz is quoted in Lowe, *Stieglitz,* p. 256.
25. Lowe, *Stieglitz,* p. 299.
26. Alfred Stieglitz to Waldo Frank, October 27, 1929.
27. Perhaps the earliest treatment by a circle member of this subject (so replete with meaning for American artists who were experimenting with new technologies) is Paul Strand's 1915 photograph titled *Telegraph Poles, Texas.*
28. Marsden Hartley, "New England on the Trapeze," *Creative Art* 8, no. 2, supplement (February 1931): Sup-58.
29. Marsden Hartley to Alfred Stieglitz, November 1, 1926.
30. Hartley, "New England on the Trapeze," pp. Sup-58, Sup-57.
31. Ibid., p. Sup-57.
32. Elizabeth McCausland, *Marsden Hartley* (Minneapolis: University of Minnesota Press, 1952), p. 9.
33. Marsden Hartley to Alfred Stieglitz, July 13, 1930.
34. Merriam, quoted in Peter J. Schmitt, *Back to Nature: The Arcadian Myth in Urban America* (New York: Oxford University Press, 1969), p. 171.
35. Schmitt, *Back to Nature,* p. 171.
36. Lewis Mumford, "Regions—To Live In," *Survey: Graphic Number* 54, no. 3 (May 1, 1925): 152. Mumford helped edit this issue of the journal.
37. Hartley, "New England on the Trapeze," p. Sup-58.
38. McCausland, *Marsden Hartley,* p. 9.
39. Marsden Hartley to Alfred Stieglitz, March 12, 1931.

CHAPTER 6. THE CITY

1. Waldo Frank, *Salvos: An Informal Book about Books and Plays* (New York: Boni and Liveright, 1924), p. 201; his ellipsis.
2. Ibid., p. 202.
3. Paul Rosenfeld, *Port of New York: Essays on Fourteen American Moderns,* with camera portraits by Alfred Stieglitz, Alice Boughton, Paul Strand, and Dana Desboro (New York: Harcourt, Brace, 1924), p. 293.
4. Waldo Frank, *Our America* (New York: Boni and Liveright, 1919), p. 171.
5. Paul Rosenfeld, "The City with a Glance at Honegger," in *By Way of Art: Criticisms of Music, Literature, Painting, Sculpture, and the Dance* (New York: Coward-McCann, 1928), pp. 182–83. This work is hereafter cited parenthetically in the text.
6. Rosenfeld's homage to Randolph Bourne (an impassioned and eloquent spokesperson

for transnationalism) in *Port of New York* reveals the circle's commitment to cultural pluralism. Bourne argued against a homogeneous "melting pot," suggesting that America was instead distinguished by its mutually invigorating, egalitarian pluralism. To Bourne (very closely following Whitman) America was "the first international nation[,] . . . the world-federation in miniature"; see Randolph Bourne, "Trans-National America," in *The Radical Will: Selected Writings, 1911–1918*, ed. Olaf Hansen (New York: Urizen Books, 1977), pp. 248–64.

7. Sherwood Anderson to Waldo Frank, [Chicago(?), after November 7, 1917], in *Letters of Sherwood Anderson*, ed. Howard Mumford Jones and Walter B. Ridcout (Boston: Little, Brown, 1953), p. 23.
8. Sherwood Anderson, "New York, the 1920s," in *Sherwood Anderson's Memoirs: A Critical Edition*, ed. Ray Lewis White (Chapel Hill: University of North Carolina Press, 1969), pp. 330–31.
9. Although some of the painted and photographed statements about modern life found in the Stieglitz circle's images of the American city are noncommittal, and others are even celebratory, Paul Strand's *Wall Street* is quite pointed in its argument, as Strand's own description of it makes clear: "I was trying to photograph the people 'rushing to work.' The great black shapes of the windows [of the Morgan Trust Building] have the quality of a great maw into which the people rush"; quoted in Calvin Tomkins, *Paul Strand: Sixty Years of Photography* (Millertown, N.Y.: Aperture, 1976), p. 144. Tomkins identifies the particular building photographed as 23 Wall Street.
10. Coolidge is quoted in William E. Leuchtenburg, *The Perils of Prosperity, 1914–1932* (Chicago: University of Chicago Press, 1958), p. 188.
11. The film's original title is unclear. According to Jan-Christopher Horak in his essay "Modernist Perspectives and Romantic Impulses: Manhatta," in *Paul Strand: Essays on His Life and Work*, ed. Maren Stange (N.p.: Aperture, 1990), there is no mention of it in the letters or documents of Sheeler's estate, nor does any of the surviving Strand correspondence from the period mention the film's title. In later years Strand referred to it as both "Mannahatta" and "Manhatta," and shortly before his death he wrote that the film was "carried along by titles which we took from Walt Whitman's poem." The film was released in the United States in 1921 as "New York the Magnificent." In 1922 in Paris it was titled "Fumée de New York" (Smoke of New York). In 1927 the film was screened at the London Film Society with the title frame "Manhatta." It is that print, preserved by the British Film Institute, that is the master copy for all surviving prints in the United States. Given this study's new understanding of the influence of Whitman on the circle (of which Sheeler was a part in 1921), it seems probable that today's title is a very common misspelling of the original title, "Mannahatta."
12. Walt Whitman, "Mannahatta," from *Leaves of Grass*, in *Complete Poetry and Collected Prose*, ed. Justin Kaplan, Library of America (New York: Literary Classics of the United States, 1982), p. 586.
13. I have singled out this particular impression of the print from many possible examples because of both its excellent condition and its unique (and memorable) painterly quality.
14. Laurie Lisle, *Portrait of an Artist: A Biography of Georgia O'Keeffe* (New York: Washington Square Press, 1981), p. 182.

15. The suite number was given in a publicity brochure prepared by the Halloran House Hotel (formerly the Shelton Hotel) in New York City, "A Brand New Beginning for New York's Most Spectacular Sixty-One-Year-Old" (1985).
16. Virgil Barker, "The Watercolors of John Marin," *Arts* 5, no. 2 (February 1924): 69.
17. Lewis Mumford, *The Brown Decades: A Study of the Arts in America, 1865–1895* (1931; New York: Dover, 1971); on the Brooklyn Bridge, see chapter 2, "The Renewal of the Landscape," pp. 44–46.
18. This verbal image probably also alludes to the poet Hart Crane, a friend of circle members, whose best-known work is *The Bridge* (1930)—a long poem that focuses on the Brooklyn Bridge as its central metaphor. Crane participated in creating the periodical *Secession* in 1921 and was a regular at Stieglitz and O'Keeffe's "salons" after 1923; see Sue Davidson Lowe, *Stieglitz: A Memoir/Biography* (New York: Farrar, Straus and Giroux, 1983), p. 261.
19. Mumford, *The Brown Decades,* pp. 105–6.
20. This oversimplification began as early as Hugh McClellan Potter's "The 'Romantic Nationalists' of the 1920s" (Ph.D. diss., University of Minnesota, 1964), pp. 196–98.
21. Paul Rosenfeld to Alfred Stieglitz, November 8, 1922, and Alfred Stieglitz to Sherwood Anderson, postscript, June 22, 1925; Alfred Stieglitz Papers, Collection of American Literature, Beinecke Rare Book and Manuscript Library, Yale University, New Haven, Connecticut. Unless otherwise noted, all letters cited are from this collection.
22. Alfred Stieglitz to Sherwood Anderson, December 9, 1925; December 27, 1925.
23. Sherwood Anderson, "City Plowman," and Jean Toomer, "The Hill," both in *America and Alfred Stieglitz: A Collective Portrait,* ed. Waldo Frank et al., rev. ed. (Millerton, N.Y.: Aperture, 1979), pp. 146–48, 123–27. These two essays form a section titled "City Plowman."
24. Sarah Greenough, "Alfred Stieglitz and 'the Idea Photography,'" in *Alfred Stieglitz: Photographs and Writings,* by Sarah Greenough and Juan Hamilton, exhibition catalogue (Washington, D.C.: National Gallery of Art, 1983), p. 26.
25. Ibid., p. 25.
26. Martin Filler, "High Ruse," *Art in America,* no. 8 (September 1984): 154.
27. Irving Sandler points out that by the 1930s the painting of Mondrian was better known and appreciated in the United States than anywhere else in the world (*The Triumph of American Painting: A History of Abstract Expressionism* [New York: Harper and Row, 1970], pp. 17–18). The early taste for geometric abstraction in the United States inspired some artists in 1936 to form a group that they named the American Abstract Artists. The neoplasticism of Mondrian was the strongest influence binding the AAA.
28. Lewis Mumford, "Regionalism and Irregionalism," *Sociological Review* 19, no. 4 (October 1927): 277–88; "The Theory and Practice of Regionalism," 20, no. 1 (January 1928): 18–33; and "The Theory and Practice of Regionalism (continued)," 20, no. 2 (April 1928): 131–41.
29. See Lewis Mumford, "Is the Skyscraper Tolerable?" *Architecture* 55 (February 1927): 67–69; and "Botched Cities," *American Mercury* 18 (October 1929): 143–50.
30. See Waldo Frank, "Straight Streets," in *In the American Jungle [1925–1936]* (New York: Farrar and Rinehart, 1937), pp. 123–27; discussed in chapter 4 above.
31. Alfred Stieglitz to Paul Rosenfeld, October 5, 1930.
32. Betsy Fahlman made this identification in a talk on Demuth given at the Los Angeles

County Museum of Art on March 13, 1988; an employee of Armstrong, which still operates a plant in the original structure on the original site, had seen the image and recognized the structure. She did not have this information when she wrote the catalogue *Pennsylvania Modern: Charles Demuth of Lancaster* (Philadelphia: Philadelphia Museum of Art, 1983).

33. The structure is identified by Fahlman, *Pennsylvania Modern,* p. 49.
34. The structure is identified by Fahlman in her talk, March 13, 1988.
35. Fahlman, *Pennsylvania Modern,* p. 67.
36. *Spring and All* is reprinted in William Carlos Williams, *Imaginations* (New York: New Directions, 1970), pp. 85–151; see especially pp. 97–98. In this serial work, first published in a edition of about 300 copies and dedicated to Charles Demuth, twenty-seven numbered poems are introduced and set within a prose polemic. The poet's most impassioned plea on behalf of the imagination is also a plea for a new realism: "Those who led yesterday wish to hold their sway a while longer. . . . They ask us to return to the proven truth of tradition. . . . Demuth and a few others do their best to point out the error, telling us that design is a function of the IMAGINATION, describing its movements, its colors—but it is a hard battle" (p. 98).
37. In a letter of 1929 from Alfred Stieglitz to William Carlos Williams, the photographer explained that he had changed the name of Intimate Gallery to "An American Place" in honor of Williams's *In the American Grain.* See Mike Weaver, *William Carlos Williams: The American Background* (Cambridge: Cambridge University Press, 1971), p. 55.
38. Walt Whitman, "Song of the Exposition," from *Leaves of Grass,* in *Complete Poetry and Collected Prose,* p. 341.

CHAPTER 7. "THE MOST AMERICAN PLACE": NEW MEXICO

1. Marsden Hartley, "America as Landscape," *El Palacio* 5, no. 20 (December 9, 1918): 341.
2. Paul Strand to Alfred Stieglitz, September 20, 1926, Alfred Stieglitz Papers, Collection of American Literature, Beinecke Rare Book and Manuscript Library, Yale University, New Haven, Connecticut. Unless otherwise noted, all letters cited are from this collection.
3. Paul Rosenfeld to Alfred Stieglitz, August 15, 1926.
4. Ibid.
5. *Clason's New Mexico Green Guide* (Chicago: Clason Map Company, 1920), pp. 3, 4. A copy of the guide is available in the Map Collection of the Doe Library, University of California, Berkeley.
6. Elizabeth McCausland, *Marsden Hartley* (Minneapolis: University of Minnesota Press, 1952), p. 30.
7. Barbara Haskell, *Marsden Hartley,* exhibition catalogue (New York: Whitney Museum of American Art, in association with New York University Press, 1980), pp. 59, 60, 72.
8. McCausland, *Marsden Hartley,* p. 30.
9. Charles Baudelaire, "Salon of 1859" (Paris, 1859); my translation.
10. See *Marsden Hartley: Painter/Poet, 1877–1943,* exhibition catalogue, University Galleries, University of Southern California (Los Angeles: University of Southern California, 1968) for other examples of Hartley's Southwest windowscapes.

11. Walt Whitman, "Democratic Vistas," in *Complete Poetry and Collected Prose,* ed. Justin Kaplan, Library of America (New York: Literary Classics of the United States, 1982), p. 984.
12. Marin is quoted in Ward Lockwood, "The Marin I Knew: A Personal Reminiscence," *Texas Quarterly,* spring 1967, p. 109.
13. Van Deren Coke, *Marin in New Mexico, 1929 and 1930,* exhibition catalogue (Albuquerque: University Art Museum, University of New Mexico, 1968).
14. Marin is quoted in E. M. Benson, *John Marin: The Man and His Work* (Washington, D.C.: American Federation of Art, 1935), p. 108.
15. John Marin to Emil Zoler, August 25, 1929, in John Marin, *Selected Writings,* ed. Dorothy Norman (New York: Pelligrini and Cudahy, 1949), p. 132.
16. Marsden Hartley, "The Red Man," in *Adventures in the Arts: Informal Chapters on Painters, Vaudeville, and Poets* (New York: Boni and Liveright, 1921), pp. 17–23; Paul Rosenfeld, "Turning to America: The Corn Dance," in *By Way of Art: Criticisms of Music, Literature, Painting, Sculpture, and the Dance* (New York: Coward-McCann, 1928), pp. 217–35, esp. pp. 225–35. See also the discussion in chapter 4; Hartley's earlier essay, "Red Man Ceremonials: An American Plea for American Esthetics," *Art and Archaeology,* January 1920, also describes the corn dance (pp. 8–11; in "The Red Man," the slightly revised version of the essay that appears in *Adventures in the Arts,* the description occurs on pp. 17–23).
17. Waldo Frank, "Straight Streets," in *In the American Jungle [1925–1936]* (New York: Farrar and Rinehart, 1937), pp. 123–27.
18. I examined the identifiable sites in the Southwest depicted and described by circle members in October–November 1985.
19. Naomi Rosenblum, "Paul Strand: The Early Years, 1910–1932" (Ph.D. diss., City University of New York, 1978), p. 156.
20. Ibid., p. 162
21. This particular version of the church by Paul Strand is in the Beinecke Library at Yale University and is labeled (verso) "Church of St. Francis Assisi." This is the formal name of the edifice, written on a wooden cross before the front portal in Spanish: "S. Francisco de Assis: Mision est. 1710."
22. Sherwood Anderson, *A Story Teller's Story* (New York: B. W. Huebsch, 1924), p. 113.
23. A handful of Progressives—notably Hutchins Hapgood, who was a friend of Alfred Stieglitz—shared the circle's view.
24. Malcolm Cowley, *Exile's Return* (New York: W. W. Norton, 1934), p. 154.
25. Thomas Hart Benton, *An Artist in America,* 3d ed. (Columbia: University of Missouri Press, 1968), pp. 234–35.
26. Paul Rosenfeld to Alfred Stieglitz, July 18, 1926. This letter later formed the core of Rosenfeld's sensuous description of southwestern landscape in his published essay on the Corn Dance.
27. Rosenfeld, "Turning to the Corn Dance," pp. 220–21.
28. Ibid., pp. 221–22. This passage confirms that the Stieglitz circle had begun the search for "the most American place," indeed for the "real" America, years before their gallery name underscored the quest. When competing groups of artists and critics in the 1930s wrote accounts of the preceding decade, they obscured this important point.
29. Paul Rosenfeld to Alfred Stieglitz, July 18, 1926.

30. Paul Rosenfeld, *Port of New York: Essays on Fourteen American Moderns,* with camera portraits by Alfred Stieglitz, Alice Boughton, Paul Strand, and Dana Desboro (New York: Harcourt, Brace, 1924), p. 92.

31. Laurie Lisle, *Portrait of an Artist: A Biography of Georgia O'Keeffe* (New York: Washington Square Press, 1980), p. 111.

32. See Vera Norwood and Janice Monk, eds., *The Desert Is No Lady* (New Haven: Yale University Press, 1988). Though the title suggests the contrary, the selections in this anthology generally agree that the desert landscape is experienced as gendered; moreover, women artists flourish in its embrace. Many, like the author Mary Austin, saw their own strengths in it; in "The Land" (1909) she wrote, "If the desert were a woman, I know well what she would be: deep-breasted, broad in the hips, tawny, with tawny hair . . . [and] eyes sane and steady as the polished jewel of her skies" (in *American Women Regionalists, 1850–1910,* ed. Judith Fetterley and Marjorie Pryse [New York: W. W. Norton, 1992], pp. 591–92).

33. Georgia O'Keeffe, *Georgia O'Keeffe* (New York: Viking, 1976), p. 58.

34. O'Keeffe recalled, "They talked so often of writing the Great American Novel—the Great American Play—the Great American Poetry. . . . Cézanne was so much in the air that I think the Great American Painting didn't even seem a possible dream." She remembered thinking of her cow's skull, "They will not think it great with the red stripes down the sides—Red, White and Blue—but they will notice it" (ibid.).

35. O'Keeffe is quoted in Henry McBride's review, "Sees Mountains Red: Georgia O'Keeffe Accused of Misdemeanor in the Southwest," *New York Sun,* January 28, 1939, p. 9.

36. Whitman, "Democratic Vistas," p. 977; see the discussion in chapter 1.

SELECTED BIBLIOGRAPHY

Abrahams, Edward. *The Lyrical Left: Randolph Bourne, Alfred Stieglitz, and the Origins of Cultural Radicalism in America*. Charlottesville: University Press of Virginia, 1986.

Anderson, Sherwood. *Sherwood Anderson's Memoirs: A Critical Edition*. Edited by Ray Lewis White. Chapel Hill: University of North Carolina Press, 1969.

Baigell, Matthew. *The American Scene: American Painting of the 1930s*. New York: Praeger, 1974.

Benton, Thomas Hart. *An American in Art: A Professional and Technical Autobiography*. Lawrence: University Press of Kansas, 1951.

———. *An Artist in America*. 3d ed. Columbia: University of Missouri Press, 1968.

Brooks, Van Wyck. *America's Coming-of-Age*. New York: B. W. Huebsch, 1915.

———. *The Wine of the Puritans: A Study of Present-Day America*. New York: M. Kennerly, 1908.

Coben, Stanley, and Lorman Ratner, eds. *The Development of an American Culture*. Englewood Cliffs, N.J.: Prentice-Hall, 1970.

Cochran, Thomas C., and William Miller. *The Age of Enterprise: A Social History of Industrial America*. New York: Macmillan, 1942.

Coke, Van Deren. *Marin in New Mexico, 1929 and 1930*. Exhibition catalogue. Albuquerque: University Art Museum, University of New Mexico, 1968.

Cowart, Jack, Juan Hamilton, and Sarah Greenough. *Georgia O'Keeffe: Art and Letters*. Exhibition catalogue. Washington, D.C.: National Gallery of Art in association with New York Graphic Society Books; Boston: Little, Brown, 1987.

Cowley, Malcolm. *Exile's Return: A Narrative of Ideas*. New York: W. W. Norton, 1934.

Craven, Thomas. *Modern Art: The Men, the Movements, the Meaning.* New York: Simon and Schuster, 1934.

Egbert, Donald Drew. *Socialism and American Art in the Light of European Utopianism, Marxism, and Anarchism.* Princeton: Princeton University Press, 1967.

Fahlman, Betsy. *Pennsylvania Modern: Charles Demuth of Lancaster.* Exhibition catalogue. Philadelphia: Philadelphia Museum of Art, 1983.

Farnham, Emily. *Charles Demuth: Behind a Laughing Mask.* Norman: University of Oklahoma Press, 1971.

Frank, Waldo. *In the American Jungle [1925–1936].* New York: Farrar and Rinehart, 1937.

———. *Our America.* New York: Boni and Liveright, 1919.

———. *The Re-discovery of America: An Introduction to a Philosophy of American Life.* New York: Charles Scribner's Sons, 1929.

———. *Salvos: An Informal Book about Books and Plays.* New York: Boni and Liveright, 1924.

Frank, Waldo, Lewis Mumford, Dorothy Norman, Paul Rosenfeld, and Harold Rugg, eds. *America and Alfred Stieglitz: A Collective Portrait.* Rev. ed. Millerton, N.Y.: Aperture, 1979.

Greenough, Sarah, and Juan Hamilton. *Alfred Stieglitz: Photographs and Writings.* Exhibition catalogue. Washington, D.C.: National Gallery of Art, 1983.

Hartley, Marsden. *Adventures in the Arts: Informal Chapters on Painters, Vaudeville, and Poets.* New York: Boni and Liveright, 1921.

Haskell, Barbara. *Arthur Dove.* Exhibition catalogue. San Francisco Museum of Modern Art. Boston: New York Graphic Society, 1974.

———. *Charles Demuth.* Exhibition catalogue. New York: Whitney Museum of American Art, in association with Harry N. Abrams, 1988.

———. *Marsden Hartley.* Exhibition catalogue. New York: Whitney Museum of American Art, in association with New York University Press, 1980.

Hills, Patricia. *Social Concern and Urban Realism: American Painting of the 1930s.* Exhibition catalogue. Boston: Boston University Art Gallery, 1983.

Homer, William Innis. *Alfred Stieglitz and the American Avant-Garde.* Boston: New York Graphic Society, 1977.

Johnson, Dorothy Rylander. *Arthur Dove: The Years of Collage.* Exhibition catalogue. College Park: [University of Maryland Art Gallery], 1967.

Kirschner, Don S. *City and Country: Rural Responses to Urbanization in the 1920s.* Westport, Conn.: Greenwood, 1970.

Leuchtenburg, William E. *The Perils of Prosperity, 1914–1932.* Chicago: University of Chicago Press, 1958.

Lipman, Jean, and Thomas Armstrong. *American Folk Painters of Three Centuries.* New York: Hudson Hills Press, in association with the Whitney Museum of American Art, 1968.

Lisle, Laurie. *Portrait of an Artist: A Biography of Georgia O'Keeffe.* New York: Washington Square Press, 1981.

Lowe, Sue Davidson. *Stieglitz: A Memoir/Biography.* New York: Farrar, Straus and Giroux, 1983.

Marchand, Roland. *Advertising the American Dream: Making Way for Modernity, 1920–1940.* Berkeley: University of California Press, 1985.

Marin, John. *John Marin.* Edited by Cleve Gray. New York: Holt, Rinehart, and Winston, 1970.

———. *Selected Writings.* Edited by Dorothy Norman. New York: Pelligrini and Cudahy, 1949.

May, Henry. *The End of American Innocence: A Study of the First Years of Our Own Time, 1912–1917.* New York: Knopf, 1959.
McCausland, Elizabeth. *Marsden Hartley.* Minneapolis: University of Minnesota Press, 1952.
Morgan, Ann Lee. *Arthur Dove: Life and Work with a Catalogue Raisonné.* Newark: University of Delaware Press, 1985.
Mowry, George E., and Blaine A. Brownell. *The Urban Nation, 1920–1980.* Rev. ed. New York: Hill and Wang, 1981.
Mumford, Lewis. *The Brown Decades: A Study of the Arts in America, 1865–1895.* 1931. Reprint, New York: Dover, 1971.
Newhall, Nancy. *Photographs, 1915–1945: Paul Strand.* Exhibition catalogue. New York: Museum of Modern Art, 1945.
Newman, Sasha. *Arthur Dove and Duncan Phillips: Artist and Patron.* Washington, D.C.: Phillips Collection; New York: in association with George Braziller, 1981.
O'Connor, Francis V. *Art for the Millions: Essays from the 1930s.* Greenwich, Conn.: New York Graphic Society, 1973.
O'Keeffe, Georgia. *Georgia O'Keeffe.* New York: Viking Press, 1976.
Phillips, Duncan. *A Collection in the Making.* New York: E. Weyhe; Washington, D.C.: Phillips Memorial Gallery, 1926.
Reich, Sheldon. *John Marin: A Stylistic Analysis and Catalogue Raisonné.* 2 vols. Tucson: University of Arizona Press, 1970.
Rosenfeld, Paul. *By Way of Art: Criticisms of Music, Literature, Painting, Sculpture, and the Dance.* New York: Coward-McCann, 1928.
———. *Port of New York: Essays on Fourteen American Moderns.* With camera portraits by Alfred Stieglitz, Alice Boughton, Paul Strand, and Dana Desboro. New York: Harcourt, Brace, 1924.
Sandler, Irving. *The Triumph of American Painting: A History of Abstract Expressionism.* New York: Harper and Row, 1970.
Schmitt, Peter J. *Back to Nature: The Arcadian Myth in Urban America.* New York: Oxford University Press, 1969.
Seligmann, Herbert. *Alfred Stieglitz Talking: Notes on Some of His Conversations, 1925–1931.* New Haven: Yale University Library, 1966.
Stebbins, Theodore E., Jr., and Carol Troyen. *The Lane Collection: Twentieth-Century Paintings in the American Tradition.* Exhibition catalogue. Boston: Museum of Fine Arts, 1983.
Tomkins, Calvin. *Paul Strand: Sixty Years of Photographs.* Millerton, N.Y.: Aperture, 1976.
Whitman, Walt. *Complete Poetry and Collected Prose.* Edited by Justin Kaplan. Library of America. New York: Literary Classics of the United States, 1982.
Williams, Raymond. *The Country and the City.* New York: Oxford University Press, 1973.

INDEX

Note: Page numbers in italics refer to illustrations.

TEXT 10/14 Scala
DISPLAY Scala Sans
DESIGN Nicole Hayward
INDEX Carol Roberts
COMPOSITION Integrated Composition Systems
PRINTING & BINDING Malloy Lithographing